ENGAGING THE HEART IN BUSINESS

In the wake of the profound upheavals that our society has been facing, the business world is undergoing change. Values such as trust, well-being, sustainability, and respect for human beings and their deeper ambitions are becoming increasingly important. Corporations and professionals can achieve and maintain success only if they can bring their relationship with their customers to a new, higher level. The condition that links the two is very similar to that created when we fall in love. The organizational models and marketing approaches based on the metaphor of war, and the inherent rhetoric of "command and control", are no longer valid; to form such a bond we need love. The authors are aware of this. Since 2013, in collaboration with international scholars, they have been studying the new market dynamics and the fundamental role of ethics in gaining commercial results. While their previous book *Sales Ethics* (2015) helped to set up and manage customer relationships based on trust and fairness, this new book will support you in building your business strategy and designing marketing tools (from customer analysis, to the definition of your offer and the style of communication, up to the positioning of prices and the management of resources) in the light of a new model, the *Loving Business Model*, which aims to make the customer fall in love with you, and you with your work. This book, like its predecessor, is the result of independent research conducted between Italy and the United States combined with the authors' many years of professional experience. It contains the most up-to-date and effective techniques available in the modern marketing landscape, supported by case studies, concrete examples and activities, which will guide you to put your newly acquired knowledge into practice.

Alice Alessandri and Alberto Aleo, partners in both their professional and private lives, are founders of the consulting and training agency *Passodue* that operates in the field of ethical sales and marketing. Many of the major Italian companies that feature among their clients have chosen ethics as a success factor. Alice and Alberto also collaborate with universities and training institutions at an international level. They are authors of the book *Sales Ethics* published in 2015. In addition to their consultancy and training work, in recent years the authors have participated as speakers at international conferences such as the Global Business Ethics Symposium in Copenhagen and Boston, the IABS Conference in Salt Lake City and Amsterdam, and the Positive Economy Forum in Rimini. Their publications and articles have appeared in newspapers and trade magazines. They are editors of the successful blog www.diariodiunconsulente.com, which contains hundreds of articles and essays that further explain their approach.

GIVING VOICE TO VALUES
Series Editor: Mary C. Gentile

The *Giving Voice to Values* series is a collection of books on Business Ethics and Corporate Social Responsibility that brings a practical, solutions-oriented, skill-building approach to the salient questions of values-driven leadership.

Giving Voice to Values (GVV: www.GivingVoiceToValues.org) – the curriculum, the pedagogy and the research upon which it is based – was designed to transform the foundational assumptions upon which the teaching of business ethics is based, and importantly, to equip future business leaders to know not only what is right – but how to make it happen.

Giving Voice to Values in the Legal Profession
Carolyn Plump

Giving Voice to Values in Accounting
Tara J. Shawver and William F. Miller

Giving Voice to Values as a Professional Physician
Ira Bedzow

Authentic Excellence
R. Kelly Crace and Robert L. Crace

Ethics, CSR and Sustainability (ECSRS) Education in the Middle East and North Africa (MENA) Region
Edited by Noha El-Bassiouny, Dina El-Bassiouny, Ehab K. A. Mohamed, and Mohamed A. K. Basuony

Engaging the Heart in Business
A Revolutionary Market Approach Based on Love
Alice Alessandri and Alberto Aleo

ENGAGING THE HEART IN BUSINESS

A Revolutionary Market Approach Based on Love

Alice Alessandri and Alberto Aleo

LONDON AND NEW YORK

First published 2021
by Routledge
2 Park Square, Milton Park, Abingdon, Oxon OX14 4RN

and by Routledge
52 Vanderbilt Avenue, New York, NY 10017

Routledge is an imprint of the Taylor & Francis Group, an informa business

© 2021 Alice Alessandri and Alberto Aleo

The right of Alice Alessandri and Alberto Aleo to be identified as authors of
this work has been asserted by them in accordance with sections 77 and 78
of the Copyright, Designs and Patents Act 1988.

All rights reserved. No part of this book may be reprinted or reproduced or utilised
in any form or by any electronic, mechanical, or other means, now known or
hereafter invented, including photocopying and recording, or in any information
storage or retrieval system, without permission in writing from the publishers.

Trademark notice: Product or corporate names may be trademarks or registered trademarks,
and are used only for identification and explanation without intent to infringe.

British Library Cataloguing-in-Publication Data
A catalogue record for this book is available from the British Library

Library of Congress Cataloging-in-Publication Data
Names: Alessandri, Alice, 1970– author. | Aleo, Alberto, 1972– author.
Title: Engaging the heart in business : a revolutionary market
approach based on love / Alice Alessandri and Alberto Aleo.
Description: Abingdon, Oxon; New York, NY: Routledge, 2021. |
Series: Giving voice to values | Includes bibliographical references and index. |
Identifiers: LCCN 2020010969 (print) | LCCN 2020010970 (ebook) |
ISBN 9781138610781 (hardback) | ISBN 9781138610804 (paperback) |
ISBN 9780429465604 (ebook)
Subjects: LCSH: Marketing–Moral and ethical aspects. |
Customer relations. | Organizational behavior. | Values. | Business ethics.
Classification: LCC HF5415 .A3965 2021 (print) |
LCC HF5415 (ebook) | DDC 174/.4–dc23
LC record available at https://lccn.loc.gov/2020010969
LC ebook record available at https://lccn.loc.gov/2020010970

ISBN: 978-1-138-61078-1 (hbk)
ISBN: 978-1-138-61080-4 (pbk)
ISBN: 978-0-429-46560-4 (ebk)

Typeset in Bembo
by Newgen Publishing UK

In memory of
W. Michael Hoffman

CONTENTS

Foreword by Prof. Antony F. Buono   xi
Preface: A new model for business   xv
Acknowledgments   xviii

Introduction   1

1   The context   7

2   Reference models for *Engaging the Heart in Business*   18

3   Engaging the heart in business   28

4   Love *yourself*: branding and identity   41

5   Love *why* you *do it*: having clear and shareable goals   54

6   Love *who* you do it *for*: who your customers are and
    what you can do for them   69

7   Love *what you do*: the offer system and the creation of value 85

8   Respect your *rivals*: how to manage your relationship
    with the competition   100

9   Love *who* you do it *with*: getting the best from people   119

x Contents

10 Love *how* you *do it*: the value journey and managing
the relationship   137

11 Conclusions   153

FAQ – Answers to frequently asked questions   *159*
Bibliography   *165*
Index   *168*

FOREWORD

Prof. Anthony F. Buono

BENTLEY UNIVERSITY

We are witnessing the emergence of a new narrative about business, one that is increasingly removed from traditional images of shareholder supremacy and a myopic focus on bottom-line short-termism. As the Business Roundtable (BRT), an association of chief executive officers of America's leading companies, recently announced, "business as usual" is no longer acceptable. Companies, the BRT notes, have far greater responsibilities to a broader array of stakeholders than has been recognized in the past.[1] While many observers have questioned whether such statements reflect more rhetoric than reality,[2] change is clearly in the air. Ever since Milton Friedman's declaration that "the social responsibility of business is to increase its profits,"[3] shareholders have dominated the economic paradigm. Moving forward, however, this new narrative is beginning to shift the factors that guide managerial planning and decision-making, moving from short-term to longer-term thinking, away from a focus exclusively on profit and power to a more inclusive emphasis on people and impact.[4]

Yet, while this narrative appears to be exerting influence on business practice, one can readily question the extent to which this story will truly transform business as we currently know it. In essence, is this stakeholder-oriented paradigm sufficient given the challenges and demands that we face? Instead of casting business practice in traditional economic and financial terms, can we create a more human and humane perspective? Can we develop a different kind of business model, one that has the potential to create the type of results that business people and their stakeholders have long sought? Might passion and love – terms that are not typically associated with the business world – provide the basis for this new paradigm? *Engaging the Heart in Business* makes a compelling case that this could – *should* – be the essence of business practice.

I first met the volume's authors, Alice and Alberto, in 2013 at Bentley University when they attended a program I facilitated in my role as director of the school's

xii Foreword

Alliance for Ethics and Social Responsibility – our annual Global Business Ethics Symposium and faculty development teaching business ethics workshop. Referred to as the "Gadfly" initiative, the program's goals were to (1) share the latest thinking and application of business ethics and (2) encourage faculty from a broad range of fields and disciplines to address ethical issues and questions of corporate responsibility and sustainability in courses across the curriculum. The Gadfly reference dates back to Socrates, who described himself as a "gadfly," whose purpose was to "sting" the citizens of Athens out of their ignorance and intellectual complacency. By "seeding" different universities and academic departments with such gadflies, the goal was to develop a core network of faculty who would prod and influence their colleagues to incorporate informed discussions of ethical issues and corporate responsibilities in their discipline-based courses.

Although the symposium each year has a mix of academic and practitioner speakers from the profit and non-profit worlds, participants in the workshop are typically academics. From time to time, business people also took part in the workshop, sharing ways in which they were incorporating these concepts in their companies. Through our conversations at the 2013 program, I was quickly enamored with Alice and Alberto's ideas and I invited them to participate as speakers in the program the following year, which was held in collaboration with the Copenhagen Business School in Frederiksberg, Denmark. Workshop participants were delighted that the two Italian practitioners were joining us to share their thoughts and experiences. Alice and Alberto focused on sales ethics – the topic of their first book – enlightening the workshop group with the possibilities of ethical sales negotiations, creating a reciprocal exchange of value and elevating the sales role with a combination of dignity and awareness. Alice and Alberto can be characterized as "idea practitioners,"[5] thought leaders who make management concepts a reality in the business world. Their insights, passion and commitment to the application of ethical practice in the context of well-established marketing theories and business frameworks provoked workshop participants and provided them with ample material to share in their courses. I've always thought that when good people with good ideas get together, good things happen.

Since publication of their first book, Alice and Alberto's conceptualization of business has continued to evolve, drawing out a new approach to how we think about business itself, drawing it closer to one of humanity's most enduring quests – love. Rather than focus on the "smartest guys in the room,"[6] their emphasis might be best characterized as the most *caring* people in the room, a shift far away from conflict and manipulation to one imbued with an authentic sense of character, trust, empowerment, and positive self-esteem, intertwined with values-based and principle-driven actions. Their work proposes a new business model that does have the potential to transform business as we know it.

As Alice and Alberto note in the volume, Mary Gentile's insightful work, *Giving Voice to Values*,[7] pushed their thinking. Mary's approach is based on the premise that most people know what they feel is the right thing to do, especially as reflected in their own core values, but they lack the tools and/or wherewithal to put that into practice. *Engaging the Heart in Business* begins with a similar premise and approach – rather than trying to convince the reader that love is the way to go, they focus on real-world examples supported by various tools and techniques that operationalize the ideal of love in ways that enhance business practice. They draw out the value in relationships as one engages the heart, creating a true bond of trust that is the basis for ongoing exchange and mutual benefit.

Reflecting on my own work with my colleague Raj Sisodia,[8] this kind of conscious approach to business takes stakeholder engagement and business performance to a new level. In addition to creating financial wealth, through their actions conscious companies create other kinds of societal wealth as well – from more fulfilled employees, and happy and loyal customers, to innovative and committed suppliers, to thriving and environmentally healthy communities, and more. As a growing body of fieldwork suggests, this approach creates a virtuous cycle that consistently delivers superior financial performance as well as a broad array of positive impacts.[9]

Engaging the Heart in Business is rich with stories and case vignettes that capture the essence of their paradigm, bringing it to life for the reader. Although the focus of these stories is on small- and medium-sized businesses, its application can be to business of any size – their point is that this approach does not depend on substantial budgets and large numbers of personnel. Along the way, Alice and Alberto insightfully draw together an array of management concepts, from Gentile's *Giving Voice to Values* and stakeholder theory, to Maslow's hierarchy of needs in the context of contemporary marketing theory imbued with ethics. As a brief example, they translate the traditional marketing mix into a "love mix" that transforms our basic approach to marketing and selling. Shifting from product to an *offer system* composed of a set of products and services, values, and behaviors, from price to *value*, from place to an engaging and positive *customer journey*, and from promotion to kept *pledges* – this love-marketing mix reflects the foundation of a more humane and values-based business framework. All this material is well supported with thoughtful insights and guidance into how to translate these ideas into practice.

As one reads and reflects on Alice and Alberto's message, it becomes readily clear that economic thought and good intentions need not be viewed as strange bedfellows. Perhaps the best example of their framework in practice is their own consulting and training company – *Passodue* – the living embodiment of a loving approach to business and their own partnership. Casting business transactions in terms of mutuality and reciprocally beneficial exchanges in ways that integrate "I" and "We,"[10] the intertwined nature of *being* and *loving* becomes increasing clear as one reads the volume, the core of what the authors refer to as the "circle of trust." Imagine a world where these sentiments dominated business practice. Just imagine…

xiv Foreword

Notes

1 See www.businessroundtable.org/business-roundtable-redefines-the-purpose-of-a-corporation-to-promote-an-economy-that-serves-all-americans. Accessed February 14, 2020.

2 See, for example, Winston, Andrew. "Is the Business Roundtable Statement Just Empty Rhetoric?" *Harvard Business Review*. https://hbr.org/2019/08/is-the-business-roundtable-statement-just-empty-rhetoric. Accessed February 14, 2020; and Bahnsen, David L. "Business Roundtable Pretends to Redefine What a Corporation Does." *National Review*. www.nationalreview.com/2019/08/business-roundtable-pretends-to-redefine-what-a-corporation-does/. Accessed February 14, 2020.

3 Friedman, Milton. "The Social Responsibility is to Increase Profits." *New York Times Sunday Magazine*, September 13, 1970.

4 Ludema, Jim, and Amber Johnson. "The Purpose of the Corporation? Business Roundtable Advances the Conversation, Now We All Need to Contribute." *Forbes*. www.forbes.com/sites/amberjohnson-jimludema/2019/08/20/the-purpose-of-the-corporation/#63080efd3846. Accessed February 14, 2020.

5 Davenport, Thomas H., and Laurence Prusak. *What's the Big Idea? Creating and Capitalizing on the Best Management Thinking*. Harvard Business School Press, 2003.

6 McLean, Bethany, and Peter Elkind. *The Smartest Guys in the Room: The Amazing Rise and Scandalous Fall of Enron*. London, UK: Portfolio Hardcover, 2003.

7 Gentile, Mary. *Giving Voice to Values: How to Speak Your Mind When You Know What's Right*. Yale University Press, 2010.

8 Buono, Anthony, and Rajendra Sisodia. "A Conscious Purpose." *EFMD Global Focus* 5 (2011), no. 2: 56–59.

9 See, for example, Sisodia, Raj, David Wolfe, and Jag Seth. *Firms of Endearment: How World-Class Companies Profit from Passion and Purpose*. New York, NY: FT Press, 2007; Mackey, John, and Raj Sisodia. *Conscious Capitalism: Liberating the Heroic Spirit of Business*. Harvard University Press, 2013; and Davidson, Adam. *The Passion Economy: The New Rules for Thriving in the Twenty-First Century*. Knopf, 2020.

10 See, for example, Etzioni, Amitai. *The Moral Dimension: Toward a New Economics*. Collier Macmillan, 1988.

PREFACE

A new model for business

People don't look each other in the eyes, they don't hold hands, they don't try
to feel the other's energy. It is not allowed to flow freely.
They just get by, fearful, cold and numb inside
a straitjacket. In Latin, there is a saying: "Agere sequitur esse",
doing follows being. Don't try to change your actions; search to
discover your being and the actions will change. The action is something you
do, being is something you are. The action comes from you, but it is only one
fragment. If you put all your actions together,
they would only represent your past. And the future? Your being
contains your past, your future and your present: it contains your
eternity. Once you have seen yourself in your entirety, you acquire the ability
to entirely see
others too.

Osho[1]

It was Thanksgiving Day 2014 when our first book, *La Vendita Etica*, was officially
launched by the FrancoAngeli publishing house in Italy (the English edition, *Sales
Ethics*, was published in February 2015 by Business Expert Press). In the intense
period of preparation, we had dedicated all our available resources and energy to
setting out our ideas on how to conduct ethical sales negotiations. Our desire was to
aid salespeople to experience their role with dignity and awareness in the certainty
of creating a true exchange of value.

Today a new urgency has prompted us to start this publishing adventure: the
desire **to give all the people who wish to imbue their job with a sense of
mission a model that will inspire them to achieve results, generate value
and help build "a better world"**. The model we have created and implemented
is the result of an apparently surprising mix obtained by combining well-established

xvi Preface

marketing theories with our direct experience both of market dynamics and the profound values that guide us as people and as professionals. Our reflections and analyses are based on three fundamental questions:

1. Why do some companies that on paper appear destined to succeed then fail while others, which may appear weaker, are successful?
2. How can we evolve some of the best-known theories of business ethics by adapting them to the business reality and to a world that is changing so swiftly?
3. Is it possible to experience your work as an opportunity to improve yourself and carry forward your mission in life?

The search for a complete and comprehensive answer to the questions above has guided our journey, leading us to codify a new model of approach to the market based on the most profound, noble, complete and all-incorporating experience a human being can have, **love**.

In the business world, and far beyond its confines, people use countless aggressive metaphors of conflict, of fighting for survival and gambling,[2] all situations in which only one side wins: the strongest, the smartest or those willing to "do whatever it takes". The economic crisis that began in 2008 shook the markets to their foundations, so deeply indeed that some were inspired to revise their approach to business relations and rethink the need for respect and trust.

The time has now come to give voice to people like us, and you the readers of this book, people who wish to express a sincere passion for what they do by offering their customers an authentic proposal and helping to create collective well-being. This book aims to accompany you along a journey to explore the strategies you can adopt so that clear promises and authentic behavior underpin your customer–company relationships.

In a world where professional relationships are predominantly based on a philosophy of "giving to have", we propose an approach that develops through **being, offering and receiving**. This approach is based on a simple consideration: all relationships, regardless of the context in which they develop, be it personal or professional, are **between people**. To commit fully and to express our true essence, we must focus on **being** by asking ourselves who we really are, then progress to deciding what we can **offer** in a **spirit of service**, i.e. not forcing the other person to accept a pre-determined offer but tailoring our offer to our interlocutor's needs. Thus, **receiving**, unlike exchanging, becomes an act of openness towards others where we recognize and accept the tangible and intangible benefits that we receive both directly and indirectly over a longer period of time that goes beyond the single moment of the transaction.

Summer 2017. We are writing these opening lines in Puglia, in the white city of Ostuni that nestles between the sandy beaches of the Adriatic Sea and the green countryside dotted with ancient olive trees. We have traveled many kilometers and conducted dozens of meetings in Europe and the United States to prepare for this moment, for the journey with you through this book, but we chose to sit down and start writing here in Italy, because the foundations for this project are rooted in our native country; a country generously loved throughout the world and, apparently, little valued by its own inhabitants. We live in a land steeped in history, culture and art that also boasts excellence in the realms of food and wine. Yet this incredible beauty is so familiar to us that we may take it for granted. Our own approach to business has undoubtedly been influenced by our travels abroad, by our research and the reading carried out in different countries; these elements have combined to enrich our work. However, the roots lie in Italy, in the warmth of the people and their capacity to strike up relationships as well as in the passion and ancient culture of which they are bearers.

This book, like the previous one, will be written by the two of us, working together. We are united both by the *Passodue* project and the love that united us over 15 years ago. We are increasingly seeing "working couples" running companies and professional studios; we believe this union represents that integration of masculine and feminine energy, Yin and Yang, impulsiveness and ponderation, the incisiveness and acceptance that can produce a new autonomous form, an "androgynous" identity that contains both parts and is greater and more powerful than the two halves that make up the whole. Furthermore, in a company's mission the "loving couple", united by the shared values that first brought the two individuals together, can create through love something that goes beyond themselves. Whether you are alone, in a couple or with others on this journey, remember that you can let love be the guide to build a loving business!

Notes

1 Osho. *Love, Freedom, and Aloneness: A New Vision of Relating*. St. Martin's Griffing, 2001.
2 See D'Egidio, Franco. *L'impresa guidata dai valori*. Sperling & Kupfer, 1994.

ACKNOWLEDGMENTS

Like any serious journey, there were a host of moments, places and people that combined to make this book what it is. The challenge of not forgetting anyone in this short text forces us to re-open the album of accumulated memories that spans the almost two years of the book's gestation. In April 2017, Luca Montaguti and his wife Chiara Molinari opened the doors of their house in Donicilio, perched on the hills between Romagna and Tuscany, within whose solid stone walls we took refuge to gather the notes and ideas that had emerged from dialogues with entrepreneurs, university professors, managers and anyone whose interest was aroused by our project. Among those who have encouraged us to pursue the project and make it feasible, we cannot fail to mention Prof. Leigh Hafrey of the Sloan Business School and Massimo Folador of the LIUC of Castellanza who wrote the preface to the Italian edition of the book.

Our next stop was Ostuni, the "White City" that dominates the Valle d'Itria in Puglia. A magical place, rich in history, and home to some fascinating Italian traditions. Our mentor and source of support here was Mario de Liguori, who then took on the task of being among the first readers and revisers of the text.

From the south we then moved northwards, to the splendid scenery of the Dolomites, where we lived as happy hermits dedicating ourselves to intense days of work and discussion with Riccardo Trevisani, who also oversaw the section dedicated to the brand and revised the overall framework of the book aided by his refreshing youthful vision and up-to-date viewpoint. These trips alternated with long periods of work in our studio in Cesena, debating with colleagues and partners who helped us along the way; of these, we must mention Serena Calderoni (also among the text editors), Marzia Mazzi, Canzio Panzavolta and the whole team of Camp Me Up. A special thanks goes to those who lent us their story to be included in the book as case studies, such as Massimiliano Montalti, Rita Pederzoli Ricci, Maurizio Pensato, Antonio Capristo and Raffaella Casadei.

When we finally returned to Boston, we found our invaluable American editor and mentor Prof. Mary Gentile who, together with her wife, has now become part of our overseas family, including Chiara Montaguti, her husband Luigi Tarlazzi and their two splendid children who generously hosted us in their wonderful home in the woods of Boxborough. Our relationship with Boston was rendered even more loving thanks to people like Prof. Monica Borgida from Northeastern University who allowed us to share our knowledge and experience with her students and who always stimulates us by suggesting useful reading material and providing advice, not to mention her delicious burgers. In that part of the world, we know we can trust in the support of people like Prof. Tony Buono, an outstanding figure in the world of business ethics, who with rare goodwill and openness never backs down when it comes to helping us; he also wrote the preface to the English version of the text.

Special thanks to Prof. Joshua Margolis of the Harvard Business School for his support with the case studies.

Once the book was drafted, we placed the manuscript in the expert hands of our skillful readers, three of whom we have already mentioned and to which we must add Elisabeth Cellie, an enlightened manager whom we wished to involve in the project both for her skills and for the humanity she has always demonstrated. The drawings and graphics were penned by Nicole Oriani, who has contributed with her artistic touch to enliven the pages of *Engaging the Heart in Business*. Thanks also to Franco Farnedi and his team for technical support in the design of the text download contents. The international nature of the project is also the result of the translation work done for us by Sarah Suzanne Keating, who has been following us and supporting us for many years.

Our thanks must go beyond the well-known and familiar faces and places to include fleetingly experienced corners of the world, magical moments and the people we passed on our journey; they may not have been mentioned here but they have contributed to the success of this adventure. We will thus thank the koi carp in Lele's pond, old vinyl records and taverns where time passes unnoticed, Vespas, classic Atari video games, the many "Iced-Coffee-with-cream-no-sugar" of Dunkin' Donuts, the silent snow, the ocean beaches, the train that goes towards the sea, the long walks, the constructive debates and everything that has populated our lives during these long months spent processing our project. Really everyone and everything have been fundamental because, as Massimo Maggiari states in his beautiful book entitled *Al Canto delle Balene*, "The most arduous journey is not the one that moves you across the earth, but the one that starts in your mind and reaches your heart".

INTRODUCTION

Who this book is for

This book is aimed primarily at anyone who is thinking of starting a new business or wants to redesign their professional activity by introducing an authentic approach, aligned to their values and respectful of all the people involved in the process.

Whether you are an entrepreneur, a manager or a freelancer, these pages will provide you with everything you need to design a complete and precise marketing plan through the metaphor of love and, progressing from this, to change your company.

We hope that by reading this book and applying this method you may awaken in other people the desire to act according to new parameters and thus do your part in changing the dynamics of business by firmly placing people back at the core of the system.

How this book can help you, and how to use it

Engaging the Heart in Business deals with an approach to modern markets that focuses on the profound identity that each company bears. The aim of this book is to assist you in **outlining a business model** based on love that will stimulate you to evolve the entire operational structure of your business. We will be discussing love not only as a noble sentiment, but in strategic terms as a tool for building an effective and replicable organizational and procedural structure that will enable your business to flourish: Yet its impact will be wider, improving the entire market and expanding opportunities.

The **Giving Voice to Values** method[1] created by Prof. Mary Gentile, an invaluable mentor and editor of the English version of this book, starts from a simple but enlightening consideration: people generally know what is right to do in ethical terms and respecting their own core values but often they fail to act accordingly, either because they lack the tools to do so or because they fear the outcomes could run counter to their professional objectives.

In this book, we start with the same assumptions. Instead of trying to convince you that it is "good and proper" to act according to a model based on love and what you feel you have inside, we will devote much of this book to providing you with operating tools that can be applied. We will thus demonstrate how useful such tools are to generating results. You might think the terms love and business are incompatible (though perhaps you regret this) and that your humanity and your feelings must be put aside when working. Hence, we consider it essential to give you the tools to act and to complete an activity that is not only in line with your values, but literally guided by them: the results obtained will convince you that following the path of love bears fruit.

Firstly, let's immediately make it clear that ethics and love are not the only approach to doing business; however, they are undoubtedly a means to achieve success that can generate benefits both for those who implement them and for those who are involved in any way. We have no wish to demonstrate that without them it is impossible to obtain results, but simply to propose them as a possible way to achieve your goals.

Always remember that the value of relationships adds to the value expressed by products, services and the brand, thus amplifying it. A powerful ripple effect is created when every part of the organization acts in agreement with the others.

What is the link between business ethics and engaging one's heart?

Ethics is a philosophical discipline that deals with behavior and can be taught through the actions we take. While involved in sales, we discovered that trust drives good commercial transactions and the actions that characterize them. We therefore committed ourselves to studying such mechanisms, proposing a negotiating process that would build trust, one stage after another, and maintain the confidence between the customer and the seller over time. The role played in *Sales Ethics* by the bond of trust generated between people will now be played instead by love. In fact, if you think about it, companies actually attempt to make their customers "fall in love", as we will explain later. Indeed, only a certain form of love can fully justify otherwise incomprehensible buying choices. Hence, we asked ourselves whether it would be possible to teach and develop love as we did with trust. This is because we strongly believe that both these states of mind are useful not only for selling or attracting customers, but also for reforming and guiding the market in an ethical direction. By analyzing data and research, experimenting, verifying

Introduction **3**

and investigating with the contribution of experts, collaborators and customers, we became convinced that it is possible to create the conditions and identify the steps that can develop love in business. From there, love can be further fostered and maintained, thereby obtaining results for ourselves, for the organization of which we are part as well as the customers and all the other actors involved in our activity. Explaining how to do it, step by step, is the goal of this book.

We invite you to read the book slowly, giving yourself time to internalize its contents, complete the suggested activities and give space to the insights that will emerge. Don't worry if everything isn't immediately clear: the journey along the path itself will stimulate reflections that will allow you to learn more about yourself and your work, to recognize your true passions and your real skills, as well as teaching you to leave aside the things that do not reflect your true essence. Bear in mind that everything, all your planned strategies, objectives and operating models, will be updated over time because business is in constant evolution, just like life itself.

How the book is organized

You can decide to use this book in two ways: as a guide to building your marketing plan or as an in-depth manual.

If you have decided to redesign your **marketing plan**, we suggest you follow the topics in the order in which they are presented. In fact, you will be guided, chapter by chapter, to create its supporting structure and to gradually add all the details that will eventually enable you to define your project in detail: brand and identity, mission and vision, customers, offer system, customer journey, competition and people management. If you are only interested in exploring specific topics, you can easily jump from one chapter to another to find solutions to your particular doubts.

Each chapter will contain **stories** and case studies drawn mainly from the everyday life of small and medium-sized companies. This selection is not intended to suggest that large organizations do not adopt or cannot adopt this model (we will cite some virtuous cases). Rather, we wish to demonstrate that everyone can engage the heart in business: it does not require massive budgets and innovation is not a prerogative of large companies.

We would like to specify here that the constituent elements of the strategic plan (study of the customer, choice of positioning, competition analysis…) and the tools we will teach you to use (SWOT analysis, hierarchy of logical levels…) are largely drawn from the economic literature as well as from psychology and neuro-linguistic studies. On the other hand, the interpretation of the results of the analysis and the use of the tools in each specific context, based on the metaphor of love, are the result of our own approach. Indeed, the meaning of a fact can change depending on the viewpoint adopted. Specifically, an approach in which the company is conceived as a fighting force, and the market action as conflict, interprets everything in terms of *opposition*, namely "me against my customers, against the market and against competitors". By contrast, *love* is inclusive: "me together with

Introduction

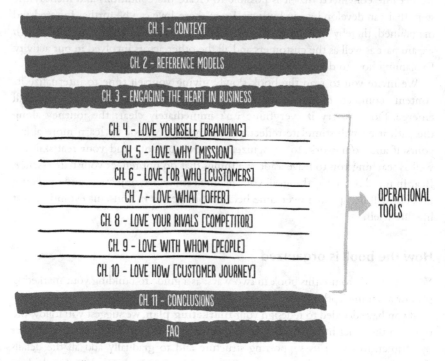

FIGURE 0.1 Illustration of the book's structure

my customers, with the market and with competitors". As we will see, in fact, while the word *compete* is generally interpreted as striving against someone, the word derives from the Latin prefix *com-* indicating 'together', while the root is *petere*, meaning 'to seek', or 'aim at'. Hence, the most literal meaning would be 'seeking together'. We invite you to choose this latter interpretation and to use this approach from time to time when evaluating which actions to take.

The structure of the chapters

Each chapter of the book is organized according to a precise structure to promote clarity and to help you to fully understand the contents.

The discussion opens with a **quote** that introduces the main theme; an **abstract** will briefly explain why you should read the chapter and which topics will be developed. You can thus decide whether you want to read on in that chapter, and it will be easy for you to find a specific topic as required. A **case study**, based on a true story, will help you understand the doubts, dilemmas and challenges that companies must tackle in the context of the specific topic addressed in the chapter.

This will be followed by a detailed explanation of **an element of the marketing plan** and how to "design it" in line with the *Loving Business Model* presented later.

ILLUSTRATION OF THE CHAPTER STRUCTURE

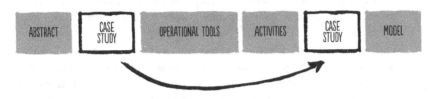

FIGURE 0.2 Illustration of the chapter structure

For each technique presented we will give you practical tips and activities to apply it to your business.

At the end of the chapter you will find out how the case previously presented **concludes**. Some supporting data, provided directly by the companies involved, will help you understand what results have been obtained thanks to the use of the tools presented. Finally, you will find a summary of **what you have learned** and how to add a piece to your business model!

The book is divided into 11 main chapters plus this introduction and the FAQs, i.e. the answers to the most frequently asked questions that may have arisen. The first three chapters describe the analyses and considerations that were necessary to build a business model based on love, from the fourth to the tenth chapters you will discover the seven steps for building your operational plan, while the last chapters contain our conclusions and a rich bibliography for further reading. Here is a more detailed description of the individual chapters:

> **Chapter 1 – The context** will enable you to discover the origins of love in economics and the signs of change taking place in the market today: the factors that we believe justify a transformation in the approach and, in particular, the construction of a business model based on love.
>
> In **Chapter 2 – Reference models for** *Engaging the Heart in Business*, we describe the theories that serve as pillars for this model that legitimates love as a strategic tool. From the *Giving Voice to Values* approach to stakeholder theory, through the Maslow's hierarchy and modern marketing trends, everything will flow into a single vision with a beating heart at its core.
>
> The operational model is presented in **Chapter 3 – Engaging the heart in business** in which the *Loving Business Model* is introduced, the components of the marketing mix are outlined (which we interpret as a love mix) together with the phases of the marketing plan.
>
> From this moment on, each chapter will address a specific operational component of the plan, starting from **Chapter 4 – Love** *yourself*: **Branding and identity**, where the reinterpreted SWOT analysis, together with a method for verifying behavior-value alignment will help you identify the soul of your business and brand identity.

6 Introduction

With this new awareness you will be ready to tackle **Chapter 5 – Love** *why* **you** *do it*: **Having clear and shareable goals**, namely fixing the goals at which you are aiming, identifying your mission and what you want to contribute to building, while producing prosperity for yourself and the system of reference.

To remain in the market, you need customers and in **Chapter 6 – Love** *who* **you do it** *for*: **Who your customers are and what you can do for them**, you will first find out how a reciprocal appeal can be applied to marketing and then redefine the concept of "target" by going back to talking about people whose specific needs and motivations intersect with your mission.

How to shape your value when creating your offer system and the definition of price strategies will be the focus of **Chapter 7 – Love** *what you do*: **The offer system and the creation of value**.

In the business model transformed by love, the relationship with competitors becomes cooperation, backed by a comparison on value and a differentiating promise, as you will discover in **Chapter 8 – Respect your** *rivals*: **How to manage your relationship with the competition**.

People, along with time, represent the most precious element in the business value chain and are fundamental to achieving your desired results. In In **Chapter 9 – Love** *who* **you do it** *with*: **Getting the best from people**, you will discover how to guide and value them.

In **Chapter 10 – Love** *how* **you** *do it*: **The value journey and managing the relationship**, you will learn to build a special and memorable experience for your customer through your design of the customer journey and the touch points, i.e. each interaction and chance to meet.

As you near the end of this journey, you will find in **Chapter 11 – Conclusions** our reflections and further stimulation to become an actor of the changes you desire in your life and in the context that surrounds you.

The **FAQ and Bibliography** will complete the discussion and will indicate further in-depth studies.

An important clarification before starting the journey. In the download area of our site you can download all the activities designed for each chapter so as to complete your personal *Loving Business Model*. Enter the address https://diariodiunconsulente. it/en/engaging-the-heart-in-business-extra/ and enter the confidential password[2] BinL_reader19.

Happy reading and may the journey begin!

Notes

1 We will present this method later in the book, in Chapter 2.
2 We must remind you that the contents of this book, as well as the activities and diagrams available in the download area, are subject to copyright and may only be used in association with this book.

1

THE CONTEXT

Abstract

In a changing market, it is necessary to adapt your paradigms to ensure that your business models remain competitive. In this chapter, we analyze together the main changes that have taken place over the last few years in society and in economics. We believe such alterations support using the new metaphor of love in the current context. Read this chapter if you want to understand why love releases energy that can help your business grow.

Love is in the air: signs that change is underway

Have you noticed that things are changing? In addition to the ongoing political and social upheavals we are seeing throughout the world, the lives of individuals have also changed: your life and our lives, so to speak.

In fact, we now spend much of our time online; we use social media to get news, to share our opinions and exchange news stories though we are frequently unaware of the sources and may not even know how truthful they are. The mass production of news has led to a vast amount of low-cost content and an inevitable decrease in quality. In addition, the aging of populations in Western countries suggests another, fundamental paradigm shift, because with age comes greater reflection and a search for meaning that is further intensified by the fall of dominant ideologies and the now structural crisis of the major religions.

These two apparently separate phenomena may feed into each other, as the increasingly superficial modes of communication underscore an unsatisfied need to find meaning in our lives. This can lead to people adopting positions and convictions based on little or no substance: the trend of a moment becomes a dogma. This use of a vast array of untrustworthy media to satisfy our thirst for meaning necessarily impacts on the economic sphere. We can go beyond accepting and integrating these social needs when creating business models, by attempting to generate a positive impact that will direct market action towards the common good, promote greater awareness and prompt a renewed sense of responsibility. However, it is necessary to ask ourselves what human need unites and explains these phenomena. We believe the common denominator that leads people to frantically interact in search of meaning, and to sometimes choose superficial and pre-packaged answers to this quest, is based on every human being's essential desire **to love and be loved.**

We communicate and interact to have human contact and feel protected by the "network" that we continue to create.

We look for meanings and we weave conversations with the aim of forming bonds with others, to feel accepted and welcomed, exchanging emotions and feelings and thereby giving value to our lives. All these are manifestations of love or, if you prefer, of a search for love.

If it is true that we, indeed all of society, are "love-driven", why not tackle the issue directly even when talking about business?

Economics is a social science. It thus deals with people, communities and scarce resources that must be managed efficiently for a single purpose: to generate well-being. Well-being, not just wealth! Today, people are happy when they are relating to others, when they have access to evolutionary knowledge and information and when they can participate and give meaning to their existence thanks to all this. If this is the case, then economics should deal with love. There is nothing new in this proposition because, as we will discover in the next paragraph, economics and love have been linked for several centuries. Moreover, companies have already begun, more or less consciously, to give signs of movement in this direction; indeed, you need only turn on your TV to recognize the "romantic", intimate and emotional tone of most advertising and content. Feelings are already "selling" goods and services; however, we have not yet proceeded beyond exploiting their attractiveness to actually explore using feelings as a guide to redesign current business models. Why? Our answer is that sentiments, and love especially, are challenging. While it is easy to declare love and rattle it under the nose of a potential lover (or customer), proving and exchanging love, and establishing a true relationship based on this, is a different kettle of fish. Yet the statistics demonstrate that those who succeed can achieve surprising and lasting results. For example, Prof. Raj Sisodia, professor of business ethics at Babson College, demonstrates in his book *Firms of Endearment*[1] that companies that "practice love" on average obtain better results, and faster and for longer, than those that are ruthless. One of the largest consulting companies in the world, McKinsey, has published a study on the negative effects of the selfish or "short-term" corporate vision, dispelling the myth that only the bad guys win in the market.[2] These analyses clearly show that the performance of companies that pursue self-interested behavior is comparable in the short term to those that adopt a more ethical vision of business; however, after just five years the differences in results are in favor of the latter. Over a longer period, this gap becomes an abyss: over a period of 15 years, for example, the results of ethical businesses become ten times better, while the more ruthless organizations struggle, and generally fail, to pass the test of time. We have collected some statistics too, using a sample of about 50 organizations among the clients we meet each year, with an average of 800 people involved in training activities on sales and marketing ethics. Well, what we observed during the two years we were preparing this book is that 83% of the participants declared a significant improvement either in personal performance or in that of their organization after taking part in initiatives that were directed at making their work more humane and respectful of their values. Specifically, almost 20% of them claimed to have achieved an increase in commercial results (higher sales, customer loyalty, word of mouth increase) from the first months after the activity.[3]

So, why do we continue to believe that economics and good sentiments are bad bedfellows? Sometimes we may lack the proper tools to measure results correctly. If you only consider the short-term results, neglecting the side effects and indirect outcomes of your actions on the market, you might overlook the effectiveness of certain behaviors inspired by ethics, respect and love. Moreover, numbers alone fail to highlight the negative effects of misconduct. This may provide an explanation for the seemingly inexplicable flop of certain enterprises that appear destined for success, while other entrepreneurial ideas that initially had trouble finding investors become multi-billion businesses.[4]

If the market and its dynamics could be fully represented through data and figures, a "super algorithm" would have been invented to predict phenomena such as the 2008 crisis or to create the perfect money-making machine. Moreover, as Albert Einstein said, "Not everything that can be counted counts and not everything that counts can be counted".[5]

Of course, introducing love into the business paradigm makes things seem more complicated and not everyone likes the idea. To get good results by applying a business model focused on love – like the one presented in this book – you have to work hard. The prize for those who persist will not only be greater and longer-lasting results. Above all, it is also the achievement of a state of well-being that is more than economic, but closely resembles the happiness that many of us seek. In our opinion, this is the true objective that the social science of economics is called to serve.

Let's summarize the key elements[6] we have identified in the market and in society, which will help you understand why the time has come to change the paradigm:

- **Failure of mechanistic models** – Data, numbers and mathematical theories no longer seem to fully describe the business and its results. Phenomenal cases

10 The context

of success and failure only become clearer if an experiential and emotional component is introduced into customer choices, employee performance and market.

- **Spread of *feminine principles*** – Listening, acceptance, soft skills, or as some authors call them, "feminine principles",[7] have become a must in modern organizations. Personnel managers, and managers in general, seek them in applicants and are committed to developing them among their collaborators.
- **Use of emotions in communication** – Emotions reach the brain before logical words and thoughts.[8] They are, therefore, more important when it comes to convincing someone to buy. This is why advertising uses them so lavishly.[9] Even if you operate in a business to business market, selling to other companies and not to the final consumer, you have to take this into account because it is people who are making the choices.
- **Democratization and transparency of information** – Whether we like it or not, social media is part of our lives, meaning that everything we do now is easily accessible and perhaps more transparent than we would like. People and companies must consider that they cannot fully control who, where, how and when people are talking about them: if you behave incorrectly, sooner or later people will know.
- **Increase in touch points** – Consumer interactions with business have multiplied and diversified. Professionals and managers need a greater number of connections to do their jobs effectively. This omnichannel complexity is a must-have for anyone who wants to remain in the market.
- **Crisis of confidence** – Since the events of 2008 (Lehman's bankruptcy filing and the market crisis) onwards, distrust has become the consumers' fundamental tactic of self-protection. Access to information through the Internet and social networks enables us to collect data and potentially verify in real time the truth and completeness of any information provided by sellers. For companies, a betrayal of their customers' trust can lead to realizing their worst nightmares and risking dangerous negative effects.
- **Importance of loyalty and word of mouth** – The distrust we discussed above is best overcome through word of mouth and loyalty. If someone recommends a product or service impartially, we are more willing to listen to them. Returning customers are also easier and "cheaper" to manage. Research indicates that, on average, selling to a new customer costs five to six times more than an already active contact. Any marketing plan that makes sense must, therefore, focus on encouraging loyalty and positive word of mouth.
- **Sustainability** – There is much talk of environmental and social sustainability, but the concept extends also to the economic sphere.[10] Multinationals, for instance, may sometimes affect the environment and society much more than governments. The application of principles of business ethics in companies can therefore radically improve the conditions in which human beings exist, but to have the means to do so, profits are necessary. There can be no ethics without revenues because there would be no resources to act.

The context **11**

- **Return to spirituality** – From the 1960s onwards, we have witnessed a progressive decline in values and in religion. The resulting identity crisis has led to what Zygmunt Bauman[11] called a "liquid" society in which the only moral reference is one's own interest and ego. More recent generations have, however, begun to react to the loss of moral certainties and to the sense of insecurity that derives from this, with an increased interest in spirituality. New forms of religiosity and renewed awareness have begun to appear in society and, consequently, also affect the markets: customers and companies may be united by common values.
- **Aging populations** – The West is aging; this is a fact. As people get older, they naturally seek deeper meanings and consider their spiritual legacy. Contributing to improving the world or being part of a project that goes beyond oneself are manifestations of a simple but fundamental awareness: we are not eternal, so it is worth trying to make sense of our existence, and our work and purchasing choices are part of the whole.
- **Human and digital integration** – The largest companies in the world are digital. Giants like Apple, Amazon and Facebook were born and developed through new interfaces and virtual modes. Their skill was to conceive new technologies as an enhancement of human relations, not as a substitute for them. Man–machine integration is possible; indeed, it promises unlimited new developments, provided that robots do not replace people in relationships. We need, and will always need, human contact because we are social beings that feed on emotions.
- **Freelancing** – The prospects and working expectations of the new generations are very different from those of previous generations. The desire to do things by oneself and to chart new territories leads to the invention of "unconventional" professional paths and the decline of the steady job as the ultimate goal. Authors like Jeremy Rifkin[12] presume that in the coming years there will be many more freelancers: they will interact on the market in the double role of producers-consumers of services and goods that are currently impossible to imagine.
- **Organizational horizontality** – The desire and the need for independence have made young people less subject to the constraints of a "steady job" and to the power game that it may entail. If we are unable to attract collaborators by continuously providing stimulus that also excites emotion, the most talented will soon leave. But there is more: to talk about feelings and produce an offer that leads customers to fall in love, you must create an organization that is coherent, moving beyond the constraints of the hierarchical structure typical of a military organization.
- **Constant push towards innovation** – The incessant market evolution requires continual paradigm changes with the creation of new standards and organizational models. Innovation, to be first accepted and then implemented, requires consensus. Change is challenging for humans because it involves leaving your comfort zone. Ethics and positive emotions exorcise the fear of the unknown, creating bonds that assure us we are not alone when venturing towards something new.

12 The context

- **Diversity and globalization** – The irreversible phenomenon of globalization has led, sometimes forcibly, to a mixture of cultures, habits and customs. Integration may be necessary, but it should not be confused with an imposition of uniformity and the sacrifice of diversity. Some time ago, a friend of ours explained the concept with the metaphor of two nearby trees whose branches intertwine and embrace seamlessly, but whose roots remain divided. As we wish to demonstrate, in the economic sphere too, loving means integrating the demands and objectives of companies with those of customers and stakeholders.

Hence, we suggest accepting these developments in the market without trying to dominate or alter them, but rather adapting our own behaviors and our reactions to external circumstances. Finance has also become aware of these forces that are agitating the markets and is starting to accept and support them. This is testified by the creation of ethical banking institutions and the renewed interest that the sector devotes to training dealing with sales ethics.[13] Trust is an essential factor when we must decide who will manage our money. Moreover, with the real estate market in crisis, savers who had previously invested in property to protect their investments began to search for reliable companies, with solid long-term business models. These are organizations that have based their success on good relations and on correct behavior, characteristics that – as the statistics confirm – will ensure longevity on the market and good performance.[14] Do you require a further example of how important ethical behavior is for the stock market? Remember what happened to the Volkswagen group when the diesel-engine scandal emerged? According to the data of the major financial newspapers, the shares dropped by 18.6%, signifying a loss in real terms of about 13 billion dollars in value in just the first few days after the news was made public.

There are, therefore, enough good reasons to encourage even the most ruthless economists to consider adopting models inspired by positive feelings such as love. In this book, we will try to guide you towards the foundation of a business that translates principles such as respect, transparency, ethics and love into facts, procedures, work models and, above all, results.

We do not want to convince you that this is the only possible option or that it works *tout-court*, but rather we invite you to experiment with some of the proposed tools in your work and in your organization and then to measure their positive effects. You can only believe it once you have "touched" the results, as many have done before you. In fact, the relationship that links economics and love began many years ago and has already been successfully explored by entrepreneurs, who are perhaps little known but no less extraordinary for that. Let's explore the history in the next section.

The origins of love in economics

What is the link between business and love? At first glance, they seem distant concepts but on deeper reflection we concluded that they share a common

The context **13**

ground: business ethics. In fact, in our opinion, the aim of business ethics is to reestablish the connection between market actions and our deepest values which are generated by the human quest for love, as we hope to demonstrate in this book. Hence, to better understand the relation of business and love, we will trace the history of business ethics.

Officially, the first department of business ethics originated in the United States in the 1970s,[15] though it had its foundations in studies that had previously explored the relationship between profit and morals. In 1976, W. Michael Hoffman, professor of Philosophy at Bentley University, decided to establish a department that would help Economics students to evaluate the moral consequences of their actions and to discern what action is right or wrong in certain situations. Over time, the departments focusing on this theme grew, both in the US and throughout the world, but they were considered fringe areas within the university curricula, optional modules that could be added, if forced to do so, to complete a study program. In the same period, Italy also saw the development of an academic movement interested in civil economics, mainly devoted to the study of alternative forms of capitalism and cooperative models of corporate organization. In fact, Italy had early experience of the introduction of business ethics with entrepreneurs such as Adriano Olivetti[16] or the thousands of successful cooperatives established in the country in the late nineteenth century.

Despite the efforts made in both the US and Europe to promote the subject, up to the 1990s, ethics and economic results still seemed unlikely companions. Some studies on the theory of strategic games attempted to bridge the gap in the wake of the research conducted by Nobel Prize winner John Nash. Nash's results, based on theories and supporting data, demonstrated that cooperation among market players that respect and preserve relational objectives and everyone's interests leads to better results than selfish or self-interested behaviors.[17] This was, however, a period when the market was booming in the final years of the Cold War and any attempt to change economic dynamics would be difficult, even when backed up by science. Only later would business ethics begin to achieve some concrete results and gain visibility thanks to experiments made by luminaries such as Nobel laureate Muhammad Yunus[18] in the field of microcredit, a model that demonstrates how trust can create economic results even in apparently impossible cases. Edward Freeman's theory of stakeholders, which we will discuss in the next chapter, adds another important piece to the overall picture. Nonetheless, the discipline integrating economics and ethics, results and good practices seemed destined to remain confined to a few isolated episodes and the odd, fortunate entrepreneurial experiment that was difficult to replicate. Then came 2008, and the most devastating market crisis that recent history has ever seen.

The crisis blew up in the financial world and then immediately spread to the industrial world before hitting the political world, infecting the whole of society. The now infamous "market crisis" swept like a tsunami over the lives of all, bringing changes and upheavals that spared painfully few. The academic field recognized that the integration of economic studies with ethics could no longer be postponed.

14 The context

Business ethics professors emerged from the academic basement to help others find a possible route to escape the impasse of a market plagued by crises of trust and values; meanwhile, companies, or at least the most enlightened companies, experienced a strong need to rebuild the pact of trust with their customers and with society, through good practices and correct behavior. This is how, at first slowly then increasingly more quickly, ethics and economics resumed a common path. The early effects of this renewed relationship are there for all to see: advertising campaigns replete with good feelings and romanticism, but also corporate missions and visions brimming with declarations of the will to fight poverty, defend the environment and protect flora and fauna, or other equally noble initiatives albeit, at times, lacking credibility. Certainly, an impulse to align with the economy's ethical trend has grown from the exceptional results of virtuous companies such as Whole Foods Market or Patagonia in the US, and Cucinelli or Illycaffè in Italy, to name just a few.

In the current economic and social environment, business ethics is a proven and increasingly used approach to the market; its growing success has prompted the establishment of institutions, bodies and companies for its promotion and development.

In the long term, we will find out who has invested seriously in these issues and who has merely used the principles of ethics, sustainability and love as a window-dressing to communicate attractive content that lacks substance. Sooner or later there will be a selection based on coherence because, as you will discover, being ethical has costs in terms of commitment, choices and resources.

You will have noticed that during this brief, and certainly limited, excursus on the history of the relationship between business and ethics that we associate with love, we have often used the expression "rediscovered relationship". In fact, the history of the ethical economy, which integrates social aims and targets the complete evolution of the human being by pursuing an idea of well-being that goes beyond material gain, was born many years earlier, to be exact, at the dawn of economic thought. The birthplace of this concept, at least in its most concrete application,[19] was Italy. As Massimo Folador tells us in his illuminating text *L'organizzazione Perfetta*,[20] the first structures that had the declared objective of being economically self-sufficient, focusing on the evolution of the individual and of the community, were the Benedictine monasteries. In AD 534, Saint Benedict decided to form communities of monks around a simple formula: *ora et lege et labora* – pray and study and work – based on the premise that we are composed of spirit, mind and body. Benedict's primary purpose was to save the Western Christian culture from the imminent attack of the "barbarians", who were invading the Italian peninsula after the fall of the Eastern Roman Empire. His formula was so successful that it grew exponentially: at one time, his order had approximately 75,000 monasteries, in some of which over 20,000 people were working. These communities were scattered throughout the world and have contributed over the centuries to promote social growth, the improvement of living conditions and the creation of wealth, thanks also to the development of farming, weaving, distillation and managerial

The context **15**

techniques. Basing his precepts on the needs of humans, Saint Benedict managed to establish a "corporate" organization whose success has continued to the present day.

Where there is love there can be no fear

What model, then, should inspire tomorrow's company? If, as we have seen in the previous paragraphs, business ethics seems to provide a solution to reviving markets and building a prosperous future, what should entrepreneurs, managers and professionals do to design their business accordingly? This book contains our answer to these questions.

Since 2011, the year in which we founded our studio, we have provided over 200 organizations with courses and consultancy, involving a total of about 5,000 people in our activity. We have seen businesses set up that were perfect on paper,[21] but then abruptly disappeared; we have also seen apparently utopian business projects flourish and prosper. Some of the projects we followed are presented as case studies in this book, while we lacked the space for many other equally relevant cases: from the most ruthless "for profit" companies, which initially approached ethics as a fad and then found they were better and richer, to social cooperatives that, by making peace with profit, were able to finance additional services dedicated to the weakest, and finishing with those "ethical companies" that, in many cases, had to discover the difference between declaring oneself as ethical and then acting coherently.

We wish to conclude the chapter by reflecting on the current emergence of extremist policies. So, is the world moving away from cooperation, ethics and love? We believe that the examples cited in the section on the changes currently underway are real and active and can become right or wrong depending on their interpretation and the way they are implemented. When discussing the return of emotions in communication strategies, for example, we must not forget that hatred and fear also belong to this category. The same is true for this aspect as for each of the trends highlighted at the beginning of the chapter: desire for independence, return to spirituality, crisis of confidence, horizontality, failure of mechanistic models, etc. They can all fuel positive or negative behavioral models. If you think about it, our present situation is similar to that experienced by Saint Benedict when he decided to establish his order to face possibly threatening changes in society. Now, as then, the answer is to start from organized and self-sufficient groups that lead the world towards something better, gathering around a common and noble goal. In the past, these communities were monasteries; today, they could be companies.

We are convinced that the answer to individualism, selfishness and division cannot simply be do-goodism and altruism, but rather that we need to introduce more structured concepts such as **mutuality** that does not neglect our interests but integrates them with those of others, and the **ethics** that are based on strategically studied, valuable actions that are performed with competence and ability. For ethics to be useful in business, they must not only involve prohibitions presented in rules and deontological codes but indicate what it is right to do and how to do it in order to achieve respect for people, the environment, society and economic balance.

Being ethical is not choosing the easiest option, but doing the right thing and this can be incredibly difficult if you are not prepared. In this we are perfectly aligned with the thoughts of Mary Gentile, author of the *Giving Voice to Values* program, promoter of the idea that it is essential to deliver concrete tools for those who do business to act effectively and ethically; otherwise, business ethics will remain a luxury for a few or an academic utopia.

What you have learnt

The social, cultural, environmental and economic context in which your business operates is important: you, therefore, must consider it as an "interest bearer" that must be listened to and respected, or even better as a "value bearer". We, therefore, advise you to carry out a preliminary analysis of the environment in which you operate, perhaps starting from what you consider its limitations; if framed in a new perspective, they might become a source of inspiration and innovation.

Notes

1 Sisodia, Raj, David B. Wolfe, and Jagdish N. Sheth. *Firms of Endearment: How World-Class Companies Profit from Passion and Purpose.* Pearson, 2003.
2 McKinsey Global Institute. *Measuring the Economic Impact of Short-Termism*, January 2017.
3 The data are taken from our internal statistical survey available on the website www.passodue.com. For more information and full details, contact the authors of this book.
4 Any examples? Just look at Apple, a company whose products were initially rejected by the major corporations in that sector, but succeeded thanks primarily to the tenacious love, bordering on obsession, that founder Steve Jobs had for his creations.
5 Handwritten sign in Einstein's study at Princeton University.
6 To explore these considerations on the current economic context and the Italian situation further, we suggest you read *Un futuro da costruire bene: Ventiduesimo rapporto sull'economia globale e l'Italia*, edited by Deaglio Mario for the Luigi Einaudi Research and Documentation Center.
7 Winters, Carol. "The Feminine Principle: An Evolving Idea." *Quest* 94, no. 5 (November–December 2006): 206–209, 215.
8 As reported by Poli Erica Francesca in the book *Anatomy of Healing*, the reaction times of the amygdala, an area of the limbic system responsible for the impulsive response to stimuli, is 12 milliseconds, while the cortical response, which allows a logical reflection, is in the order of 25 milliseconds.
9 During the journey that led us to the writing of this book, we decided, in a light-hearted way, to document our research: we photographed and collected examples of communication that used words like love, feeling, care, respect, well-being or others with "emotional" associations. We collected a lot of them, and we realized that, in some merchandise sectors, at least one out of three communications contain them! To see some of these images visit www.facebook.com/diariodiunconsulente/

The context **17**

10 The reference is to the concept of sustainable growth officially sanctioned by the United Nations in August 2015 with the launch of the Sustainable Development Goals.

11 Bauman, Zygmunt. *Liquid Life*. Polity Press, 2005.

12 Rifkin, Jeremy. *The Zero Marginal Cost Society: The Internet of Things, the Collaborative Commons, and the Eclipse of Capitalism*. Reprint ed. St. Martin's Griffin, 2015.

13 Even *Passodue*, our consulting agency operating in the fields of ethical sales and marketing, in 2017–18 recorded a significant increase in training and consulting requests from companies and institutions operating in the banking or financial sector.

14 Wall Street, the largest financial market in the world, has seen a significant increase in "responsible investments", i.e. the purchase of shares of ethical companies. Morgan Stanley confirms that investments in this sector have grown by 23% only in the two-year period of 2014–16 according to Audrey Choi, the company's chief sustainability officer, at Barron's first Impact Investing Summit held in 2018. The growth of ethical finance is available on www.gabv.org and www.febea.org, websites of organizations that in Europe and across the globe bring together banks and institutions operating in the sector.

15 We should clarify that although there was not previously a "department" of business ethics, the subject matter was part of both business education and some of the economic writings for much longer (e.g. Adam Smith, *Theory of Moral Sentiments*).

16 For further information, see www.fondazioneadrianolivetti.it

17 Nash, John F. *Equilibrium Points in n-Person Games*. National Academy of the USA, 1950.

18 For further insight, see the following book: Yunus, Muhammad. *Banker to the Poor: Micro-Lending and the Battle Against World Poverty*. PublicAffairs, 2008.

19 Aristotle, Plato and other classical philosophers had already dealt in theoretical form with the relationships between economics and ethics.

20 Folador, Massimo. *L'organizzazione Perfetta. La regola di San Benedetto. Una saggezza antica al servizio dell'impresa moderna*. Guerini Next, 2016.

21 Just to have a measure of how often apparently infallible companies turn out to be ephemeral, just think that 52% of the organizations that were present in the Fortune 500 in 2000, the list that brings together the best US companies, no longer exist today.

2

REFERENCE MODELS FOR *ENGAGING THE HEART IN BUSINESS*

Abstract

Everything we will deal with in the following chapters is the result of our own experience and research, but it is rooted in consolidated theoretical models that have been applied and tested by experts in economics, sociology and psychology. Whether they are university professors, therapists or entrepreneurs, each of the people who created these approaches achieved excellent results for both themselves and for others when they were applied in practice. In this chapter, we will clarify the inspiring principles of this book, indicating the sources to which you can refer to better investigate the assumptions on which it is based.

From theories to facts: the *Giving Voice to Values* approach

Our work is inspired and guided by the approaches to business ethics that gained wider dissemination in the aftermath of the 2008 economic crisis, as described in the previous pages. Business ethics deals with introducing ethics to management practices and to the economy in general. Today, practically every self-respecting business school has a department, faculty and/or course dedicated to this subject. Those teaching these courses are involved in helping their students to understand what is right and what is wrong to do in certain situations, but also to recognize an "ethical dilemma" when they are faced with one. While highly noble objectives, they risk remaining theoretical if they cannot be clearly applied in practice. In fact, research has shown that many of the courses provided by universities on the issues of ethics in economics are perceived by students as being impractical, or even far removed from the realities of business.[1] Paradoxically, the methods used to provide courses created to promote a more ethical approach to doing business have, in some cases, convinced participants that ethics and business are incompatible and that the application of the principles expressed by business ethics makes corporate life both complex and cumbersome, at the expense of results. A few years ago, Mary Gentile noted this paradoxical effect and became convinced that it was necessary to redesign the entire teaching method on the subject, transforming it into a tool for making operational decisions. This is how the *Giving Voice to Values* (GVV) program was born.[2] The method is founded on the belief that people often behave incorrectly, not because they do not know what is right or wrong when faced with an ethical dilemma, but because they do not know how to act according to their values effectively. Hence, providing courses to explain what should be done, without helping the participants understand how to act concretely, was both useless and potentially frustrating for them.

Mary has since been occupied in developing communication and negotiation techniques that enable people to act effectively and coherently once they have decided what is right to do. As Figure 2.1 shows, GVV represents the missing piece in the approaches proposed by business ethics and finally transforms the principles into actions.

What have been the results of this approach? We can describe them indirectly through the great diffusion that GVV has had in over ten years of existence. To date, the program has generated many scientific articles and a series of books detailing its application in various fields. Mary and her collaborators have lectured at many of the world's major universities, as well as being involved in the teaching and dissemination of online courses and speaking at international conferences and symposia.

GIVING VOICE TO VALUES MODEL

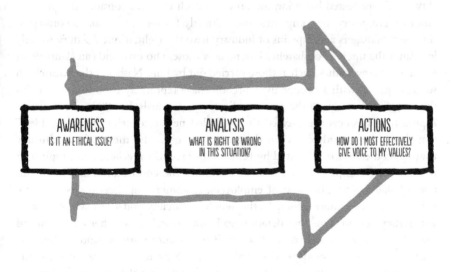

FIGURE 2.1 *Giving Voice to Values* model

20 Reference models

Articles dedicated to the GVV approach have appeared in the *Financial Times*, the *New York Times*, *Forbes* and the *Harvard Business Review*, to name just a few. Over 1,170 educational institutions, companies and organizations on seven continents have piloted GVV and/or turned to Mary for advice and suggestions to help them evolve their internal procedures.[3]

Mary Gentile was the editor of the English version of our first book, *Sales Ethics*, having immediately felt the affinity of our method with that of GVV. What could be more effective to spread the principles of business ethics than to offer practical tools that show how ethics can become a factor of success, rather than a hindrance, in sales negotiations?

Our relationship with Mary further convinced us that, to make a real contribution, we had to conceive of each act in terms of applications, asking ourselves "What operational indications can we provide for people? What step will they be ready to take tomorrow?" This book has also been designed with this in mind.

Ethics derives from the Greek *Ethos* = practical behavior. Thus, you cannot be ethical on paper alone, just as you cannot be "theoretically" in love. As Bernardo Bertolucci's movie *The Dreamers* reminds us: "Love does not exist; only proof of your love exists". We interpret this as a clear invitation to act coherently. Everything that follows is, therefore, inspired by the approach created by Mary Gentile and supported by other sources. Let us explore together the other theories on which this book is based in the sections that follow.

Plurality and interdependence: stakeholder theory

Classical economics based its thinking on the ideas of authors such as Adam Smith and Milton Friedman, advocates of profit maximizing and the efficiency and rationality of self-interested behavior, the only approach that was considered capable of ensuring prosperity for companies and, indirectly, for society overall. According to this view, managers and captains of industry have the right, if not the duty, to only look after the interests of shareholders, namely those who own and can claim rights to capital. Many studies, such as those carried out by John Nash and the research on strategic games with a cooperative outcome, have repeatedly tried to counter this thinking based solely on the interest of a few individuals. In 1983, an alternative approach to business was created that included new categories of "stakeholders" that should be considered when designing strategies. The thesis of **stakeholder theory**, as the approach created by R. Edward Freeman is called, is as simple as it is irrefutable: companies cannot survive without the contribution and input not only of shareholders, but also of employees, customers, suppliers (called primary stakeholders) and, more generally, the whole of society and the environment in which they operate. This consideration leads immediately to another: organizations must take care of the welfare of all actors if they want to prosper and continue to exist. This strategic interdependence also creates a protection network for companies that not only allows them to operate efficiently but also ensures the support of a large network.

Over the years, Freeman's idea has been studied and expanded, and in some cases even applied, becoming a successful operational model.

Today, stakeholder theory has moved beyond the theoretical stage to become an actual business model adopted by hundreds of successful organizations, e.g. B Corporations,[4] which are aware that to receive value it is firstly necessary to generate it and offer it to customers and those who work with us. The market players directly involved in our processes do not drain our organization. Rather, they are value producers; they are interconnected by bonds that when well-structured can form a "chain" that will generate benefits for everyone. If you create competition between stakeholders (for example, by creating situations that undermine good relations between the company, employees and customers), you reverse this circle, transforming it from a "virtuous" circle to a "vicious" one, thereby generating inefficiencies and waste that will threaten the very existence of your organization. In this new perspective, management is no longer accountable solely to shareholders, who are just one of the interest groups and sometimes not even the most "powerful", given that customers often decide the fate of a business. Our strategies should, therefore, include the greatest possible number of advantages for the greatest number of actors. Stakeholders must be considered assets or strategic pillars of our organizations: the more stakeholders we can involve in our market activity, the greater guarantee that we will have a network of supporters who will support us during the "race" for success.

Measuring evolution: Maslow's hierarchy of needs

Many years ago, psychologist Abraham Maslow made a surprising discovery: all humans are different, but they share the same quest to satisfy needs. In his research, Maslow went on to identify a pyramidal hierarchy of these needs. According to his classification system, as human beings we first deal with satisfying our physiological needs (eating, sleeping, reproducing etc.); we then ensure our safety and security, after which our attention focuses on belonging to a specific group of people within which we will be recognized and protected. Once this is achieved, we strive to develop our individuality and uniqueness, generating self-esteem and esteem from others. Not until the end will we pursue happiness, or self-actualization, corresponding to the highest step in the hierarchy. The further we can progress up the **hierarchy of needs**, the more we will evolve and achieve our deeper goals, contributing to the improvement of our condition and those of the people around us.

Companies are made up of people; hence the system described above is equally applicable. In an interview for our blog diariodiunconsulente.com, entrepreneur Luigi Zoia, president of the Conscious Business Group (an association that deals with spreading awareness in the world of work), reminded us that for a company Maslow's level of physiological needs can be compared to the search for profit; the search for safety is comparable to the need for stable cash flows over time; belonging corresponds to positioning within a specific market sector; esteem translates into

Reference models

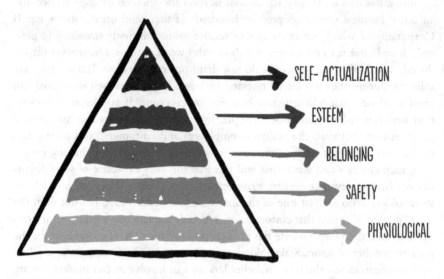

FIGURE 2.2 Maslow's hierarchy of needs

the reputation that permits a company to be recognized and differentiated from competitors. Self-actualization, on the other hand, correlates with mission and vision, the goals that an organization targets and that go beyond economic interests to include a large number of people or even the entire community.

Therefore, evolution for an enterprise means setting ever-higher goals, i.e. scaling Maslow's hierarchy of needs. Zoia also argues that an organization's growth can be measured from the quality of the objectives it sets itself. A company that only deals with making profit is at the beginning of the path that leads to generating value for itself and for others. On the other hand, as Prof. T. Levitt states, "Believing that entrepreneurs do business only for profit would be like believing that human beings exist only to eat", a sentence that seems to contain an undeniable truth: human action, and market action in particular, cannot be attributed exclusively to the achievement of material objectives; there is much more. Organizations cannot survive for long without meeting the more advanced needs. When creating our operational model, we will take into account Maslow's studies, using his system of ranking needs not only to define the business objectives but also to understand how to ensure that we satisfy our stakeholders, be they customers, employees, suppliers or whatever stakeholder we meet along the way.

The love code: a path to happiness

Is there a valid theory of love? Before writing this book, we asked ourselves this question. If a sufficiently plausible one existed, we could refer to it to construct

Reference models **23**

an effective business model by analogy. In fact, as we have made clear previously, modern marketing makes generous use of the concept of "love", now considered more effective and substituting for the aggressive style used in the preceding models. Marketing, like business in general, cannot operate without a reference structure. Yet who can explain to us how love works clearly enough to permit us to derive practical indications?

The host of psychological and sociological studies that have investigated the subject do not seem to have reached a common conclusion. However, our research has brought to light certain considerations that we wish to share because they will allow us to define the structure of business based on love.

Let's start from the reflection that "to love" is a verb and as such should be placed in one of the two macro categories in which verbs are classified according to the English language: state or motion. Then let's try to understand to which one it belongs. We could define love as the condition in which we feel a deep and lasting feeling for another being. If we accept this definition, it would seem that "to love" is a verb of state, i.e. it describes an inner condition. But if we delve deeper into the concept, we discover that true love aims at happiness both for ourselves and for our loved one. A condition, that of being happy, which must be sought, and which therefore implies action. Loving then seems to pass into the category of dynamic activities. It is, therefore, both a verb of state and a verb of motion.

This strange, dual nature leads us to reflect on another verb that has a similar duality: **to be**. Being is again a verb of state but also of movement: life is, in fact, intrinsically dynamic.

To love and *to be* thus appear linked by a common destiny as it is difficult to place either in pre-set categories. This "anomaly" suggests a similar DNA. This is so pronounced that we suspect that, in the end, *loving* and *being* actually mean something similar.

Another aspect highlights this convergence of meanings: the goal that both these actions/states possess. The desire of those who love, and the condition for which we strive when we feel love for someone, is happiness. If happiness is the goal of love, we should then consider what the goal of being is. A big question, whose answer seems to be contained in one of the most significant documents in history: The United States Declaration of Independence, a symbol of freedom and self-determination.

Let us recall the words of the founding fathers: *"We hold these truths to be self-evident, that all men are created equal, that they are endowed by their Creator with certain unalienable Rights, that among these are Life, Liberty and the pursuit of Happiness…"*.

Happiness is, therefore, the basis of being and loving.

Whatever the connection between loving and being might be, we have discovered that if we deal with happiness (their ultimate goal) we can better understand the nature of both of them.

In our exploration of the concept of happiness, we will be helped by Dr. Erica Poli, a psychologist and psychotherapist who has investigated the subject deeply with field research and scientific experiments.

24 Reference models

Her analysis suggests three levels of happiness:

Competitive happiness – Linked to the possession of things and, as the term implies, leads us to compete with others to grab more goods.

Conditional happiness – Depends on others and the circumstances in which we find ourselves. Like the preceding level it also "comes from outside" but is satisfied not with material objects but with relationships.

Unconditional happiness – A dynamic state (which Poli, in fact, calls "flow") of profound inner well-being that feeds on the condition of being and experiencing life.

The first two levels can be described as the search for something that is not yet fully satisfied, and as such they refer more to the "motor nature" of being and loving, while the last level describes a condition of the soul, thus giving full legitimacy to the dual nature – of state and of motion – of happiness and consequently of loving and being. Achieving unconditional happiness means dynamically remaining in a fulfilling condition of being, which corresponds to unconditional love for oneself, for others and for what surrounds us, and more generally everything that happens in our lives.

The connection with Maslow's hierarchy of needs, described above, is immediately evident as in both cases there is an evolutionary path, only here the progression is not from the bottom upwards, but from the **outside to the inside**.

How can we complete the evolutionary steps that will allow us to reach full happiness and love unconditionally? What attitudes and skills must be developed to make this journey?

There is an ingredient without which love, like any other form of relationship, cannot evolve and remain over time: trust. Indeed, much of our research has been devoted to the dynamics of the building of trust and we illustrated this progression with the **Circle of Trust**. When we were writing our book on sales, we studied and analyzed the negotiation techniques and behavior of successful salespeople and we discovered that, more or less consciously, they endeavored to build, increase and maintain trust with their customers. In doing so, they had to advance through different levels of difficulty: a progression dependent on the use of specific techniques and requiring attention. From the collection and observation of hundreds of real negotiations, we designed the six rings of the *Circle of Trust* which describe precisely the phases of the relationship between customer and seller, but which – by extension – can also be applied to the relationship between consumers and companies. Love must be based on trust, yet the bond between these two concepts goes beyond this initial requirement.

Love forms the very core of trust; it is not just a premise for loving. To further explore the links between love and trust, let's consider their opposites. What feeling is the opposite of trust? The fear of being betrayed, of not being accepted, of being used or otherwise deceived. What is the opposite of love? We would be tempted to say hatred, but we only hate out of fear: fear of what is different, fear of suffering, fear of not being accepted, of being betrayed... As is true of trust, the opposite of

Reference models   25

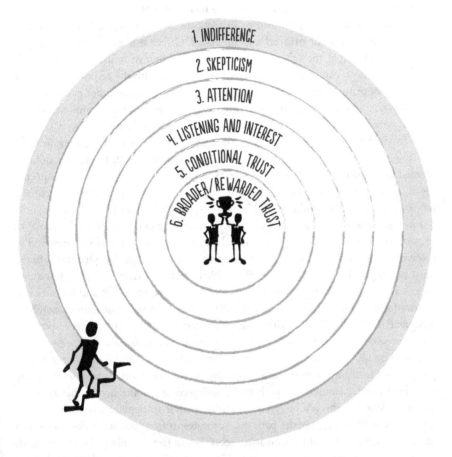

FIGURE 2.3 The *Circle of Trust*

love is also fear. Fear acts in a way that clashes with a positive drive: while love and trust lead us to act towards evolution, recharging our energies, elevating our spirit and bringing us closer to others, fear blocks us or encourages involution; fear enmeshes us in the search for control and the power connected to it. It takes us further away, separates us and empties us of vital energy.

In these pages, you will learn that many mistaken choices in business are dictated by fear or the actions that it determines such as anger, greed or the search for power and abuse.[5]

In our previous book, we emphasized how trust is regulated by the law of reciprocity: first, you offer trust, and then you receive it. This is a concept we must bear in mind as the same thing happens with love. You must be the first one to offer trust and love if you hope to be reciprocated. But how do we offer something we don't have? The levels of the *Circle of Trust* represent real "passages in an evolutionary state" that we must also develop within ourselves. As long as we feel indifferent and skeptical, are inattentive, uninterested and uninvolved in the exchange with the other person, then we will be unable to feel (and therefore offer) trust or love.

We wish to call your attention to our choice of terms: trust, like love, is not given and not taken but **offered** and **received**. Offering is a ritual gesture that is respectful and simple; the other person may freely accept or refuse; the offer, therefore, requires both careful preparation and compliance with the response. The other person is not primed to receive but will await the offer. On the other hand, you can give or take without necessarily involving the other party, but you cannot offer and receive without the other person exercising their power of choice.

We would like this awareness to accompany you while you read *Engaging the Heart in Business* because we have often heard people remark, "Well, I gave but nobody seemed to appreciate it", or "Yes, I received something in return but I really expected more". Offering means choosing what to offer to the other person based on their interests, not just giving them something and expecting them to like it. Learning how to offer, as we will try to do together, will, therefore, mean designing our proposal to respect the needs and values of your interlocutors, so that they will be interested in receiving it. Similarly, anyone receiving something in exchange for what they offered must be prepared to accept a value that is likely to take a different form. Just as we cannot impose on others how to love us, but must learn to accept and let ourselves be loved according to the abilities of the other person, so we must train ourselves to recognize the "return" value with which the market and our customers respond to our offer: a necessary skill if we are to fully evaluate our business action.

Based on all these theories, we have created a business model that can generate prosperity, the common good and happiness. Its structure will be characterized by two fundamental elements: a path to be followed and some actors that must be involved. Whether this is a hierarchy to climb, a circle to penetrate or a set of levels through which to progress, the path that separates us from our happiness (which in economic terms we could define as "success") is, in fact, populated by people with whom we will share it and stages to tackle. Then follow us in exploring what we have called the *Loving Business Model*.

What you have learnt

We learnt about the theories and ideas on which this book is based. Bear these theories and these steps in mind all the time you are reading. You will need them to understand the reasons and the choices we make in terms of methodology and the use of the tools. Should you fail to understand the connection between what we are saying and the metaphor of love, you can go back and read this chapter again. Other questions and doubts will be dispelled in the FAQ section at the end of the book.

Notes

1 For more information on the subject, you can consult the studies conducted by Dr. Peter Edward of Newcastle University Business School; we also recommend the following articles: Haidt, Jonathan. "Can You Teach Businessmen to Be Ethical?" *The Washington Post*, January 13, 2014; Stark, Andrew. "What's the Matter with Business Ethics?" *Harvard Business Review*, May–June, 1993.

2 Mary developed the program thanks to the support of the Aspen Institute, which also served as an incubator, and of the Yale School of Management; from 2009 to 2016 GVV was supported by Babson College and currently by the UVA Darden School of Business.

3 For further information, see www.givingvoicetovalues.org and www.givingvoiceto valuesthebook.com

4 Honeyman, Ryan, and Tiffany Jana. *The B Corp Handbook*. Berrett-Koehler Publishers Inc., 2014.

5 For further reading on this subject, we suggest the following book: Casella, Sergio. *Vincere la paura in Azienda*. Tecniche Nuove, 2019.

3

ENGAGING THE HEART IN BUSINESS

Abstract

The path we have set out for you to follow will lead you to reflect on some important issues and thus define your own business model inspired by love. We have called the development of this path the *Loving Business Model* and we will present it in this chapter. Reading this chapter will enable you to frame the work you are going to complete as you progress through the book within a precise project. This chapter is central, or perhaps we should say, the "heart" of the book.

Love as a choice: the *Loving Business Model*

The previous chapter analyzed the theories and concepts that will provide support as we define a new business model based on love. Yet it is built on more than theory! Both the model and the related operating techniques have developed from our fieldwork and the independent research we conducted between 2016 and the beginning of 2018, involving 75 organizations and roughly 1,300 people coming from sectors such as information technology, plumbing and heating, insurance, banking, cooperation, logistics, pharmaceutics, design and furniture, trade associations, business services and consultancy. The research was carried out empirically, i.e. through the direct observation of good practices and by investigating the tools and business models used by the companies that obtained better results. We also studied cases of failure, from which we derived much useful knowledge.

At this earlier stage of study, we also implemented experimentation to test the effectiveness of the approach we were developing. Roughly 25% of the companies with whom we worked during the period indicated chose to completely redesign their marketing strategies and actions according to the *Loving Business Model*. The feedback obtained through our questionnaires showed 90% satisfaction of all the 75 companies with which we worked, with a significant improvement in results in terms of increased sales performance, reinforcement of reputation and positive word of mouth, as well as greater strategic vision and an improvement in relationships at all levels, accompanied by increased motivation.

We realize that our work cannot be considered complete or exhaustive, as is true for all serious research, but these encouraging numbers led us to codify this approach in order to make it available to those folks who, like you, want to improve the effectiveness of their organization and their relationship with the market. What we learned as we investigated further is the validity of a simple formula: if you love what you do, you can involve your customers, collaborators and partners at a deeper emotional level while in return receiving prosperity, in both tangible and intangible terms.

Before presenting the model, we must clarify exactly what *Engaging the Heart in Business* means.

Being in love with your business and your work is a situation that enables you to create a "love bond" between you and the people involved in your business, whatever their role.

> You are in love with your business when you receive energy from it, in the form of tangible and intangible assets, as well as getting an emotional return.
>
> You are in love with your business and your work when it enables you to express your true values, and it is by doing so that your results improve. The more you feel you are reflected in what you do and the way you do it, as well as your motivations for doing it, the more those around you – your customers, collaborators, partner companies and the environment – will understand and appreciate your contribution.
>
> You are in love with your business when you stop fearing your competitors and attempting to control what is happening around you, but follow your own path, your own mission, certain of the unique and unrepeatable contribution that you can give to the market.
>
> You are in love with your business when you go beyond telling a fascinating story but become part of this story and bring it to life every day.
>
> You are in love with your business when you do not hide behind others but take full responsibility, evolving yourself while comprehending how to transform others, all the others, including your competitors, into bearers not only of interest but also of value, altering their condition from that of stakeholder to the much richer role of *valueholder*, in the certainty that they will contribute, directly and indirectly, to achieve an evolutionary project that is beyond and above all of us.

30 Engaging the heart in business

What could be more powerful for the success of a business than nurturing such a profound and benevolent feeling? We are talking not only about its effect on economic results: *Engaging the Heart in Business* is a "state of grace" in which everything functions well, both outside and inside the organization. When you have achieved it, your professional projects will produce results in a natural way, your emotions will become valuable, and as Adam Grant[1] would say, "the more you give, the more you will get". Achieving this condition is far from easy. Moreover, it is a dynamic process and thus requires a constant input to be maintained and balanced.

We want this book to teach you how to manage the relationship with your work and your business so that it is in keeping with your true essence, in a continuous exchange that will teach you to love and respect, personally and professionally, yourself and others.

At the roots of *Engaging the Heart in Business*: the pillars of the operational model

We have given you a definition of *Engaging the Heart in Business*, but we have not yet said how you can achieve this condition. If what you have read so far has convinced you to use love as a tool for success and to transform your business, what you need is an operating model to inspire you to rebuild your organization and rethink the tools you use to interact with the market. We are now going to propose an approach that is effectively a synthesis of the different models that we have observed, studied and applied with our customers.

We believe there are **eight pillars**, or principal elements, that define the life of an organization, be it a company, a firm of professionals, a cooperative or any other body that interacts with the market:

1. Yourself, your identity or brand
2. The environment and social context in which you operate, i.e. the set of stakeholders
3. Your customers
4. Your objectives and mission
5. Your offer
6. Your internal customers, namely those working in your team
7. The competitors
8. The relationships that link all these factors that are organized into an experience or journey aimed at creating value

You must control and manage all eight of these elements in the best possible way, i.e. "with love", in order to claim to be *Engaging the Heart in Business*. These elements are also interconnected and interact with each other, as shown in Figure 3.1, and together constitute what we will now call the *Loving Business Model*.

Each chapter will deal with one of these pillars. For the moment, let's find out a little more about each one.

Engaging the heart in business 31

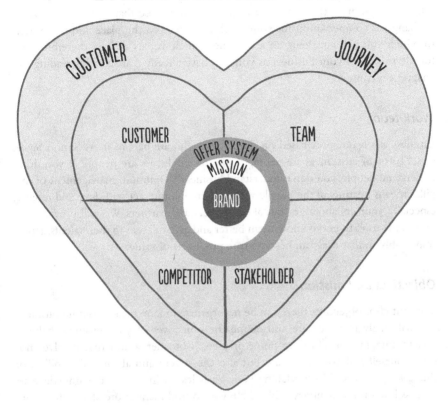

FIGURE 3.1 *Loving Business Model*

Yourself: brand

Taking care of this first "pillar" means learning to love yourself. So, you will have to ask yourself "Who am I?" And then, in the light of this awareness, shoulder your own responsibility, in order to respect and enhance your uniqueness with coherence and transparency. We will later see that there is a series of tools that will help you set off along a path that aims to build an identity based on self-love and then "lovingly" make it available to others and to the market. The brand is central to our model because it embodies the essence of an organization from which every market action originates.

Context and the stakeholders

Every business exists within a social, economic and environmental context. The system in which you operate must be known and respected, and you must assume full responsibility for the exchanges in your relationship with it. Within each

32 Engaging the heart in business

section we will offer you tools to interact with the market and society, in order to "give back" some of the value you have generated. Your identity, the tangible and intangible resources that you need to produce and those that you will receive in exchange as compensation for your work are linked to the place and the system to which you belong. Being an active and conscious part of it is, therefore, vital for the success of your business, as you will have already realized after reading the chapter on context.

Work team

Business is a team sport based on the people who are part of it. As Simon Sinek says, "100% of customers are people, 100% of employees are people. If you don't understand people, you don't understand business". Optimum management of this pillar means treating all the people with whom you interact with love and respect, especially your collaborators, but also suppliers and partners. We will provide you with some tools to get to know them better and give full rein to their talents, acting responsibly so that they can become true producers of value.

Objectives and mission

Without clear objectives there can be no organization, no project and no business. We will analyze the nature and define the objectives of your business, helping you to integrate an altruistic point of view, a broader vision that involves not only yourself and your company, but also the system and all the other pillars of the *Loving Business Model*. Making your goals less "selfish" will not impede your success but, on the contrary, will enable you to find many more allies when pursuing your results. As you can see from the illustration, the objectives and the mission are positioned in the central rings precisely because each element of the model plays a part in achieving the objectives and contributes, in various ways, to the fulfillment of the mission.

Offer system

What we offer to the market is not purely tangible; it also has an intangible component. We are not referring to the services that are now linked to the sale of any product; rather, we are referring to the emotional involvement that – through the offer – connects companies and customers. We wanted to distinguish the offer from the "self" of the company to emphasize how important it is not to identify with what we create for others. Once generated, the offer, just like a work of art, becomes separate from its creator: a common heritage shared with others, who interpret it and regenerate it by adding value. Love also exists independently of us and creates something new and wider than the sum of the individual parts, exactly as happens with the offer system.

Competitor

Your competitors participate alongside you to reach shared goals. The role of competition and rivalry is fundamental to make the market efficient, to drive innovation and continuously stimulate you to do better. Competition, like sales, is not a zero-sum game where one person wins and another loses, but rather a system that trains and exercises merit. In this sense, your competitors help you to add value to your offer, allowing you to stand out and compete based on what you do well.

Customer

Contrary to what you might expect, the customer does not occupy a central place in the *Loving Business Model*. Despite being one of the undisputed protagonists of the activities of any company, the customer's point of view cannot be the only one taken into consideration when designing the operating model. We believe that, in the interests of all the players involved, including the customers themselves, the strategic choices must be addressed. This should take into account both the needs of the final consumer and the system of relationships of which the organization is part, as well as the coherence with its objectives, values and identity. Thus, we do not want your company to be untrue to its true self or, worse still, to make false promises with a view to attracting more customers. Rather, it is essential to build a balanced and generative relationship with your customers.

Customer journey

What binds all these elements together? The experience that customers and consumers will have during the use of your products and services. During this journey, they will get to know your brand and your offer, they will interact with the people who work for you and with you, but they will also come into contact with other customers and with your competitors, who will offer them alternatives. This connective tissue is represented in our illustration in the form of an outer frame that contains and connects all the elements. We will address the customer journey in Chapter 10 and find out that it consists of a series of specific moments. Each business is characterized by different phases that you will learn to identify and manage better.

Brand-Mission-Offer System are concentric and placed at the center of the model but it does not imply that these are more important than the others. However, we invite you to think from the start about what you are, what your goals are and what your offer is in order to make them available to others and the system in which you work.

Each of the elements that make up the *Loving Business Model* interacts either directly or indirectly with the others, exchanging value according to the rule of reciprocity. However, you have already seen that there is a step preceding *offering*

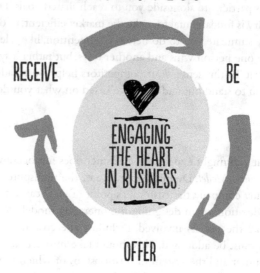

FIGURE 3.2 Circular flow

and this step is *being*. When we move on to discussing the relationships between the elements of this model, always bear in mind this progression: *being-offering-receiving*.

The diagram that represents this process (Figure 3.2) is circular because receiving leads back to being, which through the experience of love evolves and changes.

From marketing mix to love mix

We have chosen to begin our discussion of love by starting from marketing as we believe that in any enterprise this is the subject that, more than any other, encapsulates the essence of what we do with the market, namely distributing and delivering the results of our entrepreneurial activity. The tools of marketing are a bridge between the identity and values that an organization expresses, the form that these then assume through the creation of an offer and the methods of interaction and communication with customers, employees, suppliers as well as the stakeholders and society overall. Marketing plays a fundamental role in achieving the "higher" goals of an organization and in translating good intentions into actions. The holistic and integrated idea of marketing on which our approach is based is borrowed from the description of this discipline given by George G. Brenkert in his book *Marketing Ethics*[2] quoted below:

> Marketing is a complex set of connected activities, values and norms that form a practice... is the creation, communication and conveyance of something of value to designated groups through voluntary exchanges... the integrated

marketing concept enjoins marketers to integrate the various aspects of marketing in a strategic manner that provides the greatest value to those they target while making allowance for the background conditions within which they operate.... It directs marketers to look to their own resources, competences and values in determining the nature of superior performance at which they should aim... it is mistaken to think that marketers can simply develop any set of excellences... firms have different competences and capacities.

We will go on to explain these concepts, applying them and activating them by using specific tools and techniques. We will start immediately by redesigning, according to Brenkert's new perspective, what is probably the best-known strategic tool: the **marketing mix**.

As set out in 1960 by Jerome McCarthy in his book *Basic Marketing: A Managerial Approach*,[3] it initially contemplated only four elements, the famous "4 Ps": *Product, Promotion, Price* and *Place*.

Over the years, at least another three elements have been added: *Process, People* and the *Physical Environment* where the enterprise operates. These important additions highlight how sensitivity on certain issues is now widespread. Yet how do these elements change when we are talking about *Engaging the Heart in Business*?

So, let's review the seven elements of the marketing mix to expand its meaning.

The love mix

Product

It is limiting to talk only about the product. As we discussed in our book *Sales Ethics*, we now need to talk about the **offer system**, i.e. a set of products and services but also values, behavior, style of communication and much more, which includes both tangible and intangible elements. This is what customers are really buying. The element that captures their attention and convinces them to choose you rather than another may be completely intangible: your reputation, the relationship with the people who work with you, the image and style that set you apart. Organizations need to control a range of variables in order to capture the consumer's heart and set themselves apart from the competition. In a broader sense, your entire business model makes up the offer system.

Price

The price is linked to that of value, a term that refers to something much deeper and wider than a simple economic quote. The true objective of doing business must be to create and exchange not just money but also **value**, for all your products or services and with all the actors involved in our business. Let us not forget that the economic results of the exchange, both for companies and their customers, can only be evaluated from a broader perspective that includes relationships and effects over time.

36 Engaging the heart in business

Place

This is the element that defines the "where", the scenario that acts as a backdrop to our commercial exchanges. Today, tackling this theme means asking questions about cultural roots, the *genius loci* that contains and supports your action on the market, while doing more besides. You need to design the experience in these physical or virtual places so that the **customer journey** is engaging and positive. You can do this by designing each interface so that it is coherent, representative of your essence and the culture from which you come, while also being interactive, open and transparent. The previous concept of "place" therefore assumes a new dynamism. All this involves a profound internal and external rethinking of your organization.

Promotion

It is no longer enough to advertise to the market or to make pledges, you must also know how to respect them; you must therefore be equipped to do this well and consistently. Working on promotion means understanding and accepting your positioning on the market, specializing consistently and without dissimulation. Customers are tired of bland promises and of companies and professionals who try to sell the myth of perfection. We are convinced that promoting yourself means choosing to interact in a frank and loyal way; it also means educating customers to discern true value and to orientate themselves among the various market proposals. By equipping yourself to make **specific pledges that you are able to keep**, addressed to those who can understand and appreciate them, you will naturally activate loyalty and positive word of mouth: the most powerful forms of promotion that the market currently has.

People

Customers are people, but so are your employees and suppliers: you need to be able to communicate with every individual; you must share a system of values, goals and motivations that will affect their actions whatever role they play within your business model. You must promote and encourage coherence between what you are and what you do, at all levels. You can only involve your customers emotionally and create a truly human interaction if you express your true self in every context. **Giving centrality to the individual** means accepting and valuing each person's diversity and integrating the emotional sphere to drive each person's actions.

Process

This concept involves not only doing things well, namely producing and delivering quality, but also **evolving**. If we refer to Maslow's hierarchy of needs,

Engaging the heart in business **37**

thinking in terms of process means progressing to respond to an increasingly evolved level of internal and external needs. Efficiency not only to make profit, but to help increase your happiness, the happiness of others and of the system that hosts you.

Physical environment

You cannot limit yourself to the study of what surrounds you with the sole purpose of defining the most correct operational strategy. You must **improve the ecosystem** in which you live, perform actions that indicate a path to the people who are part of it, propose evolutionary goals, and lead them in a quest for meanings that enables the "container" that hosts us to expand and discover its own motivation for continued prosperity. This implies a profound paradigm change: from competition and exploitation to cooperation and renewal of resources. The relationship with competitors must be reset to competing on value and not on price, since you can only hope to make the environment and society in which you live a better place if you strive to outdo your competitors in the production of "good".

This is the *Love Mix* we want to deal with in these pages and that we would like you to keep in mind while doing business or during your work each day. This is more than merely a way of being on the market but a way of being that you can adopt only if you are willing to transform yourself.

Spread the love: the phases of the marketing plan

In the following chapters, we will suggest you start by carefully reflecting on yourself, on your goals and on the value – in terms of the offer system – that you can exchange with all the other elements in the *Loving Business Model*. Remember that this new way of doing business is circular; winning organizations and market models that achieve success are not rigidly hierarchized, which means that you will always have to bear in mind that no single element of the model is more powerful or important than the others. This interaction and integration of the forces at stake is witnessed by the Whole Foods Market "declaration of interdependence"[4] that states:

> Our success in achieving our vision is measured by the satisfaction of our customers, the happiness and excellence of our Team Members, return on investment, in addition to the improvement of our environment, and support for our local and larger communities.
>
> …
>
> We recognize the interdependence among our stakeholders – those who benefit from or are impacted by our company. We earn trust through transparent communication, open door policies and inclusive people practices.

38 Engaging the heart in business

> ...
>
> Our Declaration of Interdependence reflects the hopes and intentions of many people.
>
> ... let us take up the challenge together to bring our reality closer to our vision. The future we will experience tomorrow is created one step at a time today.

We could paraphrase the concepts expressed here by stating that success is only achieved if shared: if your employees are happy, your customers will be too and thereby also those who invest in the business you have created. Satisfying only some of these actors, to the detriment of others, creates damage and everyone will suffer, including those who initially felt privileged. On the contrary, giving value to each of them will allow you to create virtuous and circular efficiencies that will bring unexpected "rewards". From the analyses conducted by the authors of the previously mentioned *Firms of Endearment*, it is clear that companies that nurture this idea of circularity and interdependence enjoy a variety of benefits: they save on advertising, as it is in part replaced by positive word of mouth and good references and they increase their productivity because those working in these organizations have the incentive to do better and to do more. Moreover, they are more creative and can, when difficulties arise, rely on a network of internal and external relationships that will support them. It would also be a mistake to favor a customer or the environment in which you operate at the expense of your own well-being and your own goals. If pushed to an extreme, the purely customer-oriented approach, which focuses exclusively on satisfying customers, risks compromising profit and, therefore, the existence of the business itself. By contrast, our idea is to create value at all levels and for all the people involved. This vision may seem utopian but remember that, by enlarging the lens through which we observe the results, integration is always possible.

The grid in Figure 3.3 highlights the interconnections between the various elements in the *Loving Business Model* and identifies the pivotal concept of their exchange. This will be the focus of our reflections and of the work we will do together in the following chapters.

The path that we will follow together in these pages is very similar to the path we ourselves have covered, so you will find many references to our own history and that of the customers, friends and partners who have accompanied us.

The model and the techniques we provide represent one of the possible ways you can fulfill your professional dreams and achieve your goals. We invite you to approach this method with an open mind and with an eye to flexibility; feel free to revise it and rewrite it according to your own ideas, your values and your experience. Our goal is not to present a universally valid and uniquely applicable theory, but by offering tools and advice, to help all those who see their work as an opportunity to produce shared value.

Engaging the heart in business 39

GRID OF INTERACTION BETWEEN ELEMENTS

	BRAND	MISSION	TEAM	CUSTOMER	OFFER SYSTEM	COMPETITOR	STAKEHOLDER	CUSTOMER JOURNEY
BRAND								
MISSION	COHERENCE							
TEAM	SHARING	MOTIVATION						
CUSTOMER	RECOGNITION	APPEAL	RELATIONSHIP					
OFFER SYSTEM	INTANGIBLE VALUE	ANSWER TO WHY	RESPONSIBILITY	SATISFACTION				
COMPETITOR	POSITIONING	COMPETITION ON VALUE	MOTIVATION	CHOICE	DIFFERENTIATION			
STAKEHOLDER	SOCIAL ROLE	GIVE BACK	PRIDE BELONGING	CONTRIBUTION	SUSTAINABILITY	MARKET ROLE		
CUSTOMER JOURNEY	TOUCH POINT DESIGN	STORY DOING	EMPLOYEE JOURNEY	EXPERIENCE	CONTENT	KM MARKETING	TRANSPARENCY	

FIGURE 3.3 Grid of interaction between elements

Activity – Lay the foundations

Using the instructions given at the end of the introduction, download the *Loving Business Model* diagram from the download area of our website and print it in a suitable format (we recommend A0 if you have it) so you can use it as a basis and fill it with results of the activities as we carry them out together. Make sure you have pencils and sticky-notes handy, so you can add your notes directly to the diagram.

What you have learnt

We have designed an operating model that will help you organize your work, clarifying the elements that compose it and how they relate to each other. We have also started the "practical" phase of the path that, step by step, will enable you to put what you have learned on paper and later add any considerations you gain from the reading and activities that follow. Roll up your sleeves and start designing your marketing plan because, as Benjamin Franklin said, "Tell me and I forget. Teach me and I remember. Involve me and I learn".

40 Engaging the heart in business

Notes

1 Grant, Adam. *Give and Take: Why Helping Others Drives Our Success*. Reprint ed. Penguin Books, 2014.
2 Brenkert, George G. *Marketing Ethics*. Blackwell Publishing, 2008.
3 McCarthy, Edmund Jerome. *Basic Marketing: A Global-managerial Approach*. R.D. Irwin, 1962, pp. 53, 57.
4 To read the complete text, consult "Declaration of Interdependence" on the site www. wholefoodsmarket.com

4

LOVE *YOURSELF*

Branding and identity

(In collaboration with Riccardo Trevisani[1])

Abstract

Loving yourself means knowing yourself, respecting yourself, taking responsibility for who you really are and therefore acting accordingly, fearlessly and with resolve. It also means possessing the certainty that you can find your soulmate, or attract the right customers, only if you show yourself as you really are, unequivocally. In this chapter, we will help you rediscover yourself in relation to your business and understand how to put yourself at the service of others as well as your success.

Case study: identity crisis

When we talk about identity we are talking about people. Companies are made up of people, so to study the identity of an organization one must start from the identity of those who compose it.

42 Love *yourself*

Partners, employees, collaborators and all those who participate in your business combine to create its character. If something is out of line, if either you or someone in the team does not identify themselves or recognize themselves in the organization, the company will suffer in terms of efficiency and lose part of its character.

We sometimes feel compelled to act in ways that put our values and professional goals at odds. Both companies and professionals frequently find themselves in a similar situation. Some time ago we were working with a software company that had suffered severe trauma. One of its founders, a charismatic custodian of the organization's DNA and the emissary of its personality and style of relations, died prematurely. This event sparked a profound identity crisis that impacted on both internal and external relationships, some of which collapsed, resulting in a loss of efficiency and motivation. Initially, the management set precise rules to continue throughout this difficult period and avoid inconsistent behavior, but the rules imposed had the effect of drawing an even deeper gap between "who you are and what you do". The management turned to us to find a way out of this situation. We aided them to reflect deeply on their identity and their values as individuals and as a group. We will explain the tools we used in this chapter. What happened in the end? Follow us in exploring the techniques used to reconstruct a fractured identity and reconnect the actions and practices of the entire team.

Engaging your soul in your business

There is a term that defines particularly well the path that we are going to follow in this chapter: **branding**, namely, building your company's distinctive brand. But what exactly is a **brand**? In our view, the brand is everything that represents the character and identity of a company. It has physical components, such as the logo or the name, but these alone are not enough to represent the company's personality and distinctive features, just as people cannot be described by either their physical appearance alone or by their personal data. The different components that go to make up the brand have been investigated by many authors, managers and entrepreneurs. Let's see what some of them say:

> Your brand is what other people say about you when you are not in the room.
>
> *Jeff Bezos, Founder of Amazon*

> If people believe they share values with a company, they will stay loyal to the brand.
>
> *Howard Schultz, CEO of Starbucks*

> Brand is simply the emotional connection people have with you or your business.
>
> *J. Morgan, author of* Brand Against the Machine

Love *yourself* **43**

Although each of these definitions differs, what they all seem to say is that the brand is a glue that unites entrepreneurs and co-workers, customers and companies, an attraction based on the power of values and emotions. A business model that does not tackle the questions "Who are you really?" and "What do you believe in?" cannot be deemed complete as it would fail to create connections and empathy among the various actors that populate it. Moving from the business context to that of love, imagine what would happen if when hoping to seduce the person you loved you failed to reveal your real identity or, perhaps worse, you adapted it in an effort to please. Of course, we are talking about business and companies, not about people and romantic relationships, so there may be differences; yet not as many as you may think. In fact, whatever the context in which you are operating, be it relationships or business, you are always the same person and it is your values that guide your choices and behaviors. Values are powerful forces that are continuously at play, even when you may be unaware of this. If you want to work effectively and coherently you must, therefore, investigate and rediscover what truly and profoundly moves your actions and then use this knowledge when planning your objectives, actions and results.

Why did the death of one of the partners of the software company mentioned earlier have such a profound impact on the way the whole organization functioned? Because that person implicitly embodied its values, to the extent that his disappearance weakened the inspiration and meaning of the company's actions.

Hence, we will work together to find out what values and stimuli provide the basis for your actions, and then arrange them in a credible and original way so you can express them coherently. Managing your brand, as Mary Gentile would say, means starting to give a voice to your values.

We invite you to adopt the **five principles** listed below as guidelines when reflecting on identity and branding; they have been set out by Riccardo Trevisani, an expert on the subject and co-author of this chapter:

1. The behavior and **identity of the people** who populate it will influence an organization's brand. There is inevitably an osmotic exchange of values between the organization and individuals. This means that everyone is responsible for its reputation. As a result, everyone must be aware of the role they play in building a common identity.
2. As a **communication tool** a brand is used to relate to others. Failing to communicate our identity would be paramount to not having one. For the "voice" of the brand to be heard and followed, it must avoid being overpowering, arrogant, domineering or redundant. Personality is communicated mainly through the subtle signals that identify style and details that go beyond words, stimulating attraction and respect.
3. The **character** of a brand is more than the sum of the component parts although it combines the identities of all. Therefore, treat your organization as something apart from yourself, that exists beyond you. Let your business stand on its own feet, expressing ideas freely in line with its specific essence.

44 Love *yourself*

You should be ready to step in and help but don't make yourself indispensable, enabling it to have its own life regardless of whether you are present.

4. **Adaptation** is the first secret of survival in nature: while your values will not change but will continue to illuminate your path, remember that it is necessary to adapt your behavior to circumstances so that your identity can stand the test of time. Being consistent does not mean remaining static but flowing in harmony with one's essence.

5. Like a living being, a company is an organism that can create **empathy**. Make sure that your brand never forgets to speak directly to people's hearts, be they customers, collaborators, suppliers or other stakeholders.

To discover your identity, let's start from an analysis of traits that you don't like about yourself: those commonly called flaws.

Traditional tools for innovative results: SWOT analysis

What marks us out more distinctly than our **defects**? There may be certain deficiencies we cannot offset, the imperfections we cannot hide or the weaknesses we have never been able to overcome that stick with us like faithful traveling companions. People close to us may remind us of these defects, while those who love us have become attached to them to such an extent that if we were to eliminate them, they would no longer recognize us. Why then do we continually apologize for their existence? Why not accept and claim our defects as integral elements of our personality?

There are many cases of companies that have worked on their apparent "defects" to build a successful identity. Some examples? Motorcycles that leak oil and vibrate thereby becoming cult bikes; shoes whose leather ages and in whose wrinkles generations of teenagers have traced their own development.[2]

We are not perfect; no human being is. Why, then, should companies and their products, which are designed and created by human beings, be so? Nobody falls in love with perfection, because it is unreal. Perhaps through the years of the economic boom, we could still believe in the fantasy of an ideal world, where everything and everyone is happy and smiling. Nowadays, however, we are more likely to become attracted and excited by realist poetry. If we take the example of movies today, it is evident the stories no longer have a clear development and happy ending, where the bad guys are ugly, and the good ones are always handsome. Plots are now more complex and therefore more real: heroes too may stumble, revealing weaknesses and committing errors, while their antagonists unexpectedly rediscover their humanity. Beauty has now taken on a more credible form: we no longer look for the physique and features of a Greek statue but appreciate an asymmetrical face, marked perhaps by experience or features that lack harmony but are enlivened by passion and exercise an apparently inexplicable charm. It is life in its entirety, with all its imperfections, that makes your identity ring true and your offer attractive.

Shortly, we will guide you in the use of **SWOT analysis**, which identifies strengths, weaknesses, opportunities and threats, in a way that is completely reversed compared to your usual approach! We will start with your weaknesses to build your identity around some of them. We will then consider your opportunities from a new viewpoint, not to use them but to avoid them whenever they do not express your essence. The graveyard of failed businesses is full of the gravestones of products and companies launched towards a seemingly "easy victory" that failed to assess whether the opportunity they had spotted was in harmony with their brand and brand values. Famous car makers who delude themselves that they can break into the world of fashion, motorcycle-helmet companies that invite bankruptcy by producing skis, specialists in condiments that switch from food to household cleaning products, to name but a few.[3] We should have the strength to say "No", "this does not reflect my essence", "it's not for me". Every time we give up our values and our identity and follow the mirage of easy success, we are making a mistake for which, sooner or later, we will pay the price. As the Greek playwright, Sophocles, said: "Time sees and hears all things and discloses all". This is particularly true when we are talking about brand, identity and the sense of coherence, integrity and dignity that are linked to these two concepts.

Activity – Build your SWOT to integrate defects and choose coherent opportunities

Download the SWOT analysis template from the download area or take a sheet of paper, divide it into four squares and fill in the fields, remembering that:

Strengths are what you do well or your enterprise's strategic assets (people, processes, suppliers, patents...). You can also include special behaviors, qualities or specific aspects of your organization such as a certain style of relationship, a particularly beautiful or easily accessible location, an exciting story and positive references.

Weaknesses are the aspects that make you most vulnerable. Like your strengths, they may relate either to structural aspects, assets or professional skills, but also to human competences that are lacking or render your organization, and its relationship with the market, fragile. When you describe them, as you did for your strengths, try to be very specific, bearing in mind that they too are specific aspects of your organization, elements that distinguish it from any other market player.

The term **opportunities** indicates things the market can offer that are not covered completely by competitors (types of products, geographical areas, customers...) or political, economic, social, environmental and cultural

46 Love *yourself*

changes that can favor the dynamics of the sector in which you operate. These positive conditions will not relate only to you (otherwise they would be your strengths) but are present for all or many of the companies with which you compete.

Threats are current or future situations that will raise the level of competition or prompt changes that will damage market dynamics (new laws and bureaucratic requirements, operating restrictions, the arrival of new competitors, mandatory technological adjustment costs). Like opportunities these threats must impact on the whole sector; if they were to impact only on you, they would relate to possible specific defects of your organization.

Now consider the chart you have filled with your notes and ask yourself:

- Am I using and enhancing my strengths?
- What weaknesses actually characterize my identity?
- Are all opportunities coherent?
- How can threats be avoided?

Neglect nothing when reflecting on the flaws of your business, especially the most painful and persistent ones. Bear in mind that not all your weaknesses should be included and used to give "character" to your brand. In fact, it will be necessary to address and resolve some of them. However, if you realize that certain flaws express an essential aspect of your nature then show them off with pride; claim them as your own and weave them into your company's story.

When you consider the opportunities, will you have the courage to reject those that are not coherent with the essence and values of your organization, or far removed from them? Before discarding them definitively, assess whether some apparently incompatible opportunities can be reformulated and aligned with your values. Choose which opportunities to pursue while making clear to your teams, customers and investors why you rejected some apparently good chances. If the opportunity seems as enticing as a penalty kick at an empty goalmouth but you are not happy to take it, you must face the stands and explain why. Don't be afraid: your true fans will understand you and love you all the more.

Finally, check whether, by remaining coherent and acting only on what really characterizes you, some threat has ceased to be so worrying.

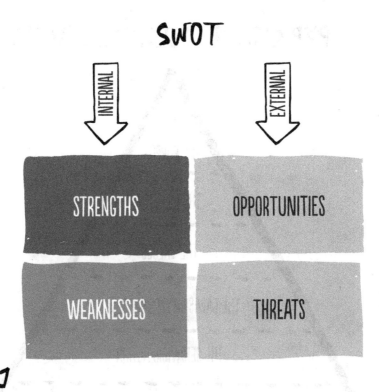

*Flaws may sometimes become **differential** qualities of character.
Not all opportunities are **coherent** with our identity and our offer system.*

FIGURE 4.1 SWOT analysis

When we used this technique with the company presented at the beginning of the chapter, we discovered that one of the company's shortcomings was that its sales activities had little formal organization as the deceased partner had handled them directly, using his network of relationships and personal experience. When he was no longer there, the sales processes were managed according to any opportunities that arose spontaneously and left to everyone's common sense, rather than following a precise operating flow. This was insufficient to achieve the sales objectives that the company had set. In the absence of a clear identity, which defined the style and means of commercial activity, effectiveness was lost. The rules imposed with the intention of replacing the previous management of sales had served only to constrain and further distance relationships with customers and the market as the identity appeared artificial. As regards opportunities, the world of information technology apparently offered many attractive ones. How could the sales team evaluate those that might be coherent with the company given that the depositary of its identity was no longer there? There was a risk of pursuing many paths but specializing in none, an ever-present danger in a fast-expanding sector, which would

FIGURE 4.2 Pyramid of Logical Levels

confuse and disorient customers. Once we had pinpointed the company's flaws, we became aware of the need to develop a new shared identity, which would take into account the sales personnel's desire to improvise and remain spontaneous, without trying to artificially rebuild something that was definitively lost. The only way to release each salesperson's ability to independently evaluate opportunities and claim their organization's specific identity on the market was to make each person an active part of a renewed identity, with a shared style of communication and character.

The company as a living being: aligning the levels

Since we have compared the brand to an individual's identity, the next tool we use derives from the study of the identity of human beings. The **Pyramid of Logical Levels** was devised by Robert Dilts, one of the world's leading exponents of Neuro-Linguistic Programming (NLP). Dilts developed this model to describe the mind's organization and hence the expression of personality and the connections that link environmental feedback with the behavior, strategies, values and identities of individuals.

We will try to understand together how this tool works and how it can help you better define your brand, starting from an analysis of each level that will begin from the lower sections, to discover the correlations between the various aspects.

The Environment – The place where we dwell, the people we frequent, our network of reference are the fruit of our choices. This is both because behaviors, strategies, values and identities lead us to live in a particular environment and because it reacts to us according to who we are, what we believe in and the skills and abilities we have acquired.

The Behavior/Action – What we do. The actions we perform affect the environment in which we live and are influenced by everything that is higher in the model. So, if we want to get different reactions, different results and change the context in which we are immersed, we will have to change the way we operate.

The Capability/Competence – These are the strategies, the acquired knowledge and the innate qualities that allow us to act in a certain way. Only by developing appropriate skills and abilities can we change our practices.

The Values – These are the profound motivations that guide us towards the development of capabilities and competence. What we believe in does not always have a positive value; sometimes our beliefs may be seriously limiting. If ideas like mistrust, fear or lust for power are rooted in you, they could influence your behavior and results in a negative way. It is, therefore, important to recognize your inner drives and transform them into positive values, which will support you along the way to achieving what you desire.

The Identity – The values, what you believe in, are born from your personality and your character, giving expression to who you really are. When someone asks you "Who are you?" it is easy to become confused, to formulate generic answers or to hide behind a role, a title or a series of achieved results. The dreams, goals and desires that inspire you are the building blocks of what we call the soul.

The Purpose – Once you are aware of who you are, you need to take one last step, asking yourself, "How can I, with this identity, these values, these capabilities and competences, contribute to the common good and to collective evolution?" It's a major question, but as you move up the pyramid, it will become easier to understand what your role in the world may be and what meaning to give to your existence. We invite you to do so, as the philosopher Daniel Dennet says, "The secret of happiness is to find something more important than you are and dedicate your life to it". The answer to this last level might look like a "vocation", a powerful word historically associated with a spiritual calling.

50 Love *yourself*

*Being called upon to accept our mission is an act of love — perhaps
the truest and powerful — towards oneself, others and life.*

To effect a change at any level of the pyramid, we need to consider the step immediately above. For example, if I want the feedback received from the environment to be different, I will have to change my behavior. If I want to act differently, I will need to develop new capabilities and competences but the drive to do so will only be triggered by a set of precise values and motivations. If I want to define them, I will have to ask myself who I am, a question whose answer is connected to my role in the world and to the meaning I want to give to my existence.

How can you apply the pyramid to a business or organization? We have coupled a marketing concept with the various levels that make up this pyramid.

1. Managing the **environment** for a company means answering the questions "Where?", "When?", "With whom?" do I do my job and what feedback do I receive? It will, therefore, be necessary to research the market and the reference sector in which you operate, including what we have called *position* in the *love mix* but also the feedback that comes from the people and the panorama of the environment.
2. Defining your **behavior** corresponds to finding an answer to the question "What do I do and how?" We are, therefore, talking about the offer, not only in terms of product but also of services and all the tangible and intangible elements that define your action on the market.
3. The **capability/competence** refers to "What makes me different?" requires studying the chain that enables you, in a unique and different way from competitors, to build value for yourself and for others, trying to understand what experiences and knowledge support you when you operate.
4. **The values** provide the motivation that drives everything you do, enabling you to overcome hurdles. The values come from the answer to the question "What guides me?", "What do I believe in?" Defining your values will help you take a position on the market and what's around you.
5. The **identity** is the brand that shapes beliefs and values, generating the sense of self and ultimately giving you the answer to the question "Who am I?" and "What do I want to become and obtain?" but also "How do I want to be perceived?" The answers you find will define the character of your company as well as its mission.
6. For an organization, a **purpose** that goes beyond immediate interests and profit entails awareness of its social role and the contribution it can make to

collective evolution. In an enterprise we usually use the term vision[4] for the company tool that deals with aspirations and answers to the questions "For who else?", "For what?" or if you prefer, "What is the company role within the society?"

When we used this tool with our client from the case study, we realized that the organization was suffering from a misalignment of the logical levels and that this generated internal and external conflicts. Going back step by step through the various levels of the pyramid just described, we realized that the desired feedback was not obtained because the behavior was not backed up by adequate capabilities and competences. The development of such capabilities was also opposed by a widespread conviction in the team of their own limitations; the team members were sure that nothing and no one could replace the deceased partner as custodian of the company's commercial identity. It was, therefore, necessary to find a new element that could bind together all the logical levels.

Activity – Launching the brand in the world

It would be very complex to venture into an analysis of the logical levels of your organization based only on a text. For this reason, we asked Riccardo Trevisani to create an activity that, in a light-hearted and fun way, could help you to reason indirectly about the main elements of the model. Besides, the results could be useful if you are planning to organize an event to support your brand! The activity consists of planning a hypothetical launch of your organization on the world market, imagining that you have infinite resources of time and money so there are no limits to your creativity.

Start by asking yourself:

- Who do I want to invite?
- What location will I choose for the event?
- What atmosphere do I want to create? How will the guests be dressed?
- What food will be served? What beverages?
- What music will there be?
- What materials will be used? What color themes?
- What fragrances will there be?
- Who do I want as the main speaker or for the celebrity endorsement?
- What phrase would best end the event?
- What would I like participants to remember of this event five years later?

52 Love *yourself*

When providing your answers, try to be as detailed as possible and bear in mind that you are not only planning something you like but an event designed to share the essence, vision and soul of your company with the world.

Once you have completed the activity, consider the final concept chosen for the launch and make a collection of "sensory materials" to create the mood board: a representation through clippings from newspapers, images found on the Internet, drawings, notes, colors, perfumes and sounds that combine to create the idea you wish to achieve. Take a look now at the final result: it's a snapshot of your company's identity and brand.

Conclusion of the case study: a new collective identity

There is nothing more painful than losing someone you love. Your life undergoes a profound upheaval, which can disorient you to the point of compromising your identity. This happens to many people, but it can also happen to entire organizations as occurred in our client's case. What is the recipe to finding yourself once again? Of course, there are no set rules or instruction manuals. We need to start from the bottom, from what is most true and concrete, whether it is painful or wrong. The knowledge of our defects – if analyzed and used productively and systematically – can be a clue or even a seed from which to rediscover a lost identity. This was our starting point with the software company; we helped them to state what could not be changed and to recreate a shared identity, to which we gave a "virtual" name and surname, to which all company employees contributed. Every single team member was involved in describing the values, capabilities, competences, behaviors and desired results. This is how the company started finding answers to many of the questions that plagued its staff. For example, when faced with questions like, "In this negotiation, should I press the client to choose this service?", "Is it right to behave like this with my colleague?", it became possible, once again, to refer to the organization's common identity to find advice and inspiration. The identity was no longer linked to a person but was a virtual and shared "self"; this does not mean it was any less powerful and concrete. The informality of the process of recognizing defects has become a symbol of creativity and flexibility that can be demonstrated to customers. The lack of organization that was apparent in the way sales activities were conducted has led to home-working and flexible hours. The company developed a new way of being that might appear imperfect in the eyes of the "old" management theories, but is much more human, engaging and even personal and attractive.

What you have learnt and adding a piece to the *Loving Business Model*

If you have drawn up the *Loving Business Model* diagram as suggested in Chapter 3, you can now complete the box that talks about the brand, by entering a brief description containing the discoveries you have made thanks to the work suggested in this chapter. Remember that once your identity has been defined, it will have to be dynamic; in particular, you will have to adapt behavior and action strategies to constantly compare them with the values and the mission your identity expresses. We thus recommend using the tools presented in this chapter both as a compass to make strategic decisions and as a test to verify, on several occasions, how the practices are aligned with what you are and with what you want to say about yourself.

Notes

1 Riccardo Trevisani is a *brand strategist* who studied at Ravensbourne University in London and at General Assembly in Boston; after a period spent working between these two cities, he returned to his native Italy where he now collaborates with a leading international branding agency.
2 The reference is to the advertisements used by the founder, Carlo Talamo, of Numero Uno, formerly an Italian importer of Harley Davidson bikes, extolling the "flaws" of the well-known American motorcycle and to Timberland, which in the 1980s and 1990s used images of shoes worn by time to promote its products.
3 The cases referred to are Ferrari and Lamborghini with their luxury accessory lines, Nava with the notorious patent *Ski System* and Heinz, a manufacturer of sauces and condiments, with its stain remover, the *All Natural Cleaning Vinegar*.
4 We will discuss the differences between mission and vision in further detail in Chapter 5.

5

LOVE *WHY* YOU *DO* IT

Having clear and shareable goals

Abstract

Now that you have clearly identified to yourself who you are and where the profound soul of your business lies, you are ready to answer a new and fundamental question: "Why do you do what you do?" Seneca said, "If one does not know to which port one is sailing, no wind is favorable". While reading this chapter, we thus invite you to consider what really prompts your actions and to set precise goals while welcoming your mission in the knowledge that it will help you fulfill yourself as well as helping to improve the system in which you live and work.

Case study: journeying along uncharted routes

Montalti Worldwide Moving (MWM) is a company specializing in logistics services; specifically, it manages the flow and storage of goods. The two owners are the third

Love *why* you *do it* **55**

generation to stand at the helm of this company that was founded by their grand-
father over 50 years ago. The market, work organization and relational dynamics
they now found themselves facing were all very different from those with which
the company had dealt in the past. In its commitment to redefining its business
model and evaluating which organizational schemes could ensure efficiency and
greater results, MWM risked losing sight of the values that had characterized the
company from its origins. The focus on revenue, without a clear value objective
shared by all the staff, risked lowering efficiency and the customers would be the
first to suffer. The salespeople were focusing on finding business opportunities but
when the new orders reached the operations team, the reaction was dismay at the
complexity of handling them and the increased workload. This misalignment was
generated by a lack of constructive dialogue based on shared values and objectives. But the conflict of vision went beyond tainting the relationships between the
sales and production departments; due to the pressure to get results, the adminis-
trative department found itself dealing with extremely complex, and sometimes
excessively challenging, contracts with special conditions that had been granted
to customers to gain their business. The overall effect was to risk growing dis-
satisfaction and complaints, with stressed suppliers and partners that were being
overworked and forced to pursue unsustainable methods and times for delivery.
The company's owners were spending their time and energy attempting to mediate
between the different departments involved in resolving conflicts and smoothing
out internal and external misunderstandings. Although all members of the company
were working hard, each had the feeling of being out of sync, stuck in a mechanism
that had lost its pace and direction. Even if the company was achieving satisfac-
tory results from a business point of view, at a personal level the strain on staff was
becoming too great. It was, therefore, time to stop and reflect, to define the destination together and chart a route to reach it.

Motivations and purposes: decide the destination

When we are involved in something that we are passionate about, we feel a vital
flow of energy that produces enthusiasm and determination; we don't feel fatigue
and our perceptive capacity is increased, giving us greater clarity and permitting
us to pick up on previously unnoticed nuances. We will thus manage to identify original solutions that will enable us to achieve our objectives. This energy
is defined in many ways – passion, aspiration, desire – but all are related to love.
Love is the force that gives you strength when doing a sport, organizing an event,
embarking on a journey, sitting an exam and, indeed, starting a business. Loving
what you do allows you to reawaken confidence in yourself, interpret events con-
structively and engage people by fully activating their talent so they contribute
to achieving the result.

   In the previous chapter, you learned to love yourself. Now you are about to
advance a further step: to clarify **what** you are pursuing, but above all **why** you
are doing it.

56 Love *why* you *do it*

The need to have a purpose is an essential part of being human. A goal gives us the strength to get up every morning and face the day and, if we look closer, it binds all the experiences of our life together, framing them in an overall design. In company practice, motivations are often confused with aims, activities with objectives and actions with tools, thus creating misunderstandings and laying the foundations for possible failures. For the sake of clarity we will be inspired by Simon Sinek who, through the *Golden Circle*, invites organizations to start from the **Why** (the central motivation that inspires every action), to then investigate the **How** (the operating methods that differentiate one company from another) and then based on the answers to the preceding questions, finally define the **What** (products and services to be offered to the market).

Therefore, we will set off to find your "Why", to discover what spurs you on and where the roots of your motivation lie. This is the only way to correctly differentiate the goals from the destinations and then, later, break them down into specific actions necessary to "close the loop".

"Why do I do what I do?" thus becomes the question to which you must devote all your attention for a moment since the answer will be the foundation on which to build the strategic plan for your business. Objectives, actions, the definition of the mission and vision will all derive from this answer. If you are already on the market and, despite having defined the tools listed above, you still feel you are not obtaining the results you deserve, it is likely you need to "retune" the whys and the objectives that follow!

In the term **motivation** [from the Latin *motivus*, derived from *motus*, past participle of the verb *movere*, what drives, what stimulates to action] you can find the reason that leads you to act, which subtly underpins your every thought or action, though you may be unaware of it. The re-discovery of this set of forces that channel your energies to reach a goal will enable you to build your present and that of your organization, involving the people with whom you will share the adventure. No feat is accomplished by a single individual; it is achieved through the sum of the motivations and the wills of all those who are directly and indirectly involved: the more these "actors" can focus on a common goal that includes everyone, the greater the chance of success.

All motivation theories start from the assumption that humans' actions are driven by needs to be met, which lead them to carry out certain behaviors. While the latter are visible to all and easily identifiable, the reasons are not so. Indeed, often they remain obscure even to us; no surprise then that others cannot fathom them. Moreover, the actions of different people can be similar, but their motivations may be completely different. For example, there are people who read all the journals from the sector in which they work because they need to feel confident when talking to customers or colleagues; others may do so because they are really curious to gain a deeper knowledge or just want to keep up to date with the latest news: confidence, thirst for knowledge and drive for innovation are very different impulses. Once you have clarified the motivation that prompts you, you can relate more effectively to those around you.

One of the most frustrating things for an individual is to feel forced to act against his or her deepest values. We can endure this condition for a while, until a survival mechanism kicks in, normally in the form of a self-boycott that unconsciously leads us to distance ourselves from a situation with which we no longer feel aligned. We invite you to reflect on the fact that sometimes people that at first sight appear to have failed might actually be living a more authentic life. So, what is your motivation?

Activity – Discovering your own motivation

 To understand what profoundly drives you, it is necessary to mentally retrace the most important choices about your business, asking yourself the simple question: "Why did I behave like this? What did I want to obtain or avoid?" Don't stop at your first answer but continue to investigate. A good technique is the one known as the "5 Whys", originally developed by Sakichi Toyoda and later used by the Toyota Motor Corporation, which consists of exploring at least five levels to determine root causes. For example, when approaching the writing of this book, our questions could have been:

1. Why did we decide to write *Engaging the Heart in Business*?
   To promote our work on ethical marketing.
2. Why do we want to promote ethical marketing?
   Because we believe it is more effective.
3. Why do we believe it is more effective?
   Because people need profound motivations and values to act, values that ethics can offer.
4. Why can ethics offer values?
   Because it goes to the root of human behaviors, helping people to reconnect with what they believe.
5. Why is it important for people to reconnect with what they believe?
   Because we all have the right to be happy and live a full and fulfilling life.

The deep motivation that led us to write is, therefore, the desire to support people in the search for an authentic and fulfilling life, the same thing we want for ourselves and our company; this is why the Passodue manifesto states:

"Our motto *'Partem Claram Semper Aspice'* (roughly translated as 'always look on the bright side') reminds us to experience everything we do with **optimism, gratitude** and a spirit of service. We are convinced that helping others to develop skills and abilities based on the integration of ethics and sales will help to make the markets more human and efficient and restore the joy of **feeling part of a bigger mission**, searching for happiness to share with all those who want **to take a step along the path towards a better world.**"[1]

Motivations differ between individuals because they are linked to the values and identity of a specific person. Within organizations, however, there is a culture, an identity and values that are perhaps implicitly shared; these elements lead to making choices according to recurring motivations. If you repeat the activity above by considering at least three different situations and reach similar conclusions, you can be certain that you are close to identifying the prevailing motivation.

Once the motivation is clear, you are ready to identify the goals or results you want to achieve through your actions. In fact, objectives and motivations are not synonymous: while the former are circumstantial, specific and can change over time depending on the evolution of your activity, the latter are the forces that underlie and give energy to all your actions. As such, they are fixed in time because they are rooted in your values and identity.[2] You could say that the motivations are the intentions behind the objectives.

We can, therefore, define an objective as the purpose we set ourselves, the goal we aim for, the result we wish to achieve. The word objective derives from the Latin *obiectus*, past participle of the verb *obicere* 'to put in front'; this meaning reminds us precisely why setting objectives is so important: they serve to trace a route, to illuminate the path we must follow to reach our desired destination.

RELATIONSHIP BETWEEN MOTIVATIONS, GOALS AND ACTION

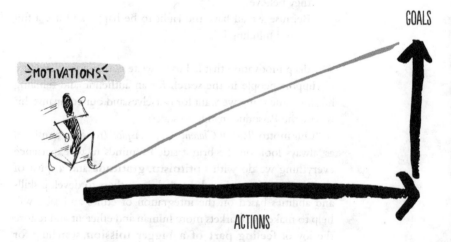

FIGURE 5.1 Relationship between motivations, goals and action

Success in achieving an objective is determined by two aspects:

1. That it is aligned with the motivation.
2. That it is correctly formulated.

Our experience as consultants has taught us that frequently, rather than having no goals, companies may have too many unclear objectives that are sometimes at odds with each other. There are several theories on how to formulate objectives correctly; we learned the one we like best from the psychologist and trainer Roberto Gavioli. For an objective to be good it must possess these eight characteristics:

1. Expressed in a positive form
2. Specific
3. Time-bound
4. Measurable
5. Achievable
6. "Ecological" (i.e. not in contrast with values or other objectives)
7. Sharable
8. Potentiating

Let us analyze these qualities one by one.

The need to express the goal in a **positive form**, which should not be confused with "positive thinking", simply means that the objective must indicate where you are headed and what you want to achieve. "I want to stop selling so little" is thus not a goal; rather, it must be expressed in the form "I want to sell more". This is a step forward but not enough; in fact, you will have to make your goal more specific or indicate precisely and concretely what status or situation you want to achieve. "I want to sell more" should become "I want to sell 100 pieces of product X". Numbers and figures will help you to add substance to your description. Walt Disney said, "The big difference between a goal and a dream is a timeline and accountability". Your assertion of will must, therefore, be **time**-bound; you will have to allow enough time to achieve your goal, but also a target time within which to achieve it. In our example, it will be "I want to sell 100 pieces of product X by 30 June 2020". The concept time-bound also includes providing moments of **verification**, namely intermediate **stages** to assess whether you are moving in the right direction or if you need to change your path, effort or resources. Having the goal clear over time will help you to be more disciplined and to organize the effort you need to make. Note that effort must not be confused with fatigue, the physical and mental state that results from doing things against your will. As we will see when we discuss management of time resources, only an authentic and profound passion for the objective you set yourself can release the dedication, commitment and discipline necessary to achieve it. Moreover, in order to avoid confusion between an objective and a more generic desire, you must be able to **measure** it by answering

60 Love *why* you *do it*

the question "How can I understand when I have reached it?" Measurement tools can refer to quantitative or qualitative parameters; the important thing is to define a criterion that enables you not only to establish when you have reached your goal but also where you are on the journey towards it. When talking about sales, it is easy to verify how many products or services have been marketed; however, when considering intangible aspects such as customer satisfaction, you will have to find a measurement system that could be a "customer satisfaction analysis" tool. "By December 31, 2020, I want to get 98% of votes between 8 and 10 on a decimal scale". An oft-overlooked aspect is that the possibility for an objective to be achievable, stimulating and capable of liberating creative skills will depend on you; you must take **responsibility** for its achievement. There are two possible side effects if you fail to do so: the alibi machine starts producing excuses like: "It's not my fault", or you may become frustrated because you feel unable to control the situation. For example, "I want satisfied customers" may not depend fully on you: maybe the customer is dissatisfied that day because he is going through a difficult time in his life. However, you can state, "our company is committed to contacting all customers who have rated their satisfaction below 8, by March 31, to understand why". The corollary of this rule is that if you set goals that are too high you will, in fact, have an excuse for not achieving them. So always ask yourself if the challenge you are about to accept is in line with you and your company. This approach does not mean looking for an "easy win"; rather, it implies taking full responsibility for your own results. Remember that a good way to tackle the most ambitious challenges is to divide them into **sub-objectives** to be addressed over a period of target dates.

Another tricky element that can hinder the achievement of a goal, even formulated well so far, is that it may conflict with other personal or business goals. Hence, you must verify that it is **ecological** or coherent and **compatible** with the other goals you are pursuing. To conduct this analysis, you will have to carry out some real tests: for example, are the two objectives "I want to sell 100 pieces of product X by December 31, 2020" and "I want to dedicate one day a week to check customer satisfaction" compatible? Depending on the answers, you may either need to redefine your goals to render them compatible or prioritize, deciding which of the two is more important.[3] You can operate in the same way at a team level, by checking if the personal and professional goals of the individual collaborators are aligned to those of the organization and if they support each other.

Point 7, namely having objectives **shareable with others**, reminds you that you must be able to clearly express your goals by explaining benefits and advantages and involving those around you to ensure you have the necessary support. Declaring that your goal is "to become a market leader" will not win many followers, whereas it is better to give yourself a more engaging goal that will convince customers, collaborators, suppliers and other stakeholders to join you in the challenge. Remember that "no man is an island"; in fact, we are all deeply interconnected. A marketing plan like the one you are about to write is just a way of setting and arguing the strategic objectives of your business and then identifying the actions that must follow. When you have drafted your plan, share it with your fellow travelers as indicated above.

Lastly, you must remember that the natural order is evolutionary and that the objectives must, therefore, **empower** both who you are and your organization, thus taking you, and all the people involved in your business, to a higher level. The phrase from Salvatore Brizzi is particularly relevant: "Your goal must force you to learn something new, to meet new people or travel to new places. What you already know can only lead you where you are already".

Activity – Definition of your goals

Review your organization's goals and ask yourself for each one:

1. Is it expressed in a positive form?
   Check if you have used words or phrases with negative connotations (never, avoid, problem...) or actual negations (I don't want..., I no longer want...). Even using conditionals (I would like) or verbs in the past (I wanted) to express a goal is a mistake to avoid.
2. Is it specific?
   Did you use generalizations to describe your goal, for example, by adding adjectives like "best" or "leading"? Try to clearly indicate the context in which you want to excel by including figures, data or numbers that will describe your leading position once it has been reached.
3. Did you consider the time factor?
   Specify two temporal limits as accurately as possible: the time within which you want to achieve your goal and how long it will take to get there.
4. How will you measure final and intermediate results?
   Create a verification system to monitor the progress and achievement of your goal. This can be anything from a simple Excel table to a series of scheduled meetings, depending on the nature of your goal. Once again, where possible, use figures and percentages.
5. Is it a goal that you and your organization can achieve?
   Make a list of who can do what to achieve the goal. If the actions and resources to be implemented are mainly outside your control, redefine the goal in order to bring it under your responsibility and that of your team. In some cases, it may be necessary to scale it back or divide it into steps.
6. Is your goal in conflict with others you consider important?
   Ask yourself what you will have to give up, or what your team must give up, to pursue this particular result. If the answer is "nothing", it means that you have not yet taken into consideration all aspects of its implementation or its

62 Love *why* you *do it*

consequences. In fact, every choice in business and life involves some sacrifice, though sometimes we may not realize it. Once the conflicts have been identified, you have two paths ahead of you: try to solve them or prioritize your outcomes.

7. Is it shareable?

Review what you wrote. Does it seem clear to you? Submit it to your team and get their opinion. The best ideas, like the best goals, are simple and easily comprehensible; otherwise, how can people give you a hand to implement them? Also, check if it is an objective that goes "against" someone's interests and then redevelop it so that it includes benefits for more people.

8. Once you have achieved this goal, will you be better, and will you have produced an evolution?

Each goal must lead you "forward", to evolve together with others. Therefore, first check if the goal you chose is compatible with the motivation you identified thanks to the first activity in this chapter. Then ask yourself if, in addition to improving your own condition, it has somehow strengthened others or the context.

The activity should be applied to all the goals you want to define for your organization. We suggest that you set goals for at least the following five macro categories:

1. Economic and financial – results, efficiency, profit and costs
2. Procedural and product – processes, organization, innovation, time
3. Relational and values – leadership, internal team, services, loyalty
4. Social and environmental – impact on society and the environment
5. Image and reputation – perception improvement, positioning

After defining your goals, you move on to the next phase, the one that allows you to precisely define the **actions** necessary to achieve your objectives. Actions answer the question "What should I do to get that result or achieve that goal?" They are operational acts and as such must have a clear time frame, a link with what comes before and after, a unit of measurement and a weight in the progress towards achieving your goals. It is fundamental to verify the actions you do every day in relation to the objectives you are pursuing, to identify inconsistencies and errors.

Mission and vision: together towards something greater

The work you completed in the previous section has allowed you to identify the elements that you will need to write your business's **mission** and **vision**, namely the two ways we describe what the organization wants to achieve and how and why it wants to do it. If well formulated, they will allow you to tell the market a credible story, to clearly articulate the challenge facing your company and convey its reason for being in an engaging way, thus motivating and engaging the people who work with you as well as potential customers.

We interpret the **mission** as defining the objectives in the short–medium term and it is aimed at customers and employees, while the **vision** looks further ahead and considers the effect of our actions on the entire market and on society. If you reflect on these two concepts from the perspective of a business driven by love, the **vision** leads you to imagine something that has yet to happen, a different future where your aspirations and your values take substance in a scenario that is evolutionary for humans: a better world thanks to you and your activity. The **mission** is an explicit reminder of the task you have to carry out in terms of the contribution you can give "here and now", of what you can offer with the capabilities and competences you have, putting yourselves at the service of your customers.

Love is by nature benevolent and generative, directed at others:
a business driven by love will have to contribute to the
common good and to the generation of new value.

In the same way, the mission and vision of an organization can be interpreted as the proposal it offers to the market, but also to its collaborators and in general to all stakeholders. People will buy into it if they realize that their relationship with the company will allow them to accomplish, in whole or at least partially, their own personal mission as well as contributing to something bigger.

Companies often use the mission and vision as pure communication tools; in fact, they are often created by external companies that try to interpret what they know about the organization so that they can then present it in an attractive form for the market. We recommend you take time to ask yourself and your team about the profound reasons and **values** that characterize your organization. What are you doing to aid the progress of humankind; how will the future change thanks to the path you have responsibly chosen to take? Only by answering this kind of question can you draft a truly attractive statement. Mission and vision are the foundations of the image the company projects, of its operational strategy and of the differential value it offers; they are also fundamental for communicating within the organization, for motivating people and focusing the group on a common goal. You can thus use them dynamically and productively to clarify to yourself and others who you are, what you do and why. Only a clear and authentic declaration – through a mission and a vision that express the deeper motivation of your organization – can enable you to find collaborators, customers and partners who recognize themselves in the same values and meanings.

Activity – Questions to draft your mission and vision statements

Below we suggest some questions to start developing your mission and vision.

Mission

- What goals do I want to achieve for my organization and how?
- How do we want to be perceived and what do we want to become?
- What benefits will the customers receive and why should they believe our promises?
- What capabilities and competences differentiate us from others, enabling us to fulfill the mission?

Vision

- Why did we choose that mission?
- What values and beliefs guide and support us in the process of achieving the objectives?
- What contribution and task do we wish to have towards the market, society and the environment?
- What stimulates stakeholders, customers, collaborators and suppliers to support us and join us?

We also suggest that you look for the mission and vision, or manifesto,[4] of other companies that you like to analyze them and to understand how they are structured so they will help you to create your own version.

Use the mission and vision to verify that all the decisions you make are coherent; this will mean they become tools that are present and active in the daily life of your business. Work with your team to put them into practice by asking what it means at a concrete level for your business to pursue this mission and vision. What can you do, day by day, to move in this direction?

Happiness and sustainability: the success you cannot buy

A business model centered on love should not be mistaken for a naïve approach that fails to consider results, but rather as widening of the perspective with which we look at the organization overall.

The word "success" refers to making things happen, so a successful company could be defined as an organization capable of making "their goals" happen. *Engaging the Heart in Business* reminds you to pursue **sustainable success**. A correct view of corporate sustainability must consider each of the three fundamental dimensions that it comprises:

1. **Environmental** – our activity respects nature and preserves the ecological system in which it operates.
2. **Social** – the company takes care of people (collaborators, customers, suppliers, partners) as well as the community of which it is part.
3. **Economic** – the company earns profit as a fundamental element for its existence and continuity over time (maintaining jobs, investments, fair compensation for collaborators, suppliers and partners).

In contemporary society, when considering sustainability people often think only in terms of the first two points, mistakenly thinking that the economic element does not fall within the ethical objectives of an organization. However, we should not confuse a holistic and wellness-oriented vision of all the actors involved in the economic process with that of do-goodism that damages the system due to a short-sighted perspective.

The company driven by love pursues **success**, knowing that it is connected to the well-being of people rather than to their well-having. The search for material results must be integrated with the pursuit of something higher, capable of enriching and adding value to people's lives through good relationships, recognition and listening to others as well as providing the possibility for each to express their talents and values. This can only come about if we adopt a **new and broader view** of the exchange with all the actors of our business. Even the measurement of a company's performance, which is traditionally entrusted to instruments such as KPIs, Balance Score Cards and financial statement indices, has begun to include new qualitative parameters that can more fully assess its success. For example, parameters such as levels of loyalty and customer satisfaction, the happiness of employees and their turnover (or rotation), as well as the reputation enjoyed by the organization are all now taken into consideration.

The approach we are proposing to you, and the path you have begun taking as you read this book, starts with, what we consider, an essential assumption:

The best form of security is to be courageous, to believe in your talents, in the capabilities and competences that you possess, in the values that distinguish you and in the mission that you want to pursue.

66 Love *why* you *do it*

In our experience, the search for certainties through external expedients – such as the accumulation of material assets, a permanent job, securities and certificates, the capitalization of every action taken – leads to people acting as "auditors", wanting to quantify short-term material gains. This attitude results from a fear of losing what we believe we have earned or what we think is owing to us, without questioning ourselves about the responsibilities and the commitment from which these results derive. Taken to the extreme, this approach transforms relationships into power games where material return is the main factor of choice: nothing could be further from creating a business that can generate strong bonds and exchange love. Approaching the market with love means opening up to others, not with superficial bravado, but with a courage rooted in the awareness of our own identity, in trust, in a broader vision of events and acting freely. Considered thus, success becomes a responsible choice made by the company and by every person within it. The happiness that derives from attaining such success is a parameter to be measured in both tangible and intangible terms. Each goal achieved represents a victory to be celebrated that releases happiness while also providing a starting point for the next goal to be achieved, in an evolutionary vision of business.

For people who are active components of a company on the move, there is no room for complaining about unattained goals: either you accept the situation, or you act to change it.

Survival vs prosperity

Once you have integrated a broader vision of success and results, you will be ready to look carefully, and with a new sensitivity, at the economic aspects of your business. Remember that prosperity in monetary terms should be considered as a means that allows the company to fulfill its mission and shape its vision, not the ultimate goal of the business. The same is true at a personal level, namely, considering wealth as a necessary element to fulfill one's mission.

Many people have a troubled relationship with money. There are some people who lust for accumulation, while on the other hand, there are many who consider money "the root of all evil". Both views are distorted and create an unhealthy relationship of slavery and dependence. Wealth is an instrument, and as such is neither good nor bad: it is the use we make of it that determines its moral quality. Only a person who is aware and responsible for his/her mission can manage money freely, as a means to pursue the common good.

Every individual's behavior regarding money is conditioned by the family and society in which they grew up, by the type of education received and by any limiting convictions that have been accumulated over time. If we fail to recognize these, we risk affecting the possibility of generating wealth and success for ourselves and for others.

If you believe that it is not possible to be rich and spiritually receptive, that you do not deserve success or that you are unable to achieve it, we suggest you work to "open up" and **reshape your personal beliefs**; if you fail to do so, any entrepreneurial effort will be nullified by negative behaviors that you are unable to consciously control.

Love *why* you *do it* **67**

When you are enslaved by money, set on either accumulating or avoiding it, and the term wealth only has material value for you, then your life becomes one of pure survival. Prosperity provides you with the freedom to use the honest fruits of your labor, the income you have gained responsibly and that you are ready to share with others to contribute, through your mission, to making the world a better place.

We advise you to take paper and pencil and write down your personal idea of wealth and well-being, then analyze what you have written in light of the considerations made in this section.

When working and living with a clear vision of the being-offering-receiving cycle, the concept of "giving back" part of what you received makes sense. The meaning of this gesture is powerful and ancient;[5] it conveys a sense of abundance and gratitude, of the connection between all the elements of the system to which we belong. Even the taxes you are required to pay to the state in which your business is located can be seen as a contribution to the larger organization of which you are part. You may well be thinking that your taxes could be better managed, but if you are unwilling to make your contribution to the State and the society in which you operate you will become one of the many people who take, indeed demand, without giving anything back.

During the year, make a habit of offering part of your time or your income to those who need it, either working for free or by making a donation. Where possible, do this anonymously: what you create is new wealth, for yourself and for others.

Conclusion of the case study: traveling to your destination

The two owners of MWM had, therefore, understood the necessity of refocusing the actions of the whole company towards a clear and shared goal, being guided by the deeper values that had characterized the company since its origins. To this end, it was necessary to implement two types of action: one directed towards the group's motivational components and the other to the objectives for performance evaluation. The considerable strength of internal ties and the history of MWM provided a valuable resource for the former: the owners' grandmother and wife of the company's founder still had an active role on the company's Board of Directors. This highly cultured and charismatic woman was willing to meet periodically with all the collaborators to reset the internal relationships on the basis of the deepest values and motivations so that they could be transferred to external relationships with client companies, partners and all other stakeholders.

At this point, it was necessary to enhance the staff's approach to customer satisfaction by helping them feel part of a unique system where the objectives of each were interconnected with those of others. Hence, the owners decided to change the system of corporate bonuses, assigned each year based on results. While previously the bonuses had been linked solely to the objectives connected to each employee's role, it was decided to include the quality of interaction with colleagues and customers, considering both quantitative and relational aspects.

For salespeople, for example, the new reward system envisaged verifying four parameters: sales margins, customer loyalty, customer satisfaction and colleagues' satisfaction. While the first two elements can be calculated numerically through economic data, the other two which deal with more intangible aspects are measured through internal and external satisfaction questionnaires. Once these changes were in place, in 2016, the company's revenue increased by 5.5% while overall the growth in the Italian logistics market in the same period stood at 1.2%.[6] This increase was the result of acquiring new customers but was also achieved thanks to more purchases by loyal customers. Data on the number of "non-conformities" due to partial shipments or other errors, as analyzed through the quality system, showed a decrease from 46% to 24%; the departments were working together better and in a more profitable way. The new bonus system enabled employees to focus more on quality, leading to fewer errors in the preparation of shipments (both in terms of goods and accounting documentation), better cleaning and organization of spaces and in general a more fluid communication between different sectors and services. The sales staff, on the other hand, paid greater attention to the phases of analysis of customer needs and pre-sales, immediately involving the operations sector to assess the feasibility of certain services when preparing a quote. The employees have a greater awareness of their own role, and of the value that each task contributes to individual and company growth, thus reducing internal conflicts and inefficiencies and generating a more productive organization oriented towards a clear common goal.

What you have learnt and adding a piece to the *Loving Business Model*

By the time you finish this chapter, you will have described your goals, mission and vision more clearly. They are central aspects of the *Loving Business Model* and occupy a privileged place in the diagrams that illustrate it. Don't worry if some of them are still at the draft stage: putting them on paper is the first and perhaps most important step to achieving them. Check the consistency with the actions in the activity and, last but not least, make a serious analysis of what you can give back for everything you have received.

Notes

1 You can read our complete manifesto at https://diariodiunconsulente.it/en/passodue/manifesto-passodue/
2 You could argue that some of our actions are motivated by fear, hatred and other negative impulses. However, further reflection will suggest that, more than true motivations that push us towards something, they are impulses that stimulate escape. In a sense, therefore, they are the opposite of motivations.
3 Defining a hierarchy of objectives does not fully resolve the contrast but at least allows one priority to be assigned.
4 *Mission* and *vision* can be united in a single text and become the company's manifesto, which may also be presented as a video.
5 It is no coincidence that many religions require the faithful to pay the "tithing" or to give the needy a tenth part of their earnings.
6 Contract Logistics Observatory of the Politecnico di Milano.

6

LOVE *WHO* YOU DO IT *FOR*

Who your customers are and what you can do for them

Abstract

The analysis of the customer and his/her needs is one of the central elements of every business model or strategic business plan. Marketing has many tools to conduct such research, but what we offer is an alternative way of looking at your customers. We will not focus on their age, nationality, buying behavior or other "tangible" parameters to define an identikit; we will talk instead about their values and the motivations that lead them to choose. In short, we will try to answer the question "Why do they buy?" and then cross it with the answer to "Why do we sell?". We will discover how the two answers are inextricably linked.

Case study: falling in love with the "wrong" customer

You have no idea how many companies, professionals and organizations turn to us asking us to change their "target" customers: they have too few or those they have

70 Love *who* you do it *for*

are not rich and prestigious enough, not ethical enough or technically competent, unkind and untrustworthy, or simply unwelcome. Customers are very often a problem for those who do business and not only because of the numbers but also and above all for reasons of quality. Some time ago, a professional architect who owns a design school that designed spaces according to the rules of *Feng Shui*, an ancient Chinese discipline for harmonizing individuals with their surroundings, turned to us. She wanted to identify the type of client most suited to her school's courses. Although she was an architect herself, she did not consider the programs that the school offered as suitable for those who had chosen a traditional academic path to prepare for the design of spaces: the school was more suited to a general audience. Considering the advanced qualifications of the teachers and the technical complexity of the topics covered, this was clearly a contradiction, though the school's manager found this difficult to take on board and this misapprehension prevented her from enjoying the hoped-for success. The school was in danger of attracting students who were no more than superficially interested in the discipline and the professional fields where it could be applied. In fact, many students attended the early modules but failed to complete the specialization course. What was the answer? To help her trigger the reciprocal appeal!

Marketing and the reciprocal appeal

You can't please everyone. We all know this for a fact: it is a kind of natural law that is valid in economics as well as in personal relationships. So, trying to attract all the customers present in the market in which we operate by looking for a "general" customer is a mistake that can lead to the opposite result: not attracting anyone! And yet for years, companies have attempted to continually widen the net to include an increasing number of people in their marketing strategies, thus contradicting another fundamental law associated with happiness: "less is more".[1]

Even when talking about customers, it is better to specialize rather than slip towards generalization.[2] So, why do companies continue to expand their strategy in the illusory hope of drawing more customers into their net? Because they think it gives them an abundance of opportunities and leads to sales.

Nature teaches us that to make a plant flourish it is necessary to prune it, cut off the dead branches or withered flowers and water it constantly but sparingly, to give it quality nurturing not just an excess of attention. Think of your company as a living organism that will thrive if you follow the rules of *Danshari*,[3] an ancient Japanese discipline that teaches us to dispose of the superfluous things you have, namely everything that is not true to your essence. Therefore, Danshari not only preaches eliminating everything you do not need but also to reach towards what is essential. Identifying, ordering and focusing are the keywords of this approach, the same ones we will use to talk about your customers. What is the purpose of all this? To live a lighter and happier existence, with a lightness that will allow you to progress and evolve more easily, happiness that will allow you to inspire and attract new customers in line with what you really are and with the promises you can keep.

Both lightness and happiness need space. One to allow movement; the other to make room for those who want to share it with you. If, on the contrary, your business is weighed down by baggage you do not need, such as customers who do not resemble you and products that do not represent you, the impact will be negative. Any business thus encumbered will slow down and stall until it grinds to a stop: it will block the doors to the innovation and beauty that awaits you.

Customers are people and people need attention; they need intimacy and to be listened to. All this will be lacking if your company resembles a crowded room. Moreover, dedicating yourself to the right customers attracts new customers who resemble the first ones: customers, in fact, participate and sustain the identity of your company by supporting it with their consistency and spreading its reputation by word of mouth. If you choose generic customers your brand will be watered down.

But how do you choose on which customers to direct your focus? By taking advantage of the reciprocal appeal.

Many authors have spoken of the strength that binds our inner reality, our deepest thoughts, to what happens to us, seemingly impacting on how we attract certain occurrences, people, wealth and much more. If we apply this principle to an enterprise, we may say that it is not enough to want to have customers of a certain type to engage them. Rather, we need to work on ourselves and our company, to fully understand who/what we are and then to evolve in a direction that will allow us to fulfill our aspirations. Similarly, if we attract customers we do not like, we must have the strength and courage to admit that, at least in part, they "reflect" our essence. Namely, we must recognize that although this is not what we want, a part of what we don't like about them can be found in our own DNA. You may feel angry when told you deserve the customers you have, for better or for worse, but if your customers are unethical, then it is time to reflect on your own ethics; if they do not pay you regularly, consider how you behave with your suppliers, and so on! The harsh reality is that you cannot change your customers' minds, but the good news is that if you work on yourself, your organization and your offer, the customers you attract will change: a challenging task, but absolutely possible.

Since we attract what we are, your brand, which is the company's personality, will play a very important role in activating the magnet that "attracts customers", just like the most intangible elements of your offer that include, for example, your style of action and the service you offer. We will analyze these intangible aspects of the offer in Chapter 7; for now, you need only be aware that both your **value components** and those of your customers must resemble each other to activate a mutual attraction.

In Chapter 4 you learned a method to identify and systemize company values, but how do you investigate your customer's values? To do this, let us discuss the concept of **purchasing motivations** that we presented in the book *Sales Ethics*.

The motivations are those profound drives that "support" the customer's entire buying process. Unlike the needs that respond to the question "What shall I buy?" they respond to the inner question "Why should I buy?" The motivations are complex to investigate because the customers themselves are often unaware of them.

72 Love who you do it for

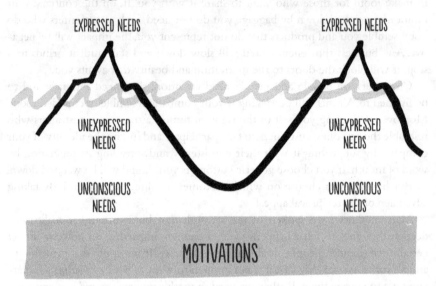

FIGURE 6.1 Connection needs – motivations

Hence, the salesperson must be able to politely question (this is not an interrogation) the customer to activate a genuinely interested dialogue, while listening closely enough to pick up any nuances and build empathy.

Our research into motivations has shown that, even if different people express them in different ways, their motivations can be divided into ten main categories[4] as follows:

1. Security, tranquility and reliability
2. Health, well-being and physical fitness
3. Savings or earning money, bargains, offers
4. Comfort, ease, simplicity
5. Speed, efficiency, optimization
6. Belonging to a group, esteem of others, acceptance
7. Friendship and bond with the seller, personalization of the relationship
8. Status and prestige, uniqueness, exclusivity, pride
9. Innovation, being updated, having the latest novelty
10. Personal growth, knowledge, evolution

All these elements may influence our purchasing decisions but some, and usually one in particular, are more powerful than others and remain constant over time, i.e. they influence all our negotiations. Such elements relate to people's values, to their identity and as such undergo few changes over time. Although the purchase needs

Love *who* you do it *for* **73**

RECIPROCAL APPEAL

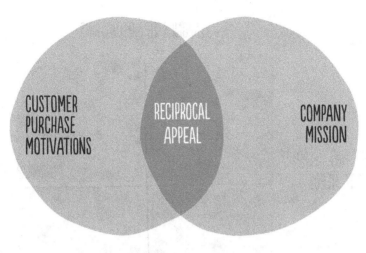

The company's values, primarily described by the Mission, encounter the customer's values, which become purchase motivations, triggering the reciprocal appeal.

FIGURE 6.2 Reciprocal appeal

change (the "things" may be different depending on the situations and moments) the motivations remain because profoundly similar goals guide all our purchasing choices. In fact, the purchase motivation acts as the **customer's mission**, the value objective pursued in the purchase. Customer mission and company mission are the expression of values and of the identity of both. For the reciprocal appeal to be triggered, they must in some way coincide, or at least have something in common.

Anyone operating in the market knows that economic exchange takes place when the demand curve and the supply curve meet. We define a price–quantity balance at that point that allows the transaction to take place. In this relationship, however, only the material aspect of the exchange is taken into consideration. But, what changes if in accordance with what we said above we also include the value components? Figure 6.3 will help you to better understand what really happens and, therefore, to understand the reciprocal appeal and its action over time.

If you respond only to the "What do you need?" elements to attract your customers, offering them an offer with features that express exclusively material benefits, you will not ensure their full satisfaction over time and will not make them fall in love with you. To achieve this, it is also necessary to respond to customers' motivations, i.e. to provide a "why" that will appeal to their value system – to their purchase motivation. Therefore, your organization's mission must intersect with the goals of the person who is buying your products or services.[5]

74 Love *who* you do it *for*

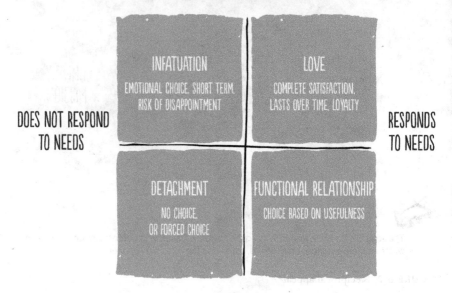

FIGURE 6.3 Needs/motivations relationship

This diagram will help you act in accordance with the *Loving Business Model*. When we talk about customers we are referring not only to "external" ones but also "internal" ones. Partners and collaborators are your first "customers", the people who must recognize themselves in your mission, which must also respond to these people's motivations. Without them, your business plan will flounder and external relations will suffer too because the people we treat poorly or who do not feel represented and connected with the organization they work for will always reflect this frustration in their relationship with the consumers; everyone will pay a price for this situation. We will discuss this point in greater detail in Chapter 9.

There is another reason why this diagram is important: it will help you analyze the most interesting and stable clients over time. Follow us in the next section to understand how.

From target to fellow human being: a new method for getting to know your customers

The analytical dimension of a business's activity is fundamental, even when it comes to a business driven by love! The data are necessary to delve deeper, to avoid bias, to broaden your experience and your vision, and exchange ideas with others, including your collaborators, based on facts. Hence, it is essential to obtain data through specific analyses, then organize them and interpret them in a new way so that they can help you liberate creativity and activate the production of value for you, for your customers and for all your stakeholders.

What kind of data does the *Loving Business Model* require?

An organization that wishes to be inspired by love cannot limit itself to analyzing its customers' personal details, their spending capacity and some other "tangible" indicators.
It must investigate further, to attempt to penetrate the consumers' "heart" where their deepest goals lie, their values and aspirations and the search for the meaning that each person wishes to give to his or her life.

Is there an investigation tool that can do this?

In recent years, marketing has developed a myriad of models for customer surveys, from the simplest such as the ABC analysis based on the Pareto principle[6] (better known as the 80/20 rule) to the use of sophisticated KPIs[7] capable of measuring market attractiveness and purchasing potential. They are all valid and interesting tools that speak to us about target customers but not about people.

To construct a useful analysis for our purposes, we must first understand how the purchasing decision-making process works, i.e. understand how and why a person decides to implement certain behaviors when selecting products and services.

Let's analyze Figure 6.4, by retracing this process step by step:

- **Identity** – More than a market player, the customers are people. Like everyone, they have their own aspirations, needs and values. These aspects of their personality affect their choices because they influence and shape the goals they will pursue in the purchase.
- **Needs and motivations** – These are the purchasing objectives. They define the "why" and the "what" we choose. Motivations are closely connected to our values and to what we are. Purchase motivations and needs are generated when we need something (tangible or intangible) or we want something to help us strengthen, support, develop or extend our identity.
- **Benefits** – Once purchasing "drives" have been generated, people go in search of something that can respond to their "whys" and the needs they generate. How do they do this? Imagining, perhaps unconsciously, their future consumption experience. Namely, they insert that product or service into a sort of personal plot in which they are the protagonists. We all imagine that what we are about to buy will do something for us and consider whether it is useful and consistent or not with our purposes. In short, we imagine a benefit and anticipate what we would like the product or service to do for us.

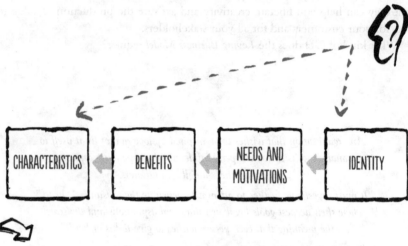

*Customers are prompted by **values** connected to the **identity**; what we sell contains a **promise** of value that attracts those who can buy it*

FIGURE 6.4 Purchase process diagram

Characteristics – As soon as we have an idea of the kind of benefit we are seeking, we begin to refer to our consumer experience or to our imagination to define which features the item we are going to buy should have. In fact, we design it by forming in our mind an idea of the ideal product/service for our purposes. Everyone does this, whether they have any technical knowledge or not; in the latter case, the unconscious process could lead us to formulate unfulfillable expectations.

Obviously, the process described above does not evolve in such a compartmentalized way and may even be completely unconscious and take place in just a few moments. However, we have based the flow chart on our experience and field research to provide a model that reflects reality. If you reverse the flow, you can go back from what you sell to the motivations and values of those who purchase, thus accessing the beating heart of your customer's choices. What do you need to do this? The data relating to your sales: information that every company should have available. And if your enterprise is a start-up? You can refer to the products that will have the greatest impact on sales, based on forecasts made when drafting your business plan.

For the sake of convenience, and to make it easier for you to follow our reasoning, we will describe the analysis while referring to the enterprise we presented in the case study at the beginning of this chapter.

Our client had already been in business for some time, so she had reliable data available. We thus started by asking ourselves a simple question: which of the school courses produces the greatest revenues?

Love *who* you do it *for* **77**

All businesses tend to have a distribution of revenues that follows Pareto's principle: this means that roughly 80% of profit comes from 20% of all the products/services sold. You should also find it simple to identify the products and services that have the greatest impacts on your own results. The turnover of our client's school was fairly consistent with the 80/20 principle; once we had identified which courses contributed most,[8] all we had to do was analyze their features by focusing on the first box on the left of the purchase process diagram illustrated in Figure 6.4.

Here is a list of the main features of these courses. As you will see, both the tangible and intangible features that distinguish a product/service must be considered when conducting this analysis:

- Ten-day courses
- Weekend sessions scheduled
- Teaching and technical materials provided to participants (specific lecture notes and work tools)
- Certification at the end of the course, recognized by an organization or professional body
- Professors with relevant professional profiles
- Classroom exercises on real cases
- Involvement of professional bodies and associations
- Homogeneity of the curriculum and professional experiences of the participants

At this point, what we had to do was identify the benefits attached to these features. Once again, we proceed in an orderly fashion, asking ourselves how the customer benefits from each feature:

What is the benefit of a ten-day course? It allows participants to study the subject in further detail by completing a learning pathway over time. If you want to become a true expert in Feng Shui, this will be your choice.

What is the benefit of weekend sessions? People can work throughout the week and then find time to attend weekend sessions without being forced to make too many changes to commitments. This is the ideal solution if you have little time to devote to training, i.e. if it must fit around your work.

What do you do with course materials? Course materials serve to complete an "instruction manual" that you can consult as needed; you can review the course contents if necessary and you will have the main tools to perform your new profession when you become a Feng Shui consultant.

And the certification? It is important if you want qualifications that you can use in your business activities if you need to prove your skills or acquire training credits to maintain your professional status.

What advantage derives from having established professionals as teachers? It gives participants direct contact with people who practice in this profession, enabling students to exchange views and ask questions and perhaps create a useful network of relationships for after the course.

78 Love *who* you do it *for*

The practical exercises based on real cases, many suggested by students themselves, enable participants to start planning while still in the classroom, while being followed by teachers and tutors. A strong advantage if you are starting to use the knowledge professionally.

Why is the involvement of professional bodies and associations advantageous? If you have limited opportunities to keep up to date with training proposals, you can more easily find out about them here; moreover, a course accredited by an association you know serves as a guarantee and is an important factor when choosing the course to ensure this context is suited to you.

What is the advantage of having a homogeneous classroom in terms of experience and skills? Again, the advantage of finding yourself among people who are similar to you and will have a comparable learning speed. There is nothing worse than having to slow down a lesson because someone does not have the skills needed to continue. Furthermore, the relationships you build with your colleagues in the classroom will be useful to you in the future.

The last step is currently missing to complete the diagram and find out who the school's ideal client is! Let's tackle it by asking ourselves: "What needs and motivation would lead you to consider the above-mentioned outcomes advantageous?" Let's investigate some of the reasons.

Why would a person wish to become a Feng Shui professional by training in our client's school? It is likely these people are looking for a new professional identity or want to add an extra skill to their curriculum as a designer. They may be looking for something original that has relatively few practitioners, meaning they can differentiate their offer. They may be curious and interested in disciplines that have a spiritual/evolutionary component, which is founded in the study of human beings. Moreover, the motivations linked to the first field could be of an economic nature (to gain better results thanks to differentiation) or linked to cognitive and personal development.

Why would students want to create a relationship with the teacher and are "practical" *answers necessary?* The time and money invested are important for many, so everything they do must lead to a result (again, economic motivation); they may also require a stronger network of contacts to consolidate their profession (belonging and security).

Why would students want to do practical activities in the classroom? It enables them to make the most of their training (speed and effectiveness) by obtaining real, even economic, advantages from attendance in the classroom. Moreover, we all know that "doing" is the best way to learn (personal development).

Why would a person want to choose courses in a familiar environment? There are so many low-level courses around but it is better to be on the safe side (safety). They make also like to be in a familiar environment (belonging).

Why is it important that the participants share similarities? They risk, otherwise, finding themselves in a place in which they do not want to be (belonging) and you avoid the risk of wasting time while waiting for less-skilled participants to catch up (money well spent and speed).

By combining all the elements that emerged from the analysis[9] we carried out with our client, we were able to produce a well-defined profile. The most common motivation is economic, linked to affirming and promoting success at work: those who attend our client's courses are likely to aim at transforming the course outcomes into sources of income and professional value! Moreover, participants like to find themselves among similar people, to be recognized as a professional among other professionals (belonging). Certainly, they are people who invest time and money in personal growth (knowledge and personal development), who are interested in disciplines related to well-being and the person (health and well-being), especially when the knowledge has ancient roots. It is a priority for these people that the course leads to the achievement of the promised results; in fact, they check the teachers' CVs and the venue where the course will be held as well as other factors related to safety.

What type of people fit this profile? The figure that sprung to our mind was that of architects, or at least designers, who wanted to re-launch themselves as professionals and promote their studios. This might be a person with strong professional pride who could worry about being ripped off or getting involved in a course that was too "mystical", perhaps interesting but hardly useful in practice. A diametrically opposed persona compared to the one initially imagined by the school manager and, above all, very similar to her own professional profile! Once again, we were able to see how attraction is reciprocal.

Activity – Reconstruct the purchase process to understand your customer

By downloading the grid in the download area, you can reconstruct your customer's purchasing behavior by moving from left to right until you identify their way of thinking and their identity.

Start by listing your differentiating features with respect to your competitors or, however, that are specific to the products or services that contribute most to your revenues. Then, ask yourself what benefits each feature brings[10] and to what purchase motivations it may refer (selecting them from the list of

CUSTOMER ANALYSIS GRID

CHARACTERISTICS	BENEFITS	MOTIVATIONS	CUSTOMER IDENTIKIT
Differentiating most sold products or services	That derive from these characteristics (what customers do with them)	That can lead to the benefits in the column on the left being considered important and valuable	With these motivations, who could this be?

FIGURE 6.5 Customer analysis grid

the ten most common ones). Are there certain elements that emerge more frequently? If so, try to compose a profile of the person that would be motivated by these reasons. Eventually, you can create more than one identikit by combining them differently each time.

Motivations meet mission: when love is triggered

Why didn't we study immediately the profiles of those who enroll in our client's courses to carry out the analysis? Would we have reached the same conclusions?

Let's start with the answer to the first question, bearing in mind that there is not always enough customer data available to do a reliable analysis, especially in the case of start-ups. On the other hand, even new entrepreneurs know the features of what they are preparing to offer because they will be part of the business plan the person has in mind. Moreover, even when the company is already up and running, the "real" customer may not always be the one who is buying more in quantitative terms. Indeed, the case of the Feng Shui school corresponded to this latter scenario: some professionals had already participated in some of the school's courses, but the training program had not been prepared with this specific user in mind.

We should add a further consideration that gives us the answer to the second question: this type of investigation gives more in-depth and stable indications because it deals not only with the customers' physical/personal data (which changes over time in line with their needs) but also considers what they really care about, their values and deeper identity: all things that characterize people over time.

Thus, even if we had had enough quantitative data to identify the typical "target" for the school, we would have missed the aspirations and desires of these people, their will to consolidate their identity through what they buy, to recognize themselves and exorcise their fears. Therefore, we would have failed to identify the motivations of the school's clients, those with whom we aligned the school's mission through the mechanism we will now describe.

According to the media company Soul Pancake that conducted a series of experiments within the project called "The Science of Happiness",

> *One of the greatest contributing factors to overall happiness is gratitude. Indeed, gratitude is a powerful state of mind that can give sense and meaning to our life, making us feel part of something greater.*

Gratitude, one of the many forms that love can take, is a true exchange: the person who feels grateful offers their gratitude to another person and receives it in return. Like love, the reciprocity nourishes its strength. If you are grateful to your customers, they will reciprocate the feeling. How can you do so? By involving them in something bigger, a goal that is not only important for you and for them, but for the system and the society in which you are immersed. This goal does not conflict with that of other competitors on the market (we will discuss the relationship with competitors in Chapter 8). What goal is so powerful in the case of the school that it can generate general agreement? This goal corresponds to our client's mission:

> *Helping to create a new generation of designers who, by integrating specific technical skills and abilities with an awareness of the relationship between humans and space inspired by the millennial principles of Feng Shui, can shape buildings and places to improve life and make people's relationship with the environment more pleasant, efficient and human.*

On the other hand, what is the customers' mission as it emerged from our earlier analysis of their reasons for purchase? We can summarize it like this:

> *To re-qualify and re-launch my profession as a designer by adding skills and abilities that allow me to differentiate myself, thus offering my clients new tools aimed at*

82 Love *who* you do it *for*

creating unique spaces and environments, specifically designed for their well-being. To this end, entrusting my training to professionals and following certified courses aimed at people like me who are proud of their role and with whom I will be able to compare my experiences and dialogue in the future.

Do you notice any similarities between these two statements? Both the clients and the school want to contribute to well-being; both want to affirm and develop the role of conscious planning and invest in extending skills and abilities by combining technical knowledge with millennial disciplines. This is how the reciprocal appeal can be triggered: in this context, love can be born between those who buy and those who sell. No compromise will be necessary because the school and its students will get results. In fact, the more faithful the school is to its mission, the better it will be able to offer the participants what they are really seeking.

Therefore, a common goal exists, a meeting of values that is not only desired but also becomes a concrete experience in the relationship between customers and companies.

Conclusion of the case study: from "I'll buy it" to "I love you"

After all the efforts made to promote your offer, there is nothing more disappointing than having no takers or only finding customers with whom you have very little in common. Unfortunately, this happens to many organizations and professionals, and it had also happened to the architect from the Feng Shui school who then turned to us. After a careful analysis of her offer, we discovered the motivations for the appeal of her course proposals and the type of people who could be really interested. We can succeed only by turning to real people, not just targets as the military metaphor of marketing would have us believe. Targets must be conquered whatever the cost, whereas people must fall in love with what we are and then accept what we offer them. Whether we are aware of it or not, our offer is born from who we are. Thus, the services and courses of our client's Feng Shui school express the essence and deepest values of the organization and the people who designed and delivered them. The purchase and supply of products and services are creative actions implemented by human beings whose aspirations, values and hopes must converge. The pathway our architect had to follow was neither easy nor immediate. Discovering, or rediscovering, her "real" customers meant performing a profound self-analysis, accepting that she was different from the initial image that she had of herself and her organization. She had to make changes to render her offer consistent with the desires and needs of the people to whom the courses are now addressed, working to refine and calibrate her marketing and communication tools. The results were excellent and are continually improving: the school has radically increased the overall number of participants (participants in the introductory courses have more than doubled, rising from an average of 30 to over 100 students) and designers in particular, from 46% to 89% of the total number of students enrolled.

What you have learnt and adding a piece to the *Loving Business Model*

Thanks to the customer analysis scheme, you have determined the identity of the people who might be interested in what you do. If you are a start-up, it may be useful to read Chapter 7 that deals with designing your offer, to identify the characteristics of what you sell and then to complete the task. Once you have obtained the client's identikit, compare the motivations with your mission as determined by the activities completed in Chapter 5. If there are discrepancies or inconsistencies, refine the work and make changes until the whole is more harmonious. Now you can add a piece to the *Loving Business Model* by entering the description obtained in the "customer" box.

Notes

1 From Robert Browning in the poem *Andrea del Sarto*, 1855; this concept is generally associated with the architect Ludwig Mies Van Der Rohe (1886–1969).
2 Those who operate in mass markets (such as the large-scale retail trade) only appear to target a generic customer: in fact, the specific customer profile at which Whole Foods Market aims is very different from that of Walmart. The only true mass markets are those linked to commodities or generic goods (for example, raw materials). These are not the subject of this discussion as the book addresses those businesses and products that can express differential value and thus have a specific customer.
3 This has recently become fashionable as "decluttering".
4 In our previous book *Sales Ethics*, we compared the customer's mind to an iceberg with the motivations forming its base. Each customer has their own and thus seems different and separate from the others. In fact, as we believe that such motivations can be identified in ten main categories, the customers all resemble each other to an extent and may have basically similar purchasing drives.
5 According to research conducted by the Corporate Executive Board (CEB), 94% of failures to activate new customers occur because the latter did not "recognize" themselves in the seller's offer.
6 Delers, Antoine. *Pareto's Principle*. 50minutes.com, 2019.
7 A *Key Performance Indicator* is a measurable value that demonstrates how effectively a company is achieving key business objectives, also referring to sales goals.
8 The 80/20 analysis is based on the revenue generated and not on the quantity of products or services sold. In the case of the *Feng Shui* school, for example, as we said the most frequently attended courses were the basic ones, but these had relatively little impact on income as they were shorter and cheaper.

84 Love *who* you do it *for*

9 To double-check the results of the analysis you can work with focus groups made up of selected clients.
10 Remember that each feature can be associated with more than one advantage. For example, weekend programming has the advantage of allowing you to work during the rest of the week without loss of earnings, but also to concentrate the learning and make it quick and productive.

7
LOVE *WHAT YOU DO*

The offer system and the creation of value

Abstract

What are you selling to your customers and what do they really want to buy from you? It seems an easy question to answer: all you need to do is consult the price list in your catalog or look at the description on your invoices. Yet it is not that simple. The offer of companies and professionals is much more complex than a list of products and services. There is something intangible, an invisible element hidden between the lines which, however, plays a very important role in the process of customer choice. The goal of this chapter is to accompany you in the precise definition of your offer system to make the invisible emerge, thus helping customers to focus on what really matters.

Case study: the challenge of standing out in a uniform world

The challenge of emerging in an increasingly uniform market is one of the most demanding tasks for every entrepreneur. The risk of the "commodification"[1] effect

86 Love *what you do*

(which we will discuss in more detail in the following chapter) that makes an offer generic, emptying it of *differential value* in the eyes of the customer, is ever-present. What is the most immediate consequence? It is much more likely that customers make their purchase choice based purely on a comparison of price! Indeed, who would blame them? If product A is apparently equivalent to product B, what other parameters exist apart from the price when you are deciding which to buy?

If there is one industry that perhaps suffers more than others from this effect, it is the sale of "mandatory" services for companies, such as work health and safety protocols and courses that must be purchased by law (at least within the European Union). Whatever the sector in which you do business, you must certify your safety procedures and equip yourself with a protocol that ensures the safety of staff and customers, keeping all risks to a minimum. In addition, you must ensure that your employees participate in certified courses in which they learn how to behave in an emergency. To comply with these obligations, companies have no alternative but to turn to a provider (institutions, service companies or freelancers) that can provide advice and training in all these fields. When you make a purchase of this kind, you are guided principally by three parameters of choice: that this costs as little as possible, that the time dedicated to these activities is kept to a minimum and that the responsibility for any claim can be delegated, at least in part. Those who are selling such services risk being crushed by a dynamic of competition that focuses on prices and short duration, even at the expense of quality. A few years ago, a company operating in this sector turned to us with a simple but fundamental question: how can I differentiate myself qualitatively in order to convince customers to choose me?

Apparently, all the health and safety services for the workplace are similar; they are generic and not personalized because they must respect precise legislative standards that inevitably tend to render them uniform. At first glance it seemed there was little space for maneuver to make this company stand out and add value, especially as customers wished to dedicate little time to these activities. Let's see together how we helped our client to add real value to their market proposal, without sacrificing efficiency and speed of service.

The offer system: "what is essential is not always visible"

If at least once in your life you have eaten at a restaurant that you liked, you will understand the following explanation regarding the "offer system".

When we enjoy a complex experience, such as eating out, there are many elements beyond the tangible ones that lead us to conclude that it has been a positive experience. A great chef will probably be better at choosing the ingredients needed to prepare his dishes; indeed, his ability to bring a positive experience to the guests is made up of a mix of elements: the ingredients, the way they are combined, the sequence of courses presented throughout the meal, the wine that accompanies it, the way the dishes are presented, the service, the table settings, the atmosphere and

Love *what you do* **87**

much more. Everything helps to create a difference in value when compared with other offers. Think of your business as a restaurant. In your new role as head chef, would you like to promote and give visibility only to the individual ingredients that you place on your customer's plate or would you attempt to argue all the rest? Just as for a restaurant, a company's offer is "systemic", namely it is composed of various elements, both **tangible and intangible**, which are put together in a precise order and together create **differential value**. The individual elements that make up what we call the offer system may be very similar if taken alone, or even identical, to those of any other organization. However, it is the wise use of the interplay between them that will make your proposal unique and unrepeatable. If you make the mistake of guiding your customers' attention to just one aspect of what you do, without helping them to consider the other elements, especially the intangible ones, you will not be enabling them to choose consciously.

When as buyers we are uncertain, we instinctively look for precise elements on which to base our choice. What happens, then, to customers who cannot understand how you are different from others? They will consider the only information that is always comprehensible and available: the price! Our research has highlighted that there is one principal reason that prevents the whole offer system from being considered during the purchase: information asymmetry, a condition in which some of the information is lacking. Customers can be affected by **information asymmetries** but, more frequently than you may imagine, it is companies that are subject to them regarding their own offer system. What we are saying is that those selling are unaware of what they are actually proposing to the market! And if the sellers do not know, how can they ever explain it to their customers? The information asymmetries that afflict you will sooner or later afflict the people you meet on the market too. What you must do immediately, by following the indications contained in this chapter, is fill your knowledge gaps, becoming fully aware of what makes up your offer system and the hierarchical connections between the various elements that compose it. We are talking about a hierarchy because, in the composition of your business proposal, you will discover that there is something more important and *barycentric* than any other element. The offer system can, in fact, be represented as shown in Figure 7.1.[2]

As can be seen from the structure of this diagram, one component will be central, acting as a pivot for the entire offer. Being able to identify which factor performs this role, compared to all those that make up the offer, is very important because the whole structure of your proposal to the market will depend on it. To do this you will have to ask yourself which component best represents your brand and mission and can best differentiate you from the competition. The position of the elements may vary depending on the market and the customers you are managing. An example that we often use in our courses is that of FIAT. In Italy, the company's production and business revolves around the automobile, and two specific models, the FIAT 500 and the FIAT Panda. In the other countries where the brand is present, especially in the US, the pivotal role around which the entire offer revolves

ILLUSTRATION OF THE OFFER SYSTEM

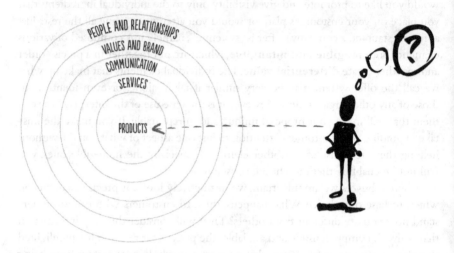

FIGURE 7.1 Illustration of the offer system

is given by its *Italianess*: a more distinctive and differentiating element in those markets. An analysis of the promotion and communication style adopted by FIAT in the two cases confirms this thesis: in Italy, the focus is on the tangible qualities of the product such as technical performance, comfort and prices, while in the US the focus is on intangible aspects such as Italian culture and lifestyle, creativity and non-conventionality of choice.[3]

Once we have completed this model together, filling out all the fields by completing the activity proposed in the next section, it will be much easier for you to argue your offer and make everything you do for your customers visible.

Structuring the offer system: giving form to your value

Designing the offer system does not mean merely adding services to your products or products to your services, nor using digital elements to "dress up" the purchase experience. Rather, it is about creating an **organized set** of valuable, tangible and intangible elements, which can satisfy not only the needs expressed by your customers but also those that are unexpressed and of which the customers themselves are unaware, as well as responding to their deeper motivations. This is the only way they will really **fall in love with your offer**!

In the process of organizing and implementing your proposal to the market, you will discover things about yourself and your organization that will enable you to more fully appreciate the value you can express, thus avoiding damaging informational asymmetries. Undoubtedly, such discoveries will lead to a greater love for

Love *what you do* **89**

what you do. Love will help you design the offer by making it attractive and shaping the tools you will learn to use in this section in the most engaging way.

Maslow's hierarchy of needs, introduced in Chapter 2, will be particularly useful to you in this context. To define an offer as "good", it must respond adequately to all levels of the hierarchical pyramid.

Such needs are present also in relations between people, in love stories and in business. Let's see together how we proceeded to keep true to the *Loving Business Model* in the case of the service company with which we started the chapter, analyzing the answer found for each level of need.

Physiological needs

What is the primary need linked to the purchase of courses and consultancy regarding safety? As anticipated at the beginning of the chapter, it is to comply with the law in the swiftest and cheapest way possible. To respond to this need, our client had to design an offer whose duration and price were in line with market demands, in order to suggest to his interlocutors, "I can supply exactly what you need". Complying with this prerequisite was necessary to get customers to consider the offer. On the other hand, if he wanted to differentiate himself in his response to this type of need, he would have two alternatives: either offering lower prices or shortening the consultancy and training (provided that the law permitted this). Our interlocutor rejected these two options.

Safety needs

It may seem paradoxical to speak of meeting the need for safety when discussing an offer for services that deal with this very theme. In fact, the question to ask is rather more complex, namely: "What is the need for safety to which a service that offers consultancy on *safety* must respond during the purchase and delivery?" The answer is to offer buyers the certainty that they will be able to shift part of their responsibilities for risks at work to the supplier. Buyers also require the certainty that the task will be carried out correctly, with no risk of problems or difficulties. What elements could the company put in its offer system to meet this need? One example would be case studies that attest its ability to manage emergencies and complex situations, guidelines provided to deal with injuries at work, toll-free numbers that can be contacted; indeed, anything that sends the customer the message: "Do not worry, I'll look after it; I have the skills and abilities to resolve such situations". To differentiate the company in this field, our client made every relationship with buyers and course participants easier and more accessible, clearly setting out all the phases and the method followed to perform consultations, while also providing data and concrete evidence to back up his promises.

90 Love *what you do*

Needs of belonging

To meet these needs, both you and our client, like any other company on the market, will need to make your purchasers feel "at home" and in the right context when they choose you. It will be helpful to present references from others in the world to which they belong (i.e. companies with similar characteristics), to receive them in suitable locations where they feel at ease, to highlight the values that you share, to create a community of users to whom they may choose to belong. In the case of our client, this meant designing an appropriate location, organizing specific references by sector and making them accessible, planning events that allowed customers to find themselves among professionals and organizations that operated in similar situations. Differentiating yourself in this sense means choosing to address a specific customer, not attempting to make a generalized appeal to all, as we discussed in detail in Chapter 6. The message you want to communicate in this case is: "You're at home, among others of your kind; you're where you want to be".

Needs for esteem

We have reached a level of needs to which your response must necessarily be more intimate and personal. To make customers feel recognized and respected – as a person and not just as a buyer – we should build an experience developed around what really interests them, based on what we have learnt from listening to them and from the motivations that we have recognized. Constructing personalized moments will mean creating the conditions that allow your customers to freely express their uniqueness, to make suggestions and advance specific requests. Our solution was to schedule a series of meetings between the provider and the purchaser, to promote a sincere style of relationship and hone the communication skills of all company employees. It was necessary to learn how to customize courses and consultancy based on the needs and curricula of the participants, taking into consideration in the design choices not only the company that bought the training and consulting, but also those who would physically benefit from it. All this with the aim of making the client realize: "I am interested in you as a person and I will take care of you".

Needs of self-actualization

These are the most complex and difficult needs to manage; in fact, not all organizations are able to find an answer to the question "How do you make the customer happy?" Happiness, as we learned from Dr. Erica Poli in Chapter 2, is an intimate condition which we reach through a process that starts from within. What we can concretely do as a company is to create the conditions favorable to self-actualization – namely, feeling good about oneself, expressing one's essence, thus contributing to creating a feeling of happiness – perhaps appealing to a sense of gratitude. We will, therefore, strive to ensure that the client, by receiving and offering gratitude, experiences the full range of emotions that give a deeper meaning to life. How can a company or a professional succeed in this ambitious task? The only way is to involve people in a greater goal that goes beyond their own interests. We are once again talking about mission and vision, objectives that include and involve all the actors of a business by making them active promoters of a higher good. For the safety service company, it meant promising:

> If you choose me, we will work together to make not only your company and your employees safer but also the entire sector in which you operate and perhaps a part of the world. Together we will try to make truly useful and engaging tools and rules regarding safety in the workplace so that you can apply them with pleasure and set a good example that others will be able to follow. Because our ultimate goal is people's well-being, not just their safety.

In line with this approach, the company decided to invest in a health and safety awareness campaign, promoting free events and training in collaboration with associations, groups of customers and other stakeholders.

Now, how about trying this yourself?

Activity – Designing your offer system

Think of all the products and services that your company offers to the market, considering both the tangible and intangible aspects that characterize it. Remember that the offer system also includes specific skills and abilities, relational style, places, references, suppliers, the history of the organization, collaborators and everything that can generate value.

Now answer the following five questions: you will need to check if you have identified all the elements necessary for complete customer satisfaction. You may need to add other components to complete your offer.

1. What basic need can you promise to satisfy with your offer and which of the elements identified earlier are relevant?
2. How can your customer trust you will fulfill your promises? What in the offer system helps to make her feel secure both in the purchase phase and in the phase of consumption?
3. How can you make your customers feel "in the right place"? Is there something in your offer system that develops the theme of belonging?
4. How can you give more value to those who choose you, highlighting their uniqueness? Which element allows you to customize the experience, making each customer feel special?
5. What can make people feel happy and fulfilled? Are there moments leading to greater involvement, where everyone can contribute?

CREATE YOUR OFFER SYSTEM

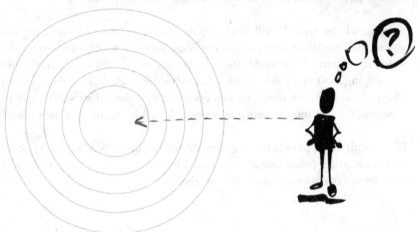

FIGURE 7.2 Create your offer system

If you have completed the activity correctly, you should have a list of items that make up your offer system. To draw the diagram that you will find in the download area, you must identify which one is central, or answer the questions: "What is the main reason for which your customers choose you? Which element, more than others, can really make a person fall in love with your company?" For this last activity, you will need to take a look at the profile of your buyer that emerged in Chapter 6. Remember to do a verification check on the hierarchy of the elements after reading Chapter 8 too, as this will help you identify your differential value compared to your competitors.

Once you have chosen the element that will occupy the central position in your diagram, you will be able to insert all the other components of the offer, up to those positioned on the periphery, namely those that differentiate you less from the competition.

We have not yet talked about price: apparently one of the most relevant factors of choice, which must be balanced with the rest of your proposal to the market if you do not want it to take on the role of the sole protagonist.

The price as indicator of value: finding your place in the market's heart

Price is a fundamental element of the offer system; if you do not manage it correctly by using an adequate strategy, it risks overshadowing all the other elements. Various

Love *what you do* **93**

factors combine in defining the selling price such as production and procurement costs, the level of margins required to achieve the company's economic objectives and remunerate the distribution system, market and competition dynamics and, lastly, and perhaps most importantly, the customers' expectations. We will focus on this latter element in the following text.

Do you know what the secret of any good pricing strategy is from the buyer's perspective? **A good offer that includes more than what the customer is actually paying for!**

Yes, you read that correctly. You must *give more* to your customers and invest in them if you want the price to become a positive element of choice rather than a source of complaints and frustration. This is also the secret of love: to give more in every moment of the relationship! Yet how can you avoid such an approach becoming uneconomical? How can we give more without losing out economically?

To answer these questions, let's take a step back in time and meet a great figure of modern economics, whose intuitions earned him the Nobel Prize: John Nash. In the course of his studies, he succeeded in proving that the best economic results are obtained by adopting a behavior that considers both your own interests and those of your counterpart, even though by doing so you may seem to have given up part of the gain. Our interpretation of this is "give more" to your customers in order to activate the **positive dynamics** that make them not only want to come back and buy more but also to expand interest in your offer to other customers through positive word of mouth.

If the goal is, therefore, to strengthen the relationship by creating added value, what are the components of the offer system that affect this aspect to the greatest extent? The purely intangible ones, such as skills, abilities, style of interaction, mission, etc. In fact, they meet the highest – and hence most valuable – needs of Maslow's hierarchy. Moreover, since the intangible elements of the offer have no direct correlation with the production costs, this means that when offering more in this area there will be no proportional increase in material costs. On the other hand, we will obtain the "imbalance" effect of the purchase price/value received, in the customers' favor. In fact, when we increase the value while maintaining the price level unchanged, the price is perceived as cheaper: just what we need for effective positioning.[4]

Figure 7.3 reminds us how the two concepts of price and value are inextricably linked in the minds of those who buy: we can define this link as a **price lever**. This means that if you want to increase the price you must necessarily increase the value of your offer, while if you lower the price, with no clear motivation, the customer will perceive a decrease in value. This direct relationship between price and value, however, is complicated by possible **information asymmetries** that are generated when you do not provide enough information on the composition of your offer, especially regarding its more intangible aspects.

Unless your customers are properly guided, they will have difficulty understanding the value/price relationship and make their choice based solely on the price. Some examples? You are looking at the abstract artworks of two contemporary artists and you are not an art expert. How can you know which of the two is "worth" more?

LINK BETWEEN PRICE-VALUE OR LEVER-PRICE

The customer perceives price and the value as directly connected; if the price goes up the value rises; if the price goes down the value of our offer system also drops.

FIGURE 7.3 Link between price value or lever-price

You will look at the price tag. If you have to choose between the offer of two safety training courses with the same programs, duration and final certifications and you have no information about the trainers' skills and style, or on any another "soft" aspect of the offer, how will you choose? You will most likely buy the cheaper course! The more the central elements of your offer are intangible, the more carefully you must manage sales arguments and pricing policies to avoid being a victim of information asymmetries. You are more likely to mismanage this aspect if you have failed to consider adequately all the intangible elements of your market proposal; indeed, you may be the first one who fails to fully recognize their importance. Before becoming external information, the price is primarily a value that you must be able to attribute correctly within your organization.[5] The different ways of understanding and structuring the relationship between price and value lead to different strategies. **Price strategies** can, in fact, be highly varied. We have chosen to focus on the one we consider to be most effective in the light of a love-based business model.

Bearing in mind the concept of "giving more" to customers to tip the price/value balance in their favor and that the price balance is influenced by information asymmetries and externalities[6] (see Figure 7.4), when defining your strategy, the first thing you must ask yourself is how you want to use the **price lever**. There are companies that use it in a "traditional" way, trying to keep the perceived value unchanged but lowering the price to convince their customers to buy, or leaving the price unchanged while increasing the perceived value (traditional price lever). On the other hand, there are companies that use the opposite strategy, i.e. raising

ILLUSTRATION OF MARKET BALANCE

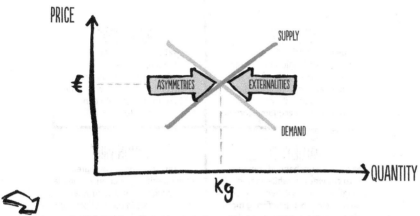

The market price is determined by the balance between supply and demand. The supply grows as the price rises: the more expensive a product is, the more profit can be made, and the more companies will want to produce it. The demand grows as the price decreases: the lower the price of a product the more people will want to buy it. However, a perfect balance is never achieved because of forces such as externalities and asymmetries.

FIGURE 7.4 Illustration of market balance

the price to help the purchaser understand the value (inverted price lever). What does the choice of one approach or the other depend on? Partly on the type of products/services and the dynamics of the market in which you operate but also, of course, on the "weight" of your brand and other factors related, for example, to the competition. Once you have made your choice, you will need to add another consideration: is the central component of your offer system tangible or intangible? Once you have identified these two aspects, namely how you will use the price lever and the extent of the tangibility that lies at the "heart" of your offer, you can position your business in the grid in Figure 7.5.

How does this diagram help you? It aids you in deciding which price strategy is most suitable for you, and the most correct ways to present this important feature of your offer system to avoid customer "disenchantment".

The upper-left quadrant contains companies that use the price lever in a standard way and rely mainly on the tangible components to make the customer fall in love with them and to stand out from the competition. The price strategy of these companies is aimed at demonstrating a single thing, namely that for the same price (data taken from the market and from observation of competitors) or less, the customer will obtain a greater quantity of product or services. This is the case with companies selling raw materials (e.g. more kg of iron at the same price) or certain consumer electronics brands (e.g. a PC costs less while providing the same functions). These companies will base their price information on strident advertising messages and promotions, enabling

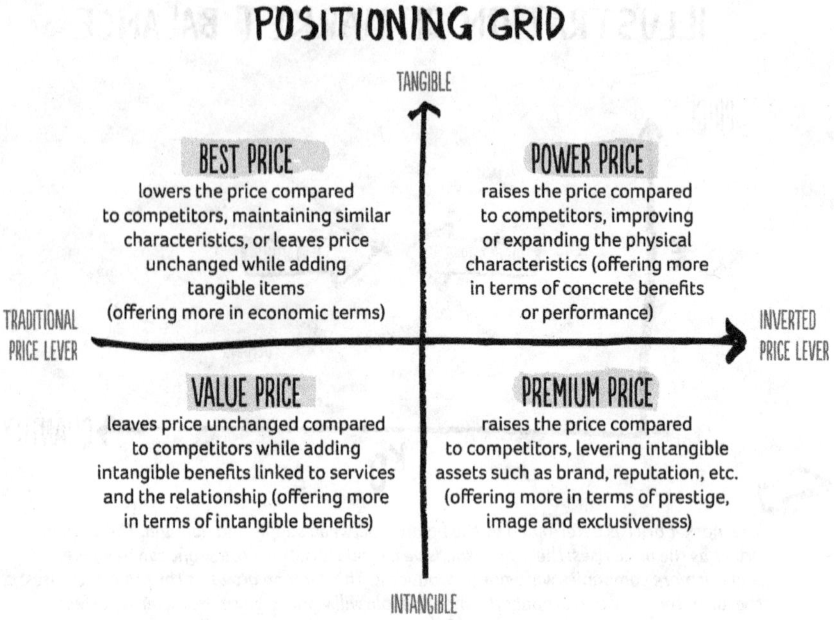

96 Love *what you do*

POSITIONING GRID

TANGIBLE

BEST PRICE
lowers the price compared
to competitors, maintaining similar
characteristics, or leaves price
unchanged while adding
tangible items
(offering more in economic terms)

POWER PRICE
raises the price compared
to competitors, improving
or expanding the physical
characteristics (offering more
in terms of concrete benefits
or performance)

TRADITIONAL PRICE LEVER — INVERTED PRICE LEVER →

VALUE PRICE
leaves price unchanged compared
to competitors while adding
intangible benefits linked to services
and the relationship (offering more
in terms of intangible benefits)

PREMIUM PRICE
raises the price compared
to competitors, levering intangible
assets such as brand, reputation, etc.
(offering more in terms of prestige,
image and exclusiveness)

INTANGIBLE

FIGURE 7.5 Positioning grid

customers to compare their offer directly with that of other manufacturers in order to emphasize that they are cheaper. On the other hand, the upper-right quadrant comprises companies with a strong tangible component that choose to use the price lever in the opposite way, namely they set the price higher than the competition: to do so they must add tangible value. This category includes brands that promise better performance, more features, longer durability, more tangible benefits, thus demanding an appropriate price. If your company is positioned here, you will have to be very good at using figures and data to communicate what more you are offering compared to the competition. On the bottom left we have companies whose offer system focuses on something intangible, such as the style of relationship, the values of their brand and so on. They do not impose their prices on the market but, with the same level of investment, they manage to add intangible value to the exchange. The example that comes to mind is that of a pharmacy in which the level of service is very high, compared to the services offered for the same prices by the pharmacy chains. The last quadrant is that of companies that use their intangible components to convince the customer to spend more, thus pursuing a premium price strategy. Luxury or high fashion brands will generally belong to this category.

The **price strategies** differ in each of the four cases and we have named them accordingly:

Best price – these are the companies that give more in economic terms. Their goal is to show that by buying from them you optimize your spending

Love *what you do* **97**

because, at the same price or even with a lower outlay, you will bring home more goods or more features.[7] The customer's attention is focused principally on the economic and quantitative aspects of the offer. Consider that if you decide to belong to this category, you will have to be very careful to avoid your very low price being perceived as an indication of low value.

Power price – these are organizations that give more in terms of performance and in meeting material needs. They want to show you that if you buy from them you are spending your money better because their products and services will satisfy more needs, faster and over a longer time. On average, they aim to have customers who know what they are looking for in terms of innovation, quality, construction technology, etc. It is thus necessary to communicate effectively all the specific aspects that justify the higher prices.

Value price – companies and professionals who, at the same price, add value in the form of services, relationships and customer care. To be understood and appreciated, their added value requires trust and long-term relationships. For this reason, they must address educated and sensitive customers, who are able to appreciate and interpret the intangible surplus received. The great challenge, in this case, is represented by the presentation, ensuring that from the early stages the customer has an appealing experience of buying and consuming, involving values that ensure the offer is not underestimated.

Premium price – these are the market's opinion leaders, the trendsetters or, we could say, the market stars. They can afford higher prices because they know their customers will receive an increase in reputation and status simply because they have bought from them. They, therefore, intend to have customers who focus on such aspects because they are looking for a sense of belonging or exclusiveness. These companies need to invest in all aspects related to the brand and reputation, and they do not consider themselves in direct technical competition with other market players.

Whichever strategy you choose to adopt, all communications with your customers must be based on transparency: tell them what price they will effectively pay and why your products/services have that specific price, thus reducing any information asymmetries on both tangible and intangible elements of your offer. In our opinion, the most effective approach is to devote the necessary time to presenting the price during the explanation of the offer's characteristics, linking it to the offer's benefits: given that customers need to know the price in order to decide, make this information as complete and clear as possible! Leaving the customer free to choose produces incredible results for all those who are true bearers of value, as W. Chan Kim and R. Mauborgne have shown in the text *The Blue Ocean Strategy*[8] and W.B. Arthur in his research on incremental return.[9]

Maybe you are now wondering which strategy we chose for our client company? We have reached the end of the chapter and of the case study. Carry on reading to find out the answer.

Conclusion of the case study: rising above the fray

After analyzing the offer system, we realized that there were two factors which would allow our client to make his buyers fall in love with him: the "style" and the "method" of providing advice and training. We, therefore, started working together on the interaction in the classroom and on the organization of the contents, as well as on the rules of engagement with clients and students during the various moments of their activity. We created an original method for delivering content that would make the experience more engaging and interactive. For example, instead of just talking about safety and health at work in their courses, they also provided advice and tips on safety at home or on mitigating the risks associated with children and pets in the domestic arena. The classrooms were set out to create a space for relaxation and networking with the other participants during the breaks, ensuring that all spaces provided a pleasant ambience. Considering the intangibility around which their differential value revolved, and not being able to raise the price because this was set by the type of market, the company decided to adopt a *value price* policy that was aligned with the competition in terms of the price but with the addition of many services to support the relationship. What were the results? Just ten months after our consultancy, the company recorded an increase of +8% in revenues with an improvement of +38% in the ratio of transformation of quotes into orders; in fact, the offer was more readily accepted.

What you have learnt and adding a piece to the *Loving Business Model*

You have more clearly identified the various elements that make up your offer, emphasizing which of them play a fundamental role; you have also decided which price strategy to adopt. Now fill in the "Offer" box in the *Loving Business Model* diagram.

Notes

1 Commodification derives from the term *commodity*; at its most basic, a non-specific good, especially raw materials.
2 The hierarchy illustrated in the diagram is just an example: the product is not always central.
3 If you are curious to see more, take a look at FIAT's advertising video for the US market: https://video.repubblica.it/motori/usa-spot-fiat-la-famiglia-italiana-diventa-un-optional/
4 It should be noted that the relationship also has a cost. However, this cost should not be considered "unproductive" but rather as an investment to which resources may be dedicated, as without such a relationship future results may be compromised.

5 As our colleague Canzio Panzavolta, an expert in budget analysis, points out, not only the customer receives value in the form of intangible elements. These intangible elements can also be evaluated, though not precisely calculated, within corporate capital. Companies generally account as costs, items that are actually investments (for example, training, reputation growth, development of new procedures, know-how, and more), which also translate into corporate value and become a surplus when evaluating assets, to be both protected and valued.

6 In economics, an **externality** occurs when the activity of production or consumption negatively or positively influences the well-being of another subject, without the latter receiving any compensation (in the case of a negative impact) or paying a price (in the case of a positive impact) equal to the cost supported/received.

7 To avoid falling into the trap of being anti-economic, companies that adopt this strategy must renounce, at least in part, offering their customers intangible value elements, for example, by saving on relationship costs. In fact, many companies in this sector entrust their commercial activities to channels such as e-commerce or other tools that permit the customer to be more independent when making the choice about which products and services to consume.

8 Chan, Kim W., and Renée Mauborgne. *Blue Ocean Strategy: How to Create Uncontested Market Space and Make Competition Irrelevant*. Harvard Business School Press, 2015.

9 Arthur, W. Brian. "Increasing Returns and the New World of Business." *Harvard Business Review*, July–August 1996. https://hbr.org/1996/07/increasing-returns-and-the-new-world-of-business

8

RESPECT YOUR *RIVALS*

How to manage your relationship with the competition

Abstract

This chapter will talk about how to manage your relationship with competitors and to adopt a healthy competition dynamic, in which you work together to build a bigger cake rather than each fighting for a slice. You will learn that real competition is not based on price, in a context where undercutting competitors can only lead in the long term to the destruction of the markets and its occupants, but on the differential value. This is the only way that competition can function usefully to increase quality, free customer choice and promote innovation. If you think this is impossible, read the chapter and think it through with us!

Case study: "friendly enemies"

A few years ago, we were contacted by a group of professionals in the field of home staging, a service that at the time had only recently arrived in Italy and that specializes in temporarily staging homes and workspaces to render them more attractive for rent or sale. As the profession was new, no professional registers existed, let alone a code of ethics that defined the quality standards to be offered to customers. One of the consequences was that competition among colleagues was ruthless, based on the continuous undercutting of prices, sometimes undermining quality and undifferentiated offers that drained the new market of value. Although the Italian Association of Home Staging Professionals had been founded a few months before, the relations between colleagues were increasingly stiff, with many clinging to divergent positions and the task of creating the team spirit required to protect, certify and support the work of the associates becoming impossible. In short, a perfect storm was about to hit the newborn market and its fury risked nipping any future opportunities in the bud. In this situation of impending danger, Rita Pederzoli Ricci, president of the association, turned to us. The goal was to find a solution that would help reset the competitive dynamics among associates, orienting them towards a more constructive form that would serve both to reinforce the perceived value of home staging services in the eyes of Italian users, and to restore order and collaboration in relationships between associates.

From competition to cooperation

"Being as different as two drops of water" is the concept that best sums up what we want to explore in this chapter. We frequently hear the "two drops of water" metaphor incorrectly used, that is, as a synonym for extreme similarity. The latest research, primarily conducted by Masaru Emoto, has instead shown that the crystals formed by this element are all inevitably different; in fact, he states that no two drops of water are the same in the entire universe.[1] While at first glance, they may outwardly seem the same, if we stop to study them more carefully, the diversities will begin to emerge. Continuing the metaphor, we could say that every drop of water is the bearer of unique information and value. The same thing happens to two competing offers: even if on the surface they may appear similar, careful observation permits us to detect the differences and distinguishing features of each.

In the previous chapter, you became aware of how the offer of companies and professionals cannot be fully described with a mere list of products and services. The organized set of tangible and intangible elements constitutes the offer system, whose composition and mix lead to the diversity and originality that constitute the "differential value" of each business. When dealing with our competitors, or performing benchmark analysis, we should, therefore, refer not only to the "physical" characteristics of their products or services but to all the elements that make up the offer. Returning to the diagram that represents the *Loving Business Model*, we could say that all the fields of which it is composed can potentially be bearers of uniqueness, because the differential value may nestle in the brand, in the objectives, in the offer, in the customer journey and in the way of managing touch points, in the internal dynamics that are activated among the people of that organization and even in the type of customers to whom they are addressed. To create a system

102 Respect your *rivals*

of comparison between competitors thus means comparing all these fields. On the other hand, our home staging professionals believed they were "as alike as two drops of water". They failed to stop and think about their differences and, consequently, were unable to point these out to customers and explain them. This lack of awareness was the basis of their "price war".

A massive information asymmetry was plaguing the entire market and it was generated by the home staging professionals themselves, who continued to fuel it: they were the first victims of their short-sightedness regarding the differences in the value they carried. The most immediate effect of a failure to differentiate the offer is a downward spiral in prices, as we saw in the previous chapter.

Training yourself to look for the differences between you and your competitors, therefore, means creating conditions that will help your customer to do the same. Undoubtedly, you will have had rivals even in your love life; they may have been seemingly more attractive and charming than you. No doubt to firstly gain the attention of your loved one and then capture his/her interest and finally his/her heart, you were forced to highlight your differences and not to be "economically more advantageous" than your rival! Of course, there are people who rely on more material aspects such as a beautiful car, gifts or other benefits, to win a partner. It would not be a long stretch of the imagination to compare this "strategy" with the price war described above. Think about it: can winning over a woman or a man in this way be the premise for a true and lasting relationship? How will he or she behave if they meet someone who can assure them a greater "economic advantage"? You would hardly be surprised if they opted for the newcomer! Price competition has the same effect on the customer. People who choose you because you "cost less" will feel authorized to change their supplier if they find someone with a similar offer at a cheaper price.[2] Indeed, they would be justified in doing so thanks to your behavior, because your strategy of undercutting the competition taught them that the best way to differentiate between professionals and companies is to see who costs less. Price competition, therefore, has the dramatic, primary side effect of destroying customer loyalty. On the other hand, the perception of added value[3] creates strong ties and this is what we will focus on in the following section.

Let us better analyze what "love competition" is all about in order to glean some more useful information for our *Loving Business Model*. Let's start by asking ourselves: what do two rivals in love really want, or should they want? The answer is to win the heart of their loved one, putting him or her in a position to **freely and consciously** choose one or the other of the suitors. Free and conscious choice is the basis on which a true relationship of love is based. Without this, the love will not be reciprocated, i.e. there will not be the offer–receive exchange that nurtures the relationship and essentially keeps it alive. Two considerations emerge from the reflections we have just made:

- The competitors aim at a common goal (the heart of the beloved).
- The real objective of the competitors is to be chosen freely and consciously (because otherwise, it would not be true love).

Regarding the first point, we can say that they both yearn for the same goal because they both love the same person. The word **compete** in fact derives from the Latin prefix *com* and the verb *petere*, indicating to "to run together towards a common goal". The origin resembles that of another term, used to express an apparently opposite concept, i.e. **cooperation**, whose etymology descends from the Latin *com-operari* or "work together with others to achieve an end". In a business model based on love, the two concepts of competition and cooperation can coexist since the contenders will com-pete for the conquest of the heart of the loved one but also co-operate so that the latter makes a free and conscious choice, selecting the partner she or he considers to be the bearer of the greatest value. As we noted in Chapter 6, when describing relationships with customers and the reciprocal appeal, this "exchange value" on which the choice of the customer-lover will be based can only be subjective. Hence, the choice does not mean that one of the competitors is objectively better than the other, but that anyone can be the best choice for a particular person at a particular time. It is important to bear this concept in mind because you will begin to differentiate yourself from your competitors from the moment you decide to turn to a specific and non-generic customer who can appreciate that differential value and that uniqueness that you feel you bear.[4]

We thus urge you to look at your competitors as key players in the market in which you operate, whose presence is necessary to achieve two results:

1. Allowing you to make the differential value of your offer clear.
2. Putting the customer in a position to choose consciously and freely.

In fact, it is only through comparison with others that what distinguishes you can be known, named and highlighted[5] and the presence on the market of other operators puts the customers in a position to seek the information that will permit them to make a choice. Data and information, provided by the various players, contribute to **educating buyers** by reducing their information asymmetries and allowing a better understanding of the real value of the offers.

The idea that market players are competing against each other to secure scarce resources, and that in a certain sense they consume these resources, needs to be replaced with the idea that they are bearers of resources and value for all. By pitting ourselves against others in ruthless opposition, triggering downward spirals, we preclude ourselves from accessing the value that our counterparts bear and impoverishing, or even destroying, the sector in which we all operate. On the contrary, recognizing the value of competition means triggering a **virtuous circle** that, if well managed, can ensure increasing margins for all.

The successful examples of this approach are numerous but, given that the case study is linked to a newly established and booming market, we want to mention a famous episode involving FIAT and the invention of the direct injection system at the dawn of the boom of diesel engines in Europe. Back in 1998, the FIAT Research Center invented the first direct injection diesel engine, later called Multijet. This was truly a technological revolution that made this type of engine more efficient both in terms of performance and consumption. The development of the project was burdensome and complex, so the manufacturer decided to "open" the patent, making it available to other manufacturers in the hope of sharing development costs and thus allowing the new technology to become established with advantages for FIAT itself, for customers, for the market in general and for the environment.[6] To date, in the various versions that over the years have evolved from the initial project, direct injection is considered a standard for engines and has been adopted by the majority of manufacturers: FIAT thus succeeded in its intent by promoting, more or less spontaneously, a dynamic of cooperative relationships with its market competitors that triggered a virtuous circle.

It may be useful to note the origin of the words **competence** and **competition**: **both** derive from the same Latin term *com-petere*. Hence, we would argue, that to consider someone a real competitor, i.e. someone with whom you can strive towards a common goal, you need to recognize their competence as being comparable and close to yours. You must not feel in competition with just anyone, but you should accept healthy competition with those you feel can contribute to the growth of the industry in which you operate. From then on, you will compete with these "market neighbors" by leveraging your differential value, specializing your offer and the promises you make to your customers. How can you do this? Follow us in the next paragraph after completing the activity.

Activity – Create your benchmark table

Keeping in mind what you've learned so far, make a list of the following items to compare with the competition and enter them in the table in the download area:

- Elements of the offer system (tangible and intangible)
- Characteristics of the organization (history, reputation, people, experience, climate, culture…)
- Brand and identity
- Type of customer to whom it is addressed
- Communication/image strategies
- Objectives, mission and values
- Relationships with the surrounding context (environment, companies, competitors)
- Price positioning

Then, compare your offer with that of direct competitors and color the boxes that correspond to excellence in a given field, both yours and others, in green. Do the same thing, but using red, for those parameters where the performance seems unsatisfactory to you.

COMPARISON WITH COMPETITORS

	US	COMPETITOR 1	COMPETITOR 2	COMPETITOR 3	COMPETITOR 4
OFFER SYSTEM					
CHARACTERISTICS OF THE ORGANIZATION					
BRAND AND IDENTITY					
TYPE OF CUSTOMER					
COMMUNICATION/IMAGE STRATEGIES					
OBJECTIVES, MISSION AND VALUES					
RELATIONSHIPS WITH THE SURROUNDING CONTEXT					
PRICE POSITIONING					

FIGURE 8.1 Comparison with competitors

Now ask yourself if the price differences are coherent with a higher capacity in managing some of the fields highlighted by the grid and on which of these aspects the economic value differences are based. Then try to understand what you can improve by learning from your most skilled competitors in certain areas.

Beat the spin doctors: building a genuine promise

As we mentioned in the previous chapter, every marketing manager fears the "commodification" of their products or services, a danger that should arouse fear in you as well.

Therefore, this appears to be the phenomenon that prompts the suicidal downward spiral of price-cutting. To explain how you can avoid this we want to add some considerations to those discussed in the previous section: the aim is to specialize your activities and distinguish yourself from the competition, avoiding the projection of a uniform offer to the customer.

We will start by distinguishing between **product-oriented** and **market-oriented**[7] companies. To understand the differences, let us pause briefly to observe how they conduct business and their attitude towards innovation.

For the first type of company, defined as product-oriented, the business is conceived with reference to internal production processes. To improve efficiency, these organizations focus on production and research and development to expand, speed up or improve their market action. This category usually includes companies with a strong artisan matrix, focused on "know-how": such enterprises dominate the productive fabric of Italy. On the other hand, market-oriented companies are organizations that look directly to the market and to their customers to raise efficiency and increase commercial performance. While the former invest in engineers and production equipment to improve, the latter dedicate resources to the promotion and communication of their products. Faced with the need for innovation, product-oriented companies will ask, "How can I do better than what I already do well?" while market-oriented companies will concentrate their efforts on questions such as "What else do customers expect from me?". These are two diametrically opposed attitudes that lead to the construction of completely different dynamics and organizational structures. We could say that the former "turn their backs to the market" by focusing on themselves and their processes to grow while the latter "turn to the market" to find solutions. If you think about it, your organization and your business belong to one of these two categories. At first glance, you might think that you have the characteristics of both types, but a proper in-depth analysis will reveal which you resemble the most.[8]

The promise that an organization can make to its customers and that will distinguish it, allowing people to get a clear idea of what to expect, is connected to the type of model being pursued. Figure 8.2 will help you to understand how.

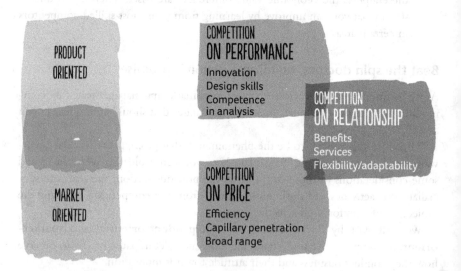

FIGURE 8.2 Production oriented vs market oriented

In our opinion there are three main types of promises that a company, a professional and anyone who approaches a market, can make:

- **Performance promise** can take the form of "I am/We are the best", "Our products have superior features/performance", "You will find no other products and services comparable to ours".
- **Price promise** uses claims such as "We are the cheapest", "With the same features, we cost less", "We have the best value for money".
- **Relationship promise** includes claims such as "We're the ones who will support you the most", "We will follow you at every stage of your relationship with the product/service", "We will involve you and you will feel part of our family".

You may be thinking that any self-respecting company should guarantee all three results. Yet it would be impossible to respect such a commitment![9] To be credible when making these promises, and to avoid betraying customer expectations, your organization must possess certain characteristics that allow it to do so. This is where the previously mentioned organizational models come into play. The diagram clearly illustrates that companies promising performance need (or are the result of) a product-oriented organization that works on itself to ensure improvement; rather than pursuing every market opportunity, it will focus on its expertise or the fact that it does certain things well, and sometimes better than anyone else. By contrast, those who promise a good price must continually study the market to compare with competing products and then optimize processes and production costs to offer the customer the best quality/price ratio available. Lastly, the promise of relationship requires a mix, an organization that can listen to the customer's requests while remaining faithful to its principles and values.

In a world populated by spin doctors, the modern customer needs **credible promises**, made by companies and professionals that are qualified to keep them. Thus, it is essential right from the start to choose to which category you belong and to evaluate the characteristics of your organization to understand if they are consistent with what you are committing to offer. Once you have chosen the promise you will make, you must consider to keep it, even in changed market conditions and with different interlocutors. Unfortunately, very often the opposite occurs, that is, the promises that companies make to their customers are generic, unclear or not differentiated from those of their competitors, or change depending on who is making them.

The fundamental errors you can make regarding promises are:

- **Chameleonism** – when faced with a customer you change your promise based on what you believe to be his/her expectations. During the purchase choice every customer will be driven by motivations and goals: it is up to companies and salespeople to understand what these are and to integrate them with their own. We chose the verb "integrate" carefully to underline

108 Respect your *rivals*

that you must not distort or change what you are; rather, you will present the aspects of your offer that share characteristics and are compatible with the goals of your interlocutor. For example, if you promise performance and the customer you are dealing with is driven by the desire to save, it is no good saying "My product is the best but also the cheapest" because this would be untrue. Rather, build a strategy of engagement that mainly attracts those who seek quality; when dealing with a person who focuses on price, discuss with them all the advantages of buying a superior item, even in economic terms.

- **Inconsistency** – as we will discuss in more detail when talking about customer journeys, an organization is made up of departments and people who contribute to customer management. Check that throughout the phases of the purchasing experience and for all those involved in them, from salespeople to service technicians, the type of promise made is clear and uniform. We frequently see advertisements that promise care and attention to the customer that clash with the approach adopted by aggressive salespeople, or products that claim to be "the best on the market" sold as a "bargain". You must be particularly careful if your distribution system or salesforce also works with other market players, thus having independent and less controllable relationship dynamics: check closely that the customer receives a consistent message from these external collaborators and that his/her experience is coherent with your promises. Inconsistency can also occur at the level of range choices. Pay attention to ensuring that everything you produce and any services provided are in line with your chosen positioning, i.e. that they concentrate on performance, relationship or price.[10]

- **Lack of differentiation** – undoubtedly, one of any company's most important needs is certainly differentiating from competitors to trigger all the positive dynamics we have discussed. To achieve this, it is essential to specialize and choose a coherent and original promise. This means you will have to study your competition carefully to understand what others are promising and to whom and how they keep that promise, as well as the features, capabilities and skills they possess to do so. Then, create your promise to highlight the difference; if the result seems too similar to that of the other players on the market, hone it further by linking it to your uniqueness. Bear in mind, we are talking about a **USP**, a *Unique* Selling Proposition.

Perhaps at this point we have convinced you of the importance of sending clear messages to the market, but you will probably be asking yourself: if everything is so clear and logical, why do so many companies make generalized promises that resemble those of competitors too closely or continually change them to keep up with passing trends? "Expanding", adapting or modifying the company's promise has always been tempting for companies and may even produce results in some cases, though only in the short term or niche markets. Some companies cast their net wide to catch whatever fish they can as specializing, or being more selective,

Respect your *rivals* **109**

seems scary. If "restricting" your promise seems to dramatically decrease your chances of engagement, why do it?

We think that anyone who believes that in today's markets, characterized by easy access to information, customers are like "fish" waiting to jump into a net, is deeply mistaken. If instead, you consider your customers as people to inform and to help and with whom you exchange value so that they make a conscious choice, then widening the net is evidently a mistaken strategy. To understand its negative effects, however, an organization must look around and try to broaden its perspective, adopting a long-term view and considering the "relational" effects of indiscriminate use of promises to the market.

To clarify the concept, let us once more use an example taken from the automobile market. You may have seen advertisements that promote a specific model with the words "Starting at ..." followed by a very attractive price. However, when you are at the dealership, you find that once they add on tax, transport costs, and all the other mandatory "options", the price soars. The manufacturers hope to entice potential buyers into the dealership with these false promises, convinced that once they have fallen "into the net", they can convince them to buy: of all the potential customers who go to look at the vehicle only a minimal percentage will buy, but why risk attracting far fewer by stating the true price of the car?

If we were consulting for these brands, we would invite them to reflect on two points:

1. What happens to the high percentage of customers who do not buy the car?
2. How would the conversion percentage vary between those who visit the dealer and those who buy if the price promised corresponded to what people actually have to pay?

According to our experience and our observation, what happens to those who do not buy the car because they feel "betrayed" or deceived by the initial promise can potentially destroy the results of that promotion both in the long and in the short term. Anyone who walks away from the car dealer feeling annoyed (most of the visitors, given that the conversion of this type of initiative has low percentages) tends to do two things: they decide not to return and tell other people of their network about the lack of clarity in the offer to which they fell victim.

To assess and measure these effects, organizations should also observe and collect data on loyalty and the reputation resulting from this type of commercial action, looking beyond the number of new sales made.

Regarding the second point, experience tells us that the conversion would pass from single-figure percentages to much larger numbers.[11] While it is true that fewer customers would enter the dealership, the ones coming would actually be interested in making a purchase and once they confirmed that the price promise was consistent, it would be easier to convince them to go ahead and buy. In addition, there would be an inversion of the negative trend described above in terms of loyalty and word of mouth: a satisfied customer, who feels he has been treated with respect and transparency, returns to buy and recommends the products to others. In turn, these others will visit the dealership because they have received a disinterested and sincere suggestion, not because they have fallen for a deceptive campaign promise!

In the next section, we will teach you a practical method to understand what you are promising to the market today and if this statement is consistent with your business's characteristics; you can then refine it to make it operational in terms of results.

> If you are on the market with the aim of staying there, as we hope, you will surely want to engage in relationships with your customers based on respect and sincerity, giving them the opportunity to choose from the start if they are interested in what you can offer them, helping them to distinguish the differences between what they can expect from you and the other contenders.

Competing on value and not on price

Hordes of sales personnel complain about the excessively high prices of the products they sell, whether sales reps or agents. Regardless of the sector in which they work and their experience in business, none of them will fail to drop the price to close a deal. The idea is that offering a discount is simpler while defending value and justifying it may be very demanding. However, there are other promises than "I will cost less" to which your customer is willing to listen and will accept, but you must be consistent and credible when making them. This consistency and credibility pass, as we have seen, from the type of organization you have behind you. Before deciding what to say to the market, you will first need to undertake a serious analysis of your company; this observation will not only allow you to understand what you can promise but, if you are already on the market, to perfect and make the proposal even more effective and clearer for the customer!

We believe that you must investigate four fields because these are the ones where companies differ most. We, therefore, advise you to probe into your behavior regarding:

1. **Positioning** and use of price
2. **Products and services** you offer
3. Choice of **people** and their relationship style
4. Production **processes** and business management

Let us analyze together each of these four fields of investigation, highlighting the differences according to the type of promise. All you must do is allow time for

BEHAVIOR/PROMISE GRID

	PERFORMANCE	PRICE	RELATIONSHIP
POSITIONING	. INVERTED PRICE LEVER . SCARCITY AND CONSTRAINTS . EXCLUSIVITY	. TRADITIONAL PRICE LEVER . DIRECT COMPARISON . EASE	. BENEFITS . STRONG VALUES . PERSONAL GROWTH
PRODUCTS/SERVICES	. DISTRIBUTION THOUGH FLAGSHIP STORES . TOP CONTENTS . NICHE . LASTS OVER TIME	. SUPERMARKETS . FUCUS ON NUMBER OF FUNCTIONS . WIDE RANGE . BRIEF LIFE CYCLE	. MANY TOUCH POINTS . EXPERIENCE . COMMUNITY . TUTORSHIP
PEOPLE	. STYLE . TECHNICAL KNOWLEDGE . CUSTOMER SEGMENTATION CAPILLARY	. SPEED/AGGRESSION . BIG NUMBERS . PENETRATION	. MOTIVATION . FLEXIBILITY . PROBLEM SOLVING
PROCESSES	. ATTENTION TO MARGINS . REFERENCES AND CASES . PRODUCT-ORIENTED	. MARKET-ORIENTED . TURNOVER . QUANTITY/€ RATIO	. TRANSPARENCY . BROADER VISION . PERSONALIZATION

FIGURE 8.3 Behavior promise grid

reflection to understand which of these actions reflect your business, and then draft your promise to the market.

Positioning

This includes all the behaviors that relate to the company's positioning on the market, both in terms of prices and in terms of image and reputation. Let's see what the main differences are, depending on the type of promise a company launches on the market.

Performance

The behavior of these organizations seems to be based on giving their customers an idea of exclusivity and rarity, in the sense that their products and services are not for everyone. The companies that belong to this category usually operate in the luxury sector or produce something very technical and specific, suitable for a niche audience that can appreciate it. As for the use of price lever (see Chapter 7), these organizations tend to raise the price to convince customers that their offer is superior.

Price

For companies belonging to this category, the positioning strategy is almost the opposite of the previous one. The idea they want to spread is that of an easy, undemanding purchase, which requires little reflection. The price lever is used in a

112 Respect your *rivals*

"classic" way and is lowered to convince the customer to choose their items, using promotions and discounts where necessary. These organizations must watch the competition on the market closely, urging their customers to compare the quantity/price ratio[12] of the various proposals.

Relationship

The companies operating in this category aim to place themselves in their customers' minds as a company driven by strong values. They tend not to speak of features and price, but of benefits. These organizations do not describe "what they do" but "what the customer will do" with what they produce. The mission and the intangible elements of the offer are generally more important than the tangible item leaving their factories. They aim to make their customers participate in their positioning, making them part of a common history, so their image and reputation depend very much on the contribution they have made to those who have chosen to buy.

Products and services

All the behaviors that concern the choices regarding the definition of the offer and the way it is brought to the market can be included here. Not only products and services in the strictest sense, but also distribution choices and the characteristics on which to focus the customer's attention.

Performance

The companies of this group try to carefully select the components and every detail concerning production. From the choice of suppliers to that of distribution partners, everything must comply with a precise standard that ensures quality and consistency. For this reason, such organizations prefer mono-brand stores (Flagship Stores) when possible, or will have direct control of the entire supply chain that reaches the end customer. The repurchase cycles of their products and services (which depend on the life cycle and the quality of what is provided) are on average longer, i.e. customers will have to buy less frequently to meet their needs.

Price

Regarding the field of products/services, the objective of those who promise price is to aim for a wide range of offers and functions that can satisfy the largest number of customers. This means that the distribution system must be as widespread and capillary as possible, perhaps selling through large-scale retail distribution. As a rule, the repurchase cycle is much faster, meaning that customers lose a little in terms of duration when choosing products from these organizations, but have the advantage of a low initial purchase cost.

Relationship

They tend to replace the idea of a single purchase with that of "investment project over time", aiming to extend the relationship with the customer beyond the limits of "here and now". For this reason, they follow the pre- and post-sales phases carefully, placing emphasis on the relational and tutorship components. Since these organizations consider the relationship the true object of exchange, they tend to build connections between their customers, activating community building processes and multiplying opportunities for encounters through a vast network of interfaces. Another fundamental aspect: they are willing to tailor products/services to customers' requirements.

People

This field includes everything related to style and the way that the personnel involved in the commercial activities of these companies manage and relate to customers. It also includes internal relationships and the way the structure is organized.

Performance

The personnel chosen by the companies belonging to this category must firstly be well-prepared technically on the products and services offered; indeed, staff may well be experts who use the products themselves. The personnel's superior technical knowledge enables them to interact with the customer as a consultant, trying to understand from the early stages of the relationship whether the characteristics and needs of their interlocutor are "compliant" with the company offer. Within the organization, relations between colleagues, managers and collaborators will be based on specialization and on a sort of "seniority" of merits and positions. They are usually organizations in which there is either a low staff turnover or changes to personnel take place in a small circle of companies with very similar characteristics.

Price

Companies with large numbers of staff are fast and, at times, aggressive in their style of relationship because they need to reach many prospective customers and must optimize and capitalize on every encounter. Their organizational charts are branched wide: recruitment is focusing on people who can generate commercial opportunities; such companies often have a high turnover. Those who work with them are required to lead the customer as smoothly as possible through the various proposals and the various elements of the offer. To make life easier for their staff, they may adopt "aids" to the relationship to accelerate the encounter and make it less expensive, especially in terms of time, like those digital opportunities (e-commerce sites, online chats, etc.).

114 Respect your *rivals*

Relationship

Everything you do for your customers must leave them with a memorable experience. You will have to know how to solve problems; in fact, in a certain sense, you must like resolving issues because you are aware that a good solution cements the relationship. Every request you receive from your interlocutors must, therefore, be analyzed and welcomed with the aim of fulfilling it or at least finding valid alternatives. Customizing and making the relationship unique is another goal of those who work here; they must always demonstrate patience and flexibility towards customers, colleagues and superiors. Internally, there is much focus on aggregation, corporate culture and flat structures that are reorganized according to the different projects to be managed.

Processes

We will now further analyze the business management style, the objectives and the ways of pursuing them as well as the tools used to do so.

Performance

Let's start by saying that these companies usually have a strong product-oriented matrix, which means that everything related to production, research and development, engineering, etc. is relevant to the rest. Their choices revolve around specific assets and know-how, key customers, key suppliers and key activities: factors that are often stated and advertised through the communication channels. The very concrete vision of their activity also translates into a strong focus on margins, rather than pure revenues.

Price

Those who fall into this category aim at obtaining large-scale quantitative results, sometimes accepting to reduce margins to increase their sales. They are organizations that maniacally study every opportunity in an attempt to exploit it and have optimized production processes to reduce costs to the bone and shorten time-to-market, i.e. the length of time it takes from a product being conceived until its being available for sale. Their structure falls fully within that previously defined as market oriented.

Relationship

Process transparency is often the choice of this type of organization. They have gone beyond (or are going beyond) measuring results exclusively on the basis of economic indicators such as margin and revenues. Instead, they focus on long-term results that also consider customer loyalty and reputation as well as the social impact of their actions. As stated above, their processes require flexibility: they are inspired

Respect your *rivals* **115**

by more open principles that revolve around group work, but also independent decision-making and personal initiative.

As you review these descriptions, where would you place yourself for each element? Clearly, we have suggested a generic and non-exhaustive picture of each of these fields, but it should be enough to enable you to start on your self-analysis.[13]

Activity – Identify and verify your promise

You can use the diagram in Figure 8.4, which we invite you to download from the download page, to complete the activity that will enable you to identify your promise.

Assign a score – 1 (low), 2 (medium), 3 (high) – to each of the four descriptive fields of behavior, i.e. positioning, products/services, people, processes, where necessary re-reading the descriptions given. As you proceed, ask yourself if they correspond little, medium or much to the behaviors that you and your organization implement. Now add up the scores for each column and divide the total by four to get the average value for that specific promise. Place the three results obtained in the diagram and join them to form a triangle.

Remember that the drawing obtained can be considered as identifying an efficient promise if it has these characteristics:

- One vertex will be more pronounced than the others, indicating to a clear prevalence in one of the three fields: performance, price or relationship.

PROMISE TO MARKET DIAGRAM

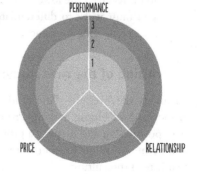

FIGURE 8.4 Promise to market diagram

EXAMPLE OF PROMISE TO MARKET DIAGRAM

	PERFORMANCE	PRICE	RELATIONSHIP
POSITIONING	1	3	2
PRODUCTS/SERVICES	1	2	1
PEOPLE	1	3	3
PROCESSES	1	2	1
AVERAGE	1.0	2.5	1.75

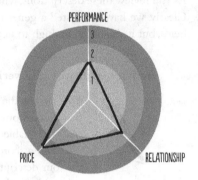

FIGURE 8.5 Example promise to market diagram

- The base (i.e. the opposite side to the more pronounced vertex) will not be too small, indicating acceptable scores also in the other two sectors.
- It will not change or rotate each time you apply the analysis to the different products and services in your range, because this would make it chameleon-like and not very consistent.
- It will stand out from that of your most direct competitors.

The ideal shape would be either an isosceles or scalene triangle, with at least two sides different and a clearly developed vertex; never that of an equilateral triangle.

When giving the scores you must answer sincerely. Ask yourself "Do I really behave like this and do I have the characteristics to do it?" You are not aiming for a diagram of the ideal organization that you have in mind, but the real one that already works for you or that you will really be able to create.

If your triangle is very small or fails to clearly indicate a promise, check which items received the lowest score; this will allow you to identify areas on which you must work to differentiate your USP from that of competitors and to start competing on value.

Conclusion of the case study: creating a new market together

Thanks to the foresight of its president, we started a training course with the Italian Association of Home Staging Professionals to help each member develop their own positioning and identify a promise they could make to the new market, thus competing on value. Furthermore, we all worked together to promote initiatives that spread the culture of home staging in Italy by first creating interest and then educating potential customers (real estate agents, investors, property owners) with the aim of enlarging the market but also of enabling buyers of this service to clearly identify their needs and consequently choose the professional with the most relevant characteristics. Italian home stagers have begun to understand that, although they all do the same job, they provide different services that can interest different people. A price war targeting generic customers who would focus only on costs was, therefore, not necessary. After months of stagnation the cooperative spirit among competitors was recovered and the demand for home staging services grew throughout Italy, leading to an incredible 70% increase in requests and an improvement in the relationship between sales made and quotes issued, which rose from one order every ten proposals to six orders every ten (average per associate). In short, our customers rediscovered that competition and antagonism are not synonymous: you can compete while remaining on good terms with your rivals. Each of them has their own method and style of reaching the goal, which in this case is winning the customer's heart. Indeed, thanks to what we have learned so far, we could say that every contender has a soulmate who tends to be different from that of anyone else, and if we stop thinking about the customer as a generic individual, we will understand that an unique customer/seller relation will never really be threatened. What people/customers ask of you is not to be "better" than your competitor, but uniquely suited to them. A lesson that our friends from the Italian Association of Home Staging Professionals have taken to heart.

What you have learnt and adding a piece to the *Loving Business Model*

Competing and cooperating are not so distant in meaning. Competition, if well managed, serves to educate customers, promote innovation, expand the market and highlight differential value. To understand what makes you unique and underline how you differ from other competitors, conduct a benchmark analysis as we illustrated. In addition, draw the diagram that describes your promise and that of three main competitors. Try to specialize your promise by increasing the scores you have obtained in the category that represents you most, trying to aim for excellence in all four aspects (positioning, products/services, people, processes) that set it apart.

Notes

1 Masaru Emoto is the author of numerous books including *The Message from Water* (Atria Books, 2005). His experiments were actually aimed at demonstrating how the water crystal changes by absorbing energy from the surrounding context, not so much to emphasize the diversity of every single drop that is a consequence of this.
2 The lack of customer loyalty is a possible side effect of those who adopt the "Best Price" strategy described in the previous chapter. To defuse this danger, companies that have chosen this strategy will have to continually invent new ways to make their offer preferable.

118 Respect your *rivals*

3 Some people consider value as spending little and, therefore, buying something particularly cheap. What really attracts these people is not the low price in itself, but the difference in terms of added value between what they feel they have purchased, and the price actually paid. It is therefore ultimately a search for greater value.

4 See note 2, Chapter 6.

5 As stated by Prof. Massimo Franceschetti, an expert in semiotics and communication, differentiation is the basis of human cognitive processes. Giving a name to things serves to define and describe, by difference, their distinctive features. So, what is different from us is fundamental to be known and appreciated in our uniqueness.

6 This process is now known as "Open Innovation" and has been widely adopted, especially in the digital world

7 Some authors introduce other categories such as that of *customer-oriented* companies. We believe that the two main categories are those described here, and all the others are offshoots of these. *Customer-oriented* (companies focused on listening and studying the customer) are nothing more than a sub-category of *market-oriented* companies because they look to the outside, to the market, for the answers they need to grow and prosper.

8 For information purposes, we have exacerbated the characteristics of both types of companies; in reality, some organizations may actually have characteristics of both, with a slight prevalence that can be identified.

9 It may appear that all three objectives must be pursued by companies, and this is partly true. However, the very organization of a company doesn't allow it to excel in all three areas. For this reason, it is improper to simultaneously promise you can offer the best-performing products with the lowest price and the highest level of assistance.

10 Some companies seem to change their promise depending on the product range. Think, for example, of the telephone sector. There are manufacturers that have both technologically advanced phones and super-cheap basic products in the range. In our opinion, however, it is more effective to change (or adapt) the promise only by modifying the brand and identity, creating for example sub-brands dedicated to low-end products.

11 Clarifying the promises made to customers by the companies we have followed over the years has led to surprising results. For example, the members of the Italian Home Staging Association, featured as the Case Study in this chapter, saw on average a four-fold increase redemption of their offers.

12 We have written about quantity/price rather than quality/price because companies that act in this way often compare the number of performances delivered in a "quantitative" way, compared to those of competitors. Their promise sounds like "there is more stuff in this, and it costs less", not focusing on quality.

13 The analysis method reported here is loosely inspired by the following article: Treacy, Michael, and Fred Wiersema. "Customer Intimacy and Other Value Disciplines." *Harvard Business Review*, January–February, 1993.

9

LOVE *WHO* YOU DO IT *WITH*

Getting the best from people

Abstract

When we talk about relationships with employees in a company, we often refer to the "management of human resources". In this chapter we want to use an evolution of this expression because considering people in terms of resources leads us to level them, losing the sense of the uniqueness and originality of each one. Even the verb "to manage" limits and distorts the relationship because "souls do not wish to be tamed".[1] In a company guided by love, everyone has the chance to give voice to their values. The leader always works firstly on himself or herself to then establish a pact with every collaborator, partner and stakeholder, which will have to be continually renewed over time.

Case study: the end of a relationship

Alice was 29 years old, with a degree in Information Science and experience as an account manager in a marketing company where she answered directly to the company's owner who fully embodied the type of leadership inspired by soldierly models: total dedication to work, very little space for emotions, language and attitudes inspired by military metaphors. It was her first and only work experience, so she imagined that the business world had to be exactly like this: traveling continuously, working all hours with very short lunch breaks, personal commitments subjugated to her job and a son who was growing up but seeing too little of his mum.

More out of desperation than by conscious choice, eventually she decided to start her own business with two partners: a marketing agency operating in an area she knew well, namely prize draws, loyalty campaigns and even a branch for in-store activities. The work took off immediately; there was great satisfaction and many customers sought the services of the new company. Thanks to her solid reputation, many who had known her in her previous job contacted her, facilitating the start-up of the new business that brought home good results in a short time. In fact, the business went so well that the company moved to a larger office with 24 workstations equipped with telephones and computers for the team of operators, who were now working shifts from nine in the morning to nine at night. With the growth of the business and increased responsibilities, however, something started to go wrong. Alice no longer had the strength necessary to exercise her leadership and committed the three capital errors that a good leader should never make: she stopped listening to her emotions, she compromised her values, and she failed to take responsibility herself for acting consistently. Over time this situation began to damage the trend towards growth and tensions arose; she found herself losing her temper even with some of her best collaborators, compromising relationships. Under pressure to obtain results, the company started accepted work from customers who in no way reflected its identity and, to make things worse, the personal relationships between the partners also deteriorated. As time passed, our young entrepreneur realized she had become, in spite of herself, everything she did not want to be, a clone of her previous boss: she had relinquished the values and style of business management which she had dreamed of implementing. Alice realized things had to change. But how?

Spread the love: the ingredients you need to get results

This is the moment when everything we have described so far must become reality. It does not take magic to accomplish this definitive transformation, but three simple elements: **willpower, time** and **people**. We have seen countless apparently perfect projects that seem bound for success wrecked because one of these elements failed or was badly managed!

Anyone who thinks they can succeed without considerable willpower, absolute dedication and constant commitment still believes in the fairy-tale of "overnight success": say the magic words and you will wake up rich and famous.

We have all heard stories about "a guy that invented an app one night and then sold it to Facebook for millions". Have you noticed how these stories are always incomplete, focusing the listener's attention on the rabbit pulled from the hat, i.e. the final success, while giving no details of all the phases that led to this result: the endless days of tests and trials, the mistakes, the doors slammed in your face before that fateful and decisive "night"?

Even the **time** variable can turn into a dangerous trap. Today we live in a world where everything happens quickly, where the most common words are *"urgent"*, *"immediately"* and *"by yesterday"*, forgetting that nature has set times, that a pregnancy lasts nine months, that wheat is sown in October and is harvested in June, that a caterpillar forms first a chrysalis and then takes wing as a butterfly 15 days later. Trying to shorten the wait to obtain immediate results is either impossible or very risky. When we accelerate work processes or demand a quick reward, we are ignoring the ancient wisdom encoded in our genes, allowing ourselves to be guided only by our craving to have more. Yet in business, as in life, we don't need haste but **pace**. Our projects require constant commitment and care; every day we have to do something to make them grow but we cannot accelerate or shorten the time needed for their development.

The third precious ingredient is the **people**. Choosing the "right" ones for our business, helping them to grow by giving them the opportunity to give optimum expression to their talents, fully involving them, recognizing, respecting and enhancing their specific capabilities and competences is fundamental for success. Putting people at the center of market dynamics means remembering that we are, in fact, dealing with human beings. If you are clear about the role played by respect, humanity and positive emotions towards the customer, now is the time to use the same sensitivity in your relationships with your collaborators. In this chapter, we will see how to adopt an attentive attitude, listening to the needs of those you have chosen for your work team and seeking to advance their satisfaction by making them actors in a shared result.

The success of a project depends not just on our employees, but also on suppliers, banks, consultants and perhaps local authorities; the quality of the relationships we build and maintain with all the people we encounter when carrying out our business will, in fact, condition the pleasantness of the exchange, the fluidity of responses, the commitment of each and, therefore, the results we ultimately achieve.

When each person takes full responsibility for what they do in their work, because they are guided by the awareness that this is the only way to liberate their ability to act, we obtain that meeting of wills that multiplies effectiveness and allows the organization to flourish.

With this attitude of openness and sharing, the responsibility of each person is added to create a larger whole that transforms into a proactive approach.

How can you choose collaborators with the right characteristics and make them fall in love with your project so that everyone works together with dedication and harmony? How can you optimize the time you dedicate to what really matters? How can you involve suppliers, thus moving beyond the concept that they are just there to be used? In the following paragraphs, we will try to address these questions together, helping you find your own, original answer.

Business is a team sport

Just as in love it is necessary to find the right person, the soulmate who understands and comprehends us. To transform our business idea into a success, we must have people who see, feel and perceive our same drive to action, who share our mission and the company's goals.

Therefore, your main task will be to clearly convey the goal which determines your business's existence and to be the first promoter of the **corporate culture** that will allow you to attract the right employees and make them fall in love with your idea, to the extent that it also becomes theirs. What parameters indicate whether a traveling companion is "right"?

In the business model driven by love, the term "right" must be relativized and humanized, becoming "right for you". You will have to look for individuals with values aligned to yours and with an approach to work in tune with that of your organization. When the corporate culture is solid and the cohesion between the elements is strong, an automatic process is activated that attracts like-minded people and drives away those with different aspirations and models. The cohesion of profound values must combine with the enhancement of diversity, to avoid producing clones of yourself: in fact, each person can work towards the same result though taking a different path that reflects their specific essence.

Anyone who bears a new and original viewpoint can stimulate creativity and bring life to the organization, helping to create a team of people with complementary abilities, but similar in their willingness to contribute and pursue a shared goal.

The entrepreneur David Hieatt,[2] author of the book *Do/Purpose*, states that employees need to know what they are helping to create and find motivation in knowing that together with us they are an active part of a positive story. So, devote time to conducting a careful **selection** phase and carefully evaluate who you want to include in your team not only in terms of competencies – what they can do –

but above all in terms of human skills (openness, desire to grow, desire to share) and the wish to play their part.

The team spirit needs to be nurtured and preserved: this is where your ability to be a true **leader** comes into play. That is, you must be able to lead and guide the group by transforming imposition into dialogue, control into motivation, orders into values and, above all, commanding into serving. Leadership thus manifests itself as a powerful driving force that unleashes each of your employees' desire to act proactively and confidently because they are free yet protected.

The love-driven leader recognizes the uniqueness of every individual, sees his or her abilities (expressed and potential) and reads each person's value in their soul. Such a leader knows when to encourage them to go it alone and when to stand by them to guide and aid them.

Feeling recognized in one's essence, being able to express skills and competences by pursuing one's personal mission and at the same time contributing to that of the organization to which one belongs, is one of the most powerful and stimulating driving forces. Cynics say that "money moves the world"; however, we would argue that trust and love for what you do moves *people*.

The **trust** within a workgroup contributes to creating a cohesive force like that within an atom that holds the particles together in a mutual and harmonious interaction: trust and love are also energy aggregators and multipliers. Consider how well you work when you feel others have confidence in you, when they praise and encourage you or even show genuine affection: you could go on tirelessly for hours, as if all this support were fueling your energy. When an environment is judgmental, dominated by control and mistrust, the stimuli will decrease, errors will increase, bonds will be broken and the whole system will become tainted and unstable. Under these circumstances, it is easier to lose employees as the internal relationships weaken.

When one of your staff resigns it is like the end of a love story. In some cases, you will discover that the conditions conducive to remaining together no longer existed because over time people evolve in different ways. However, it is always advisable when something unpleasant happens to us, such as the end of a collaboration, to ask "What could I have done differently? What did she really need?".

As we mainly deal with sales, we know that customers use excuses to break off negotiations in which they do not feel comfortable, and among the most popular excuses is the objection "It costs too much/I can find it cheaper elsewhere".[3] Just as the buyer uses the price as an excuse, so your collaborator might use an economic motivation as the explanation for leaving: "They will pay me more". Just as the intangible elements of the offer system lead a customer to give real value to products and services and to understanding what differentiates them, so your leadership will be stronger and more attractive in the development of aspects such as care, attention, dialogue and listening than in tangible elements such as salary, incentives and benefits. Let us consider, for example, the environment of the workplace itself: it is not only important to give people a desk or an office but to consider how these are positioned, to pay attention to details, noting how welcoming and comfortable the spaces are: these are all aspects that will make the difference. Customers are also influenced by the environments in which they are received, not only in tangible terms (physical space, furnishings, colors) but also intangibles and among these above all the quality of the **relationships within the organization** of which they are both witnesses and, sometimes, victims. When the internal relationships are based on respect, recognition and shared commitment, then the customers can fully benefit from the exchange. On the other hand, if the atmosphere at work is tense, with decisions imposed from above and no consideration of personal needs, the result is that the customers will directly or indirectly pay the costs. To give the customer a positive experience, you must first enjoy a positive experience within the organization of which you are part. How can we sell the value of the company if we are not the first ones to experience it, when we are the ones contributing to creating it and are part of it? Remember, therefore, that customer satisfaction is always a team effort. Referring to the chapter on brand, we can quote the words of David Hieatt, "Your people are your brand".[4] In fact, your people are an essential part of your business's **brand**. The reputation of your organization is also based on that of the individuals who are part of it and, vice versa: people's evaluation of you is colored by the reputation of the company in which you work. However, Gestalt psychology[5] reminds us that the whole is more than the sum of the individual parts: your task as a leader is, therefore, to take care of each individual according to their specific needs, so that an overall result of greater value is generated.

Activity – Mission vs motivations of collaborators

Do you remember the image we used in Chapter 6 to represent the intersection between the company's mission and the customers' purchase motivations? The same thing should happen with the motivations of the people who work with you: if you can get them to intersect with the mission, the natural reciprocal appeal will be triggered, generating more productive and more efficient relationships, an increase in involvement and the enhancement of reputation thanks to the coherence and dedication of collaborators and a lower turnover. It is thus very important to carefully select the members of your team and then create the conditions that ensure their motivations encounter your mission.

Hence, we propose an activity that will permit you to find out what personal "motivations" are most compatible with your business goals.

Start by analyzing the specific characteristics of your organization, in relation to these six fields:

1. Processes (working hours, shifts, operational methods, revenue/cost structure)
2. Internal relations (style, methods, habits and customs)
3. Required skills and competences (level of knowledge, skills, training)
4. Structural features of the company (location, dimensions, distance, furnishings, corporate structure)
5. Image and reputation (brand weight, external perception, history)
6. Offer and type of customer (products and services, buyers, distribution)

If you think it may be useful, add other features of your company even if they do not fall into any of the categories listed above.

When you have completed the list, ask yourself what kind of benefits they can generate for a hypothetical collaborator, remembering that, as with the customer, a feature can generate more than one answer.

Once you have the list of benefits, look at it and ask yourself: "What kind of personal motivation should an individual have to consider these features beneficial?" Help yourself with the ten categories of personal motivations used in Chapter 6. Of course, here we are talking about employees but if you think about it, even when we choose a job we are "buying" something, which is why we have called the employees "internal customers".

This activity should enable you to write one or more profiles of ideal collaborators. Now compare them with your mission, asking yourself if they are consistent with the organization's goals. If not, you will need to work on those features that have generated distant, or inconsistent, benefits.

It is all about pace

Life is marked by **time**, the most precious and the most underestimated variable of our existence: the hours you waste do not come back, the days do not regenerate and none of us knows when the stock of years that has been allocated to each of us will be exhausted. When seen like this, the question of time becomes rather serious, and indeed it is, even when talking about the realization of your business project.[6] Love also requires time in terms of attention, care, presence and… **pace** because you will have to do the right thing at the right time! Combining a "clicking clock" and "emotions" risks becoming complex. So, how can you best manage the time factor in the context of the *Loving Business Model*?

Being able to manage people's time well means finding a way to match their pace to that of your organization and business. Everything else, efficiency, productivity and results, will follow naturally.

126 Love *who* you do it *with*

We consider it useful to address the topic of time from three points of view:

- The time required for the process of collaborators' growth.
- The quality of time you dedicate to each of them.
- The time for yourself and the time you devote to the fundamental strategic choices for your business.

Let's analyze them together.

Giving time to the growth of collaborators

Nature, people and even investment need time to mature if they are to produce their best fruits. Let's immediately dispel two myths. The first is "treat everyone the same way", which may not only be impossible but can also be counterproductive. Every human being is unique and unrepeatable in character, life experiences, phase of life, skills matured and the willingness that they invest in what they do, so it is useless to expect a similar result from everyone.

The other misleading myth is "Everyone is useful, but no one is indispensable", which in our opinion represents the negation of individual value and the uniqueness of each person. **Everyone is indispensable in the economy of the world; all we have to do is find the right place for him or her!**

To help you effectively manage the growth path that will enable you to prepare your collaborators to accept delegated tasks and to operate independently, we will refer to the **Situational Leadership** model created by Kenneth Blanchard and Paul Hersey.[7] The concept behind this approach considers each person's level of professional and personal maturity. Professional maturity is measured by estimating their competence (born from knowledge and experience) while personal maturity relates to the psychological/personality component (in terms of commitment, involvement, responsibility and sense of belonging). The intersection of both defines the overall maturity level of the individual,[8] which can be measured according to this scale: low, moderate–low, moderate–high, high.

Each of us will tend, as a leader, to adopt the style that is most congenial to us, but if we act in a purely instinctive manner regardless of the person we need to help grow, we risk not only wasting time by spending it in a less strategic and effective way but also making irreversible mistakes like those we will consider shortly. Given that you and your team are interconnected, their time is your time![9] This is precisely why it is essential to manage yourself flexibly: in fact, what you must do as a leader is set the pace and modify your behavior in accordance with the level of maturity of each collaborator.

1. **Low maturity** – *I direct*, indicating to the person what to do, how to do it and for how long, verifying the work performed.

2. **Moderate–low maturity** – *I guide* the collaborator who has not yet completely mastered the tasks to be performed, involving her/him and explaining to the choices made, testing his/her willingness and desire to commit.
3. **Moderate–high maturity** – *I support* the person by encouraging, involving and giving importance to his/her contribution. The collaborator has the necessary experience and no longer needs to be controlled while carrying out tasks but can participate in decisions and operate more independently.
4. **High maturity** – *I delegate*, leaving the collaborator full autonomy in carrying out the assigned activities, knowing that I can count on the commitment and the willingness of this person who has embraced corporate objectives.

Whatever the features of the collaborators, the ethical leader will have to provide each person the time, attention and the sensitivity needed to foster their growth while remaining flexible.

If you are rigid in your positions, demanding that people behave as you desire, you are on a road to disaster, wasting corporate "resources" and personal energy.

We can assure anyone who thinks it is possible to take a shortcut by skipping some of these stages of growth, or dedicating less time to the relationship with collaborators, that doing so will have costs in terms of efficiency. For example, you might be tempted to delegate tasks to a new collaborator who already has experience in that field. However, we suggest that you start from the initial phase anyway, thus checking the maturity and skills of the new collaborator and making sure that she/he has time to adapt to the organization. It is possible to proceed swiftly from one phase of growth to another (within a few days or weeks) but passing through this phase will help you to set the right pace for the person to mature, giving value to the investment made.

Another common mistake is to switch immediately from the guidance to the delegation phase. This happens when we see a collaborator engage, starting to develop a certain autonomy and achieving good results. Some "leaders", who are eager to be relieved of a little more work, might then decide to promote this person to the field by delegating responsibilities and decisions that he/she had just started managing the day before: in this case, the person will not feel gratified but abandoned! The intermediate step must be used to support and develop the autonomy required to receive delegation.

The flexibility of leaders in a business driven by love is precisely that of understanding how to mix control and autonomy, emotional support and independence. We should remind you that leadership is a continuous activity; it is not

128 Love *who* you do it *with*

something that once set up you can put away in a drawer. Instead, it requires constant dedication because people change, and we also change within the evolutionary process of our lives.

The quality of time dedicated to collaborators

You have understood that your relationship with the people on your team must aim to focus them on the objectives, motivating them, ensuring that they use their time in a profitable way and obtain results for themselves as well as for the organization. As they evolve, two things can happen: the person succeeds in what they are doing or makes a mistake and gets stuck. In both cases, as a leader, you will have to step in, and each time you will have to use different tools. In the first case, you will need to use praise to highlight the results obtained; in the second, constructive criticism that transforms the error into a learning opportunity. Leaders are perceived as being right when they master both of these tools. However, our experience demonstrates that the opposite often happens: partly because of time restrictions and partly because they lack confidence when handling emotional involvement,[10] positive results are ignored or taken for granted, while the mistake turns into an opportunity to express all the frustrations that have been bottled up over time. Expressing **appreciation** of the results obtained is very important to make the other person feel valued and recognized, to encourage and stimulate improvement.[11] When complimenting a person's work it should never sound like you are passing judgment, albeit positive, on the other person; you should, instead, express your praise with sincerity, in the spirit of celebrating the result achieved and the ability acquired. Speaking of praise, you have to bear in mind that some people find it difficult to accept compliments: they may be afraid they do not deserve them, they wonder what might be asked of them in return, they are frightened of the expectations people will then have of them. The more you know how to create an environment where people feel confident about your intentions, the more they will be positively stimulated by receiving thanks or genuine appreciation and just as open to accepting when they make a mistake or fail to complete something as hoped for. It is also good to define some rules regarding **criticism** to prevent the office from turning into a courtroom.

Firstly, it is important to choose a specific time and place to deal with the issue, making sure you are alone with the person to whom you want to talk. This ensures you not only preserve the employee's self-esteem and create the right conditions for them to be open to finding a solution, but you will also avoid the risk that your negative opinion seems to be addressed indiscriminately to the group. Moreover, addressing the question in front of others could lead to the person concerned not realizing that they were the object of the criticism, while the most insecure or sensitive person on the team might feel wrongly accused! If you consider it useful, you might agree with your employee to discuss the issue later with the rest of the group so that the experience may be useful to everyone.

Another fundamental rule: if you want to be sure that one of your employees knows something, tell them! Sometimes it can be frightening **to speak out clearly**; we may fear the reaction of the other person and resort to irony and sarcasm or approach the issue indirectly by talking to another colleague and hoping that the comment will reach the interested party. Worse still, people sometimes make generalized comments in the hearing of the person they wish to tackle, inwardly convinced that they "made the message clear"! It is important to remember that being honest does not mean flattening the other person's ego or damaging their self-esteem: anything can be said if we say it in the right way.

Success in resolving an error lies in the ability to deal with it as quickly as possible. Take, for example, a new employee who arrives a few minutes late: you look at the clock, you are a bit annoyed, but you say nothing. The next day the same thing happens, your annoyance increases; as you pass near the group you make a sarcastic comment. A week passes and your employee is late every day; you decide to talk to him, but you lose your temper and storm out saying: "You are unreliable and always late". Your employee might well reply: "But you never said anything to me; I thought there were a few minutes' leeway". He is right, you did not tell him, and it is no good thinking, "He should have known", or undermining the possibility of working together in the future by arguing. If, on the contrary, you had told him the first day that punctuality was required, the whole dynamic would have changed: "I saw you arrived a few minutes late this morning. I am concerned because we do not want to keep customers waiting in the morning; they might go elsewhere. What happened today and how can we make sure it does not happen again?"

If you accuse a person directly, by using the format "You are...", you leave no margin for evolution as well as mortifying the person rather than motivating growth. If instead of making a personal evaluation you comment on the task performed, it will be easier for them to admit they encountered a difficulty, thus activating the cooperation needed to find a solution together and at the same time motivating the employee to commit to resolving the issue. To train your ability to make constructive criticism we suggest you follow this approach[12]:

1. **Specifically** describe in the most objective way possible, and **without passing judgment**, what behavior or task created a problem: "I saw you arrived ten minutes' late every day over the last week".
2. Express how you feel, explaining the **emotional impact** that behavior has on you, with a message in the first person, for example: "I am very concerned..."
3. Give evidence of the effect and **consequences** that that fact/behavior could have "...customers could go elsewhere".
4. Try to understand why your colleague acted in this way by **asking and listening**: "What happened?"; in this phase, you must limit your criticism to what can be modified, without demanding the impossible and without forcing the other to explain any deeper motivations.[13]
5. Look for a **solution** together or at least decide what new actions to take so the situation is not repeated since the goal is to help the other person overcome

130 Love *who* you do it *with*

the difficulty that caused the criticism: "How can we make sure it does not happen again?"

Analyzing this sequence of actions should clarify the importance of making one constructive criticism at a time; it is impossible if you tackle a series of issues all at once to find solutions to every problem: the emotional burden would become too great and the person would feel discouraged and overwhelmed at the idea of having to change so many different behaviors.

In general, remember that pursuing common well-being makes the difference between finding satisfaction in your professional role and turning every day into a living hell. This important objective requires dedicating time to dialogue, finding time to clear any issues that arise as they arise: in this way you will be able to build a learning environment that helps to broaden the overall vision by listening to different points of view, where joys and successes are shared but difficulties and failures are also accepted. In particular, we suggest you listen to newcomers and encourage them to share their first impressions: they are certain to be more objective than those of employees who have been with you for a while.

Time for yourself and for your business

How should you distribute your time between strategic and operational activities, listening to employees and training them, discussions with other stakeholders as well as moments for reflection and personal growth? Figure 9.1 will help you reflect on the importance of finding a balance in the management of your time and that of the team you work with.

When talking about your time, it is essential to broaden your vision to consider your life overall.

We are many things: everything comes together to generate new ideas, broaden our knowledge, stimulate connections, to enable us to evolve. Each of us, among other things, has his own pace when acting: some people prefer to anticipate where others postpone. There is no perfect strategy; in our opinion, it is essential to recognize your relationship with time and then to become more flexible in order to be more efficient.

In today's business, swift action seems to prevail, while every pause is perceived as a waste of time and opportunities. Yet love, as we all know, requires a slower pace and pauses during which waiting is also time "filled", not wasted.

It is certainly true that time is a finite resource and that we must not fall into the trap of postponing any action to the bitter end, waiting until we have absolutely all the information before making a decision. In our experience, many businesses fail because they never even start! In fact, there is no perfect moment, no time when every aspect has been evaluated and defined to avoid any possible risk: one thing is to prepare oneself, another is the manic search for unattainable perfection.

Let us embrace the approach to procrastination that Prof. Grant describes in his book *Originals*.[14] His suggestion is to prepare the activities and then to interrupt them strategically, taking a break to reflect, to see things in perspective and

LEADER AND TIME USE

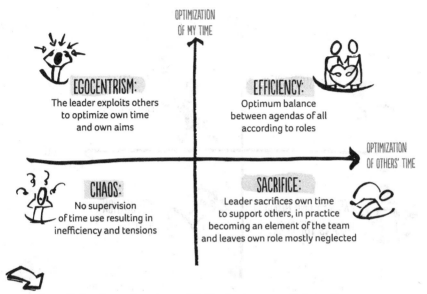

Depending on the greater or lesser skill of leaders to manage their own time and that of others, four different situations can occur as shown here.

FIGURE 9.1 Leaders and time use

give space to your creativity, perhaps modifying your approach on the basis of information that has emerged in the meantime. In reality, even if you stop doing something your brain will continue subconsciously working on the creative process, stimulating and designing innovative solutions while you are doing something else. In this sense, procrastination is not laziness but signifies waiting for the right moment!

To be a positive leader, a source of inspiration, and to respect others' time, you will have to start by looking after yourself. We advise you to choose one "**soul day**" during the week, to look after your heart and soul. To hear this inner voice, you require "silence" and a slow pace, so for 24 hours forget the hustle and bustle of daily life; dedicate this time to yourself because loving and celebrating yourself is the only way to learn to love others too.

Activity – Checking your company's climate

Look at Figure 9.2. The horizontal axis highlights the quality of personal relationships within your company, while the vertical axis indicates the intensity of commitments and challenges.[15]

Place your organization in one of the four quadrants by first analyzing the aspects related to the quality of relationships through these questions:

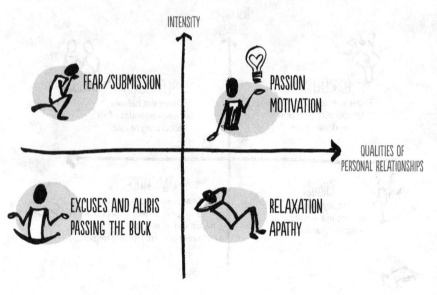

FIGURE 9.2 Company climate

- What are the relationships between me, my colleagues and employees like?
- How do they interact with each other, are there conflicts?
- Are constructive criticism and praise of results implemented?
- Is there a climate of respect and mutual trust?

It would be a good idea to involve your team in the analysis too!
When considering intensity, it depends on the use of time so you might ask yourself:

- Do I use my time and that of the team effectively?
- Are the deadlines and objectives properly adjusted in terms of time?
- Do my team and I often feel stressed or overworked?
- Are punctuality and respect for timetables the norm or a rare event?

If you managed to position yourself on the grid, but your company does not fall into the upper-right quadrant (**passion/motivation**), you will have to work on one of the following factors:

Fear/submission – Your structure has a functional use of time, but human relationships are showing cracks. Fear is the rule: threats and negative stress are leveraged to keep the organization running; people only act when they feel under threat. This situation cannot last long term. You need to look after relationships by adopting one of the suggestions in this chapter.

Love *who* you do it *with* **133**

Relaxation/apathy – Good relations and a friendly atmosphere, but few stimuli lead to laxness and boredom. The result is that efficiency decreases, everyone feels under-fulfilled and results drop. People need to be "on their game" to feel useful and valued. You need to up the pace a bit to increase the intensity.

Excuses and justifications/buck passing – "All for nobody and everyone for themselves" would be the best description of an organization in this situation. Few people do anything and when anyone does something, they make it weigh on others or expect praise and rewards for the little they have done. Where things are really bad, colleagues are suspicious or unfriendly with more diligent co-workers. It is a serious situation and to resolve it you must first work on relationships and then raise the intensity of the pace at work, perhaps by finding positive examples on which to focus.

Expanding the value chain: managing your suppliers and stakeholders

In a business driven by love, the value chain involves all the people who directly, or indirectly through the companies/institutions they represent, contribute to its creation and maintenance. The stakeholders thus also become bearers of value, and for this reason we prefer to call them *valueholders*.

In the context of the *Loving Business Model*, suppliers and partners become participants in a common project; there is space for complicity and gratitude and the responsibilities of each feed into the whole. Yes, indeed, because nobody shirks responsibility with the attitude "Now it's up to you; my task is over", but everyone's efforts converge towards the achievement of a result that is shared and meets everyone's goals.

Not only the internal employees take care of a piece of the mission by making their contribution, but also partners who are external to your company participate in achieving its objectives. When people understand that individual responsibilities release the power to act, creativity, new ideas and hidden solutions come forth. This type of approach to business, and to life in general, requires a shared culture and common values: two elements that, like beacons, will direct and guide us. Culture and values are rooted in knowledge and personal evolution, elements without which no corporate governance system can work. In fact, where people are ignorant others are bound to use fear to govern them!

In a ruthless vision of business, as a zero-sum game in which one wins and many lose, the relationship with suppliers is often experienced as a jungle dominated by the strongest and most aggressive. We have come across companies with this approach through our work and they are easily recognizable even from the smaller details. All too often the reception areas of organizations welcome customers with care and attention while suppliers receive a very different treatment. One wonders why it is so difficult to comprehend that the supplier is first and foremost a person who is also endowed with emotions and values that can serve the company's goals.

134 Love *who* you do it *with*

If we mistreat the people whose products and services contribute to the creation of our offer, sooner or later they will, either consciously or unconsciously, wish to get their own back; at the very least they will not be encouraged to do their best to aid us in "our" goals. Respect and attention produce a desire to collaborate, a commitment to keep promises and a willingness to help. This is the only way in which the attitude, "I will have to put up with this relationship because I need the business", becomes an integration of goals: "I want to work for them; I like what they do and how they do it". This is when values are shared.

The Illycaffè company, named among the most ethical in the world by the Ethisphere Institute[16] for the sixth consecutive year in 2018, provides a virtuous example in this sense. Specifically, from the company's headquarters in Trieste, the managers and purchasing staff have managed to establish a relationship with coffee producers, located in areas that are among the poorest on the planet, based on four pillars:

- *Selection* of the best growers.
- *Training* in quality and respect for the environment.
- *Value recognition*, guaranteeing a profitable price.
- *Building direct relationships* based on knowledge, exchange and growth.

Cooperation, therefore, becomes virtuous: the growers are the first to create the part of the value that the Illycaffè company[17] wants to provide to its customers, through production of excellence.

If you want quality relationships inspired by love, you must first act in this way, providing an example of a new way of being on the market and managing relationships within it. Once again, the important thing is that at the base there is a meeting of values, not necessarily equal but that can support and integrate each other, not dispersed or conflicting.

Let's go back to Illycaffè and its suppliers; the company to achieve the mission "to delight all those who cherish the quality of life, through our search for the best coffee nature can provide" needs producers who are willing to dedicate excellent care to cultivate quality. This requires extra input and more sophisticated techniques, with high production costs. The suppliers might perhaps not be particularly interested in "delighting" the end customer, with whom they have little direct contact, but they certainly want to help the community in which they work by paying adequate wages and producing innovation thanks to the higher price obtained by the company. Thus, the two requirements, one linked to the mission and the other linked to the growth of a local market, meet and integrate perfectly.

Conclusion of the case study: a new and passionate love

Great opportunities may appear in difficult moments in our lives. So, in 2011 Alice decided to close her company and started working as a trainer and consultant.

Initially, to liquidate the previous business and quickly recover her standard of living, she committed to traveling long distances between one customer and another, providing hundreds of hours of lectures and consultancy. This, at times, very tiring, commitment enabled her to encounter numerous realities and many challenges. Reflecting on the dilemmas, fears and difficulties of the people she met, she wished to learn more through reading and research to grasp the valuable lesson contained in everything she was experiencing. This is how the idea of a new negotiating model based on ethics was born. Shortly afterwards, Alberto made a similar choice; he left his job as a manager and together they established *Passodue* with the aim of helping organizations to accept and develop a new model that combined an effective approach with transparency, correctness and authenticity – putting people and their needs back at the heart of business.

As Salvatore Brizzi says: "The resources to carry out our mission are always available". If we systematically lack the means and energy to carry out a certain project, we should recognize that it is time to change course and redirect our life to its true purposes. *Passodue* provided the opportunity to experiment and create a model that encompassed a new approach to business, where everyone can enjoy the opportunity to express their talents to the fullest, where leadership is shared with free responsibility, where the values of incisiveness and determination combine with acceptance and care, and relationships are based on trust.

If the people who work with you are doing well, you will have actively contributed to making the society better, because when they return home they will be happier and willing to make good relationships, in short, to convey the value of which they feel they are part.

What you have learnt and adding a piece to the *Loving Business Model*

The people who work with you and for you are key players in your success. To guide them well, balance wisely your use of time and relationship style. From the selection phase onwards, engage and match your company's goals with their personal mission. Consider everyone, including suppliers, as valueholders who will contribute to your success. Make a list of your employees and group them according to their level of maturity, then assess the most appropriate behavior to help each person grow. It might also be useful to check the internal climate to understand what aspects of your company could be improved.

136 Love *who* you do it *with*

Notes

1 Poli, Erica Francesca. *The Anatomy of the Couple: The Seven Principles of Love*. Anima Edizioni, 2018.
2 Entrepreneur and, together with his wife, founder of the publishing house The Do Book Co. https://thedobook.co
3 As we extensively discussed in our previous book *Sales Ethics*, not all objections are true. Price is often an alibi for both customers and sellers. You can refer to the book for further insight.
4 Hieatt, David. *Do Purpose: Why Brands with a Purpose Do Better and Matter More*. The Do Book Company, 2014.
5 Gestalt psychology, born at the beginning of the last century in Germany, is a school of thought that focuses on the themes of perception of experience.
6 To realize the importance of the correct use of time on the processes and relationships within the company and on its innovative capacity, we recommend reading the following article: De Liguori, Mario, and Francesco Zurlo. "How to Measure the Positive Effects on Wellbeing of Slowdown in Product Design." Paper presented at the *Letters to the Future* conference, Srishti Institute of Art, Design & Technology, Bangalore, India, November 13, 2018, 252–263.
7 Hersey, Paul, and Kenneth Blanchard. *Management of Organizational Behavior Leading Human Resources*. 10th ed. Pearson India, 2015.
8 You could create a table in which you give a score of "maturity" to your collaborators that is the result of the sum of these two aspects.
9 We spend at least eight hours a day at work. Adding up the time in which we "think" about work and subtracting the hours of sleep, it is easy to see how our time spent with colleagues and collaborators abundantly exceeds that spent with anyone else.
10 This mistrust is often engendered by the macho and military atmosphere that dominates in many companies. Introducing the culture of *Engaging the Heart in Business* also means enabling the activation of tools such as those described in this paragraph.
11 A study conducted by McKinsey in June 2009, involving more than 1,000 managers, executives and employees from different sectors, showed that the best form of incentive is not economic but linked to factors such as appreciation, valorization and confidence.
12 This method is inspired by the following book: Rosenberg, Marshall B. *Nonviolent Communication: A Language of Life*. 3rd ed. Puddle Dancer Pr, 2015.
13 Sometimes people's behavior is the result of very intimate and personal motivations that they do not wish to share in a work environment. Forcing them to declare these would, therefore, be unethical.
14 Grant, Adam. *Originals: How Non-Conformists Move the World*. Viking, 2016.
15 The diagram shown here is loosely inspired by considerations on how to free up "The energy of an organization" contained in the following book: Sisodia, Raj, David B. Wolfe, and Jagdish N. Sheth. *Firms of Endearment: How World-Class Companies Profit from Passion and Purpose*. Pearson, 2003.
16 An international organization that defines and measures corporate ethical standards, recognizes companies that excel, and promotes best practices in corporate ethics.
17 The data and information relating to the Illycaffè company are taken from the site www.illy.com/en-us/company/company/illy

10

LOVE *HOW* YOU *DO IT*

The value journey and managing the relationship

Abstract

What binds all aspects of the *Loving Business Model* together, combining our identity with our offer, our team, our competitors and our goals? The answer is the customer journey: a movie starring the customer and with all the elements we have just mentioned as co-stars and props. This chapter will teach you how to direct it in order to build value in every frame so that it becomes a love story with a happy ending.

Case study: spontaneity vs strategy

In 2017, the Nazareno Cooperative Sociali, a group of social cooperatives, came to us with a simple but fundamental goal: to create a place that would give dignity to disadvantaged people offering them work opportunities while also encouraging citizens to gather in a structure run by the Nazareno Cooperatives by creating the restaurant, Bistrò53.

138 Love *how* you *do it*

The main headquarters of Nazareno is Villa Chierici, a 19th-century building located in Carpi in the province of Modena, set within a splendid park. A small restaurant was built here in a modern style perfectly in harmony with its surroundings. The aim was to create job opportunities for the young people hosted by the cooperative while also attracting locals to the venue to increase the citizens' awareness of the social benefits of the work the institute carried out.

A perfect program on paper, which needed a project that would allow it to compete with the various catering outlets in the area. The park and villa, moreover, are not easily accessible and are located in a little-frequented area on the city's outskirts. Finding the right job placement for the cooperative's guests in an activity such as catering was very tricky to manage, both as regards production processes and service and relationships with the customers, in part because the desire was not to create a restaurant frequented only by people moved by "charitable intentions" to contribute to Nazareno's cause, but by everyone. The desire was to have a "real business" that could attract customers with its offer, regardless of the social purpose for which it was born. To have any chance of success, the bistro needed to create and promote an independent identity. Although the Nazareno group enjoyed a good reputation throughout the vast territory in which it operates, it did not possess a unique image that would be strong enough to attract the number of customers necessary to make a success of the restaurant. The challenge was to weave all these elements together in a credible and attractive story: we thus had to design the customer journey of what would become Bistrò53!

Movie scenes, starring your customer

So far, we have defined the elements that make up the *Loving Business Model*; now we need to talk about the connective tissue that binds them all together. What is this external membrane? It is a journey that leads to the customer's complete satisfaction, indeed, in marketing literature, it is referred to as the "customer journey". However, the metaphor we will adopt in this text is that of a romantic movie centered around the customer, with the company, its employees, providers and competitors as the co-stars and the elements of the offer, products and services, but also mission and brand, as props. As the movie progresses, the customers will be guided towards the discovery of what is valid for them, but also of the value that they bear and of what the other actors can offer them if they are willing to complete an exchange.

If you want the customers to choose to exchange their value with yours, you will have to propose yourself as the director and screenwriter of this movie, willing to carefully script the unfolding of the scenes, directing the actors and selecting the locations so that the props (the tangible and intangible elements of your company's offer system) are enhanced and placed in the story you have prepared. We will call the sequences of the movie **phases of the customer journey**, and **touch points** the "locations" where they will take place. Some phases will be more important than others to developing the overall storyline of the movie, or if you prefer, of the experience that the customer will have. Figure 10.1 helps you understand how the

RELATIONSHIP BETWEEN PHASES-TOUCH POINT-OFFER SYSTEM

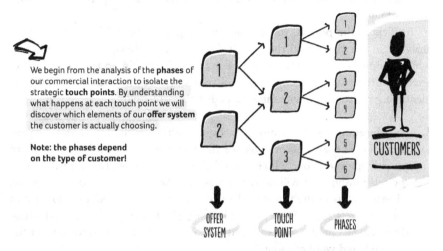

FIGURE 10.1 Relationship between phases – touch point offer system

customers, the phases of the movie, the touch points and the elements of the offer system are related.

For example, if you enter an electronics store, the products you find inside are elements of the offer system, while the location itself represents a touch point. The salespeople in the store are also a touch point, while their style and the behavior they adopt in dealing with you are part of the offer system. It is important that you clearly perceive this difference because you will need to write the script of your "romantic movie" correctly. Here are brief definitions of these three important elements:

- **Phases of the customer journey** – the different moments that the customer–company relationship goes through (e.g. first contact, negotiation, after-sales…)
- **Touch points** – the interfaces and/or location in which the relationship takes place (e.g. stores, websites, sellers…)
- **Element of the offer system** – everything, tangible or intangible, that is part of your proposal to the market (see Chapter 7).

Now get a pencil and paper because it's time to start writing the script together. First, you must imagine all the phases of your relationship with the customer, asking yourself what the movie's initial scenes are, how it might develop and finally the ending. In the middle, of course, there will be "dramatic" moments with emotional tension; these "scenes" may correspond to problems customers encounter while

140 Love *how* you *do it*

using your products or services, complaints, objections and so on. Remember that the star, i.e. the customer, is present in all the sequences of the journey but this is not equally true for the other co-stars, including you. There will, in fact, be moments in which you will not be on screen, yet the success of the story still remains your responsibility.

To identify the **phases**, you can use the diagram of the *Circle of Trust* that we analyzed in the chapter on theories. It describes the different moments through which a company and customer progress in their relationship. So, let's go over its six levels to turn them into scenes/phases in your story with the customer while also identifying the touch points or interfaces that characterize them.

1. **Indifference** – For the movie to begin, customers must be aware of your existence. The early scenes will see them exploring the market in search of something or someone who satisfies their needs or desires. In this first phase of the relationship, you will need touch points like a well-indexed Internet site, advertisements in the paper media that your customers read, the presence of your products and services in the places to which they go, and so on. Include direct email, but also sales calls and any "push" activity you need to meet the customer and word of mouth.

2. **Skepticism/mistrust** – However good you may have been in finding or being found by the customers, to overcome their distrust you will need touch points with a strong human or relational component. So immediately after engaging them, and while still in the initial stages of the customer journey, we suggest you guide them towards a physical encounter with a person or, at least, towards an interactive interface that will make them feel welcomed. This includes toll-free numbers, chat services, dedicated sales points or corners, reception staff and so on. Remember that at this point your prospective customers are still skeptical and suspicious so they will probably explore not only your touch points but also those of other competitors. Try to be reassuring and reliable, showing yourself for what you are, making promises that you can keep while avoiding any exaggeration.

3. **Attention** – After receiving and reassuring them, you will need something that captures the customers' attention. Do you know the quickest and most effective way to do this? Listen to them! This phase thus requires a touch point for listening or getting feedback, such as online forms and questionnaires, pre-sales specialists, consultancy services to help them explore their needs, or any other interface that can perform this function in accordance with the type of market in which you operate and the type of offer that characterizes your business.

4. **Interest** – You can stimulate people's interest by ensuring they recognize themselves in what they are seeing, to the extent that your product or service seems designed specifically for them. It is a matter of allowing customers to anticipate the excitement of using your offer, imagining the benefits that will derive

Love *how* you *do it* **141**

from the purchase, the values that unite them with the brand and everything that, concretely, can project them to the center of an experience. This category includes touch points such as demos, test invitations, case studies, projects, stories and references complete with statistics and numbers that support the promises made in your offer.

5. **Conditional trust** – This level of the relationship usually coincides with the first purchase choice. Thus, the customer journey you are planning requires touch points to facilitate the customers' decision, clarifying what they want to "add to the cart" and how to buy and pay for the goods. This category includes price lists, promotions, quotes, offer configurators, sales consultants who help in the choice and anything else that can help customers to choose consciously and freely in the way most congenial to them.

6. **Broader trust** – This corresponds to all the post-sales phases, in which buyers will find themselves using and experiencing what you sold them. You will then have to consider the possible difficulties or complaints that may occur. This category includes all the touch points dedicated to customer care after purchase. At this stage, there will be satisfaction questionnaires, assistance numbers or other interfaces that help customers to report a problem or a complaint, emergency personnel, assistance services, but also social pages, forums and other media where they can express their opinion and stay in contact with your company.

Clearly, these are just suggestions; you can write your phases and identify the touch points as you see fit and in the way that best represents your business.

As shown in Figure 10.1, a touch point can be designed to be effective in more than one phase. Think of your website, for example: it can help customers to find you but also overcome their initial mistrust; it can listen to them, even get them to buy something, and then provide some simple after-sales services.

We will deal with the design of touch points in the next section. In the meantime, we suggest the following activity: retrace all the points of the list that describes the phases of your customer journey and ask yourself if you have an adequate number of touch points in each of them. In addition, ask yourself what your main competitors do to be present at that precise moment of the customers' experience. If you discover that you devote less attention to certain phases than your competitors, or even totally neglect them, you will have identified an important element for improving your business. The presence of multiple touch points is important, particularly in the initial phases in which customers must be aware that you exist and desire to meet you to overcome their skepticism and verify their interest in what you offer.

Review the six phases identified above and consider your business; you will have noticed that while the customer is always the star in each phase, the co-stars can change passing, for example, from the staff answering questions via chat, to the expert consultant who guides the customer's choice through to post-sales

142 Love *how* you *do it*

colleagues. You may also find that at different moments in your relationship you will be dealing with different decision makers or with an actual "team of buyers". Hence, when we analyze the individual touch points in the next section, you will have to ask yourself not only which features they should have to function well, but also which customer will be involved and who the seller will be, where the "seller" indicates the person responsible for helping and guiding customers by offering the maximum value that can be expressed by the organization at that particular moment. For those working in a business to business to consumer market (B2B2C[1]) or using any distribution system, some of the touch points will certainly be managed by partners and will, therefore, be less directly controllable. We will call these *indirect* **touch points** and they will be considered very carefully because the fate of the "movie" may depend on them. Something similar happens with word of mouth: it is an indirect touch point since you do not manage it. So, how can you control it? A good way to keep indirect touch points monitored is to strengthen your control over what happens downstream and upstream, i.e. the neighboring touch points, as well as trying to collect data on the activities that occur within them, or in the case of word of mouth, keeping track of *who, how, when* and *how much* people are talking about you.

There are two important qualities of touch points that must be considered: their greater or lesser **strategic importance** and the possibility, or otherwise, of **controlling** them.

> **Strategic touch point** – We apply the term "strategic" to the interface from which the largest number of new customers arrive,[2] characterized by high interaction, particularly representative of your offer and consistent with the characteristics of your typical customer as well as being able to provide customers with an intense and exciting experience. If most of your first contacts are via phone, then the person who takes the phone calls is a strategic "touch point", whereas if you work in the field of digital communication your website is of primary importance. If your customers are teenagers you will consider all the social media on which they are present as strategic, while you will prefer more traditional forms of interaction if you are selling insurance policies to retirees.
>
> **Controlled touch point** – A touch point can be considered as "controlled" when you can collect precise data and information from it. You should also be able to evaluate how well it operates, namely whether it is able to maintain the customers within your movie or not. A controlled touch point profiles the people who visit it, thus providing what are technically called "contact leads". It must, therefore, be designed specifically to do this, with personnel responsible for its proper functioning and an investment budget for its development and improvement. Furthermore, its design must clearly reflect your organization, and be consistent with your corporate image, values and style: all topics that we will address in the next section.

Love *how* you *do it* **143**

The further your customers proceed on the journey, passing naturally from one phase to another of the relationship through the interfaces you have designed for them, the more they will become involved in a mutually enriching exchange.

We have compared the customer journey to a movie, but have you ever asked yourself what keeps you glued to the screen? A good movie, like a book you particularly like, expresses parts of you, leading you to identify with the story and emotions projected. The customer journey has the same purpose; you must, therefore, make them feel welcomed, accepted and important at all times because the exchange of value, the true objective of every market action, takes place throughout the entire experience.

Activity – Design your customer journey

Taking inspiration from the levels of the *Circle of Trust* described above, proceed as follows:

1. Divide your customer's experience into phases, from market exploration, to reception, then to the choice to purchase and after-sales, without neglecting the moments when you say goodbye
2. For each phase, answer these questions:
   - Who or what acts as a touch point?
   - What is the purpose of this phase? Does it achieve its goal?
   - Is the interaction "hot" or "cold"; does it excite positive emotions or not?
   - Which elements of the offer system are visible or could be so?
   - What are the risks inherent in the phase (e.g. loss of customer interest, difficulties, conflicts)?
3. Once you have identified all the touch points, ask yourself:
   - Are there enough touch points for an effective customer experience?
   - What are the strategic touch points in the "principal scenes" of the relationship?
   - Are the strategic touch points also controlled?
   - Can any improvements be made to make the customer journey smoother and more enjoyable?

We advise you to draw a diagram like Figure 10.3 that provides an example of an analysis done for a computer company; alternatively, download the survey grid in the download area. It will help you identify the touch points (remember to highlight the strategic ones) and study each phase. If you want to develop the exercise further, you can add three new columns, indicating, for each phase, who plays the role of the decision maker, who represents the company and what your best competitors do in that situation.

144 Love *how* you *do it*

CUSTOMER JOURNEY ANALYSIS

PHASE	TOUCH POINT	GOAL	OFFER SYSTEM	RISKS	IMPROVEMENTS

FIGURE 10.2 Customer journey analysis 1

EXAMPLE OF CUSTOMER JOURNEY ANALYSIS

PHASE	TOUCH POINT	GOAL	OFFER SYSTEM	RISKS	IMPROVEMENTS
EXPLORATION	EVENTS, WORD OF MOUTH, SEO	BEING FOUND, STIMULATE NEED	BRAND VALUES, REPUTATION	CUSTOMERS DO NOT FIND US	IDENTIFY KEY WORDS FOR INDEXING
INFO	SITE, REFERENCES, EMAIL OR CALLING DIRECTLY	GIVE KEY INFO, FACILITATE CONFIGURATION	PRODUCTS & SERVICES, RELATIONSHIP STYLE, EASE OF ACCESS	CUSTOMERS DO NOT UNDERSTAND	SITE CONFIGURATION, LEARNING CONTENT FOR SELF-TRAINING
KNOWLEDGE	TECHNICAL DEPT, SALES STAFF	INSPIRE TRUST, SAFETY, ENTHUSIASM	COMPETENCE AND CAPABILITY OF STAFF, MISSION	CUSTOMER IS FEARFUL OR NOT GUIDED TECHNICALLY	TECHNICAL TRAINING OF SALES STAFF
EVALUATION	QUOTE, TABLE OF INTEGRATIVE SERVICES, LIST OF SUPPLIERS	DIFFERENTIATE FROM COMPETITORS, TRANSMIT BENEFITS	PRICE, PROJECT CAPABILITY, CASE STUDIES	CUSTOMER FAILS TO PERCEIVE DIFFERENCES, DOES NOT CONSIDER US EQUALS	TAKE ESTIMATES TO VISITS WITHOUT SENDING
ACCEPTANCE	TIMETABLE, TEAM ORGANIZATION CHART, SALES ACCOUNT	REASSURANCE ON CHOICE, USE AND SUBSEQUENT PHASES	CONTRACTUAL PROTECTION, FLOW MANAGEMENT METHOD	CONSIDERS ONLY PRICE, RISK OF KEEPING PROMISE	HIGHLIGHT METHOD OF WORK ADOPTED WHEN PREPARING QUOTE TO SHOW BENEFITS
PRODUCTION	TEAM LEADER, INTERNAL TEAM, TOUCH POINT TO MANAGE INFO AND UNEXPECTED EVENTS	KEEP INFORMED, MANAGE ISSUES	TEAM COHESION, INTERNAL RELATION TRANSPARENCIES	SLOWING DOWN, CONFLICTS	SHARE TIMETABLE AND TEAM ORGANIZATION CHART
LAUNCH	TEAM TRAINING, TESTING, EXCHANGE OF TASKS	MAKE CUSTOMERS INDEPENDENT, INTEGRATE OTHER SERVICE	TRAINING, COMMUNICATION CAPABILITY, VISION	CONTINUOUS DEPENDENCE OF CUSTOMER ON US	INTRODUCE STRUCTURED TRAINING FOR CUSTOMERS
AFTER-SALES	FEEDBACK FORMS, UPDATING SYSTEM, MAINTAINING TEAM	MAINTAIN PROMISES, INDUCE LOYALTY, GENERATE WORD OF MOUTH	FREQUENCY VERIFICATION AND ANALYSIS OF AFTER-SALES, TEAM COMPETENCES	LOSS OF LOYALTY, PROMISES NOT KEPT	ACTIVATE SYSTEM OF EXTERNAL AND INTERNAL CONTROL OF SATISFACTION

FIGURE 10.3 Example of customer journey analysis 2

Love *how* you *do it* **145**

Plan every moment to make it special: touch point design

Now that you have identified the most strategic touch points, let's start designing some. We will appeal to a trio of concepts that are all aspects you must design carefully:

- The consistency of the touch point with the promises of your **brand** and the mission you have given your organization. When the customers are in your touch point, they must be certain that it belongs to you. You obtain this result by working on aspects such as colors and graphics, but also on the concepts and values expressed, for example, by the images and words you use. When designing the touch points of Bistrò53, we verified that the corporate color, a green that recalls nature and refers to the pay-off "a meadow of taste", was present in every interface. We also worked on designing a sound environment that enabled customers to enjoy the sensation of being outdoors. We chose furniture and arranged spaces so there was never too much crowding and guests were guaranteed privacy, in accordance with the organization's declared values. The link with the social objectives of the group of cooperatives to which the restaurant belongs was made clear through the involvement of the young people in the facilities, and the organization of exhibitions and events dedicated to their activities.
- A touch point must provide a positive **experience** to those who frequent it. This is the second aspect you need to consider when designing it. If you have read the chapter on competitors, you will know how the promise you make to customers must be simple and specific. So, if your pledge is based on *relationship*, everything you do in your touch points must facilitate contact, creating real human exchanges that make the value you decided to offer both permeable and interactive. In Bistrò53 we took particular care when designing access, carefully studying the places where people parked, ordered meals and waited. Companies that make a promise based around *performance* will focus instead on providing technical information, ensuring that customers feel themselves to be among their peers, experts and enthusiasts of that type of product or service. Companies whose promise is *price* will have to emphasize figures and quotes, optimize times (time is money), and facilitate direct comparisons with competing products and services. The experience imbues the promise we have made to our customers with life, by stimulating a positive emotion.
- The primary role of a touch point is to receive those coming from the previous phase of the customer journey and accompany them, in the most natural and coherent way, to the next phase. Therefore, we could say that each interface between customer and company connects and **interacts** with the others. Hence, you must clarify how the journey is to continue using an "invite to act" and clear directions on how to proceed. For the bistro of the Nazareno group, we studied a system of signposts and indications that made it easy to get around the building, to choose between the various menu options, to give feedback

TOUCH POINT/ PROMISE GRID

		PROMISE	
TOUCH POINT	**PERFORMANCE**	**PRICE**	**RELATIONSHIP**
BRAND	. FORMAL . MINIMALIST . EXCLUSIVE	. EASY . SENSATIONAL . CHEERFUL AND YOUNG	. EMOTIONAL . VALUE-BASED . WARM AND PERSONAL
EXPERIENCE	. STYLE . PROCEDURE . REFERENCES AND TESTIMONIALS	. QUICK CONSUMPTION . PRICES . PROMOTIONS AND DISCOUNTS	. PEOPLE MORE THAN INTERFACES . INTENSITY AND SMILE . BEHIND THE SCENES
INTERACTION	. SELECTED TOUCH POINTS . KEY CUSTOMERS . ADVICE ON USE	. DIGITAL SUPPORT . SHORTCUTS . SOLICITATION	. CONTACT POINTS . TRANSPARENCY . EACH-TO-EACH

FIGURE 10.4 Touch point/promise grid

on services and share it with others or simply inquire about opening times. Neglecting even one of these aspects would be like "slamming the door in the customer's face" during the customer journey: a mistake that no business can afford to make.[3]

Brand, experience and interaction will guide you in the design of your touch points. Figure 10.4 gives an overall view of how these three categories interact with the promise you are making to the market. They are not static concepts but must be developed as they appear within the different touch points.

Activity – Design and verify your touch points

We propose a series of questions whose answers will help you to be as incisive, coherent and effective as possible when designing each touch point between your company and the customer. You can enrich the previous exercise by creating a chart, for each touch point, that answers every question.

- How do I undertake branding, i.e. how does the customer realize that it is my company's touch point and understand my identity?
- How do I manage the experience; namely how does the customer experience our promise and the differential value that characterizes us?

Love *how* you *do it* **147**

- How do I fuel the interaction, that is, how do I guide the customer between the phases of the journey, in a growing and positive flow?

One last tip: remember that the most important touch points tend to be the initial ones when you receive customers, and the final or farewell touch points. Statistics show that there is a 90% chance that a negative first impression will remain, and only a 50% chance of confirming a positive one. The last scenes people will experience in the customer journey will influence their memories. Even if you were very good at the beginning, but you stumble at the end, unfortunately, there is the risk that people will focus only on that final error. Despite this, companies often neglect the final moments in the relationship with their customers. Some even consider their efforts are over once the customer has made the purchase. A telling example is the way telephone companies, at least in Italy, treat their customers, showing extreme care up to the moment the contract is signed, and then forgetting about them. Their "love" is awakened only when their customers threaten to change provider, but it is often too late to win them back. We advise you to implement adequate feedback collection to check the level of customer satisfaction so you can intervene swiftly if there are problems.

Real, not perfect: genuine communication

In this section, we want to talk to you about **communication**. To do this we wish to focus on two of the most important phases in the customer journey: overcoming indifference and building broader trust.

Word of mouth is much more effective than other tools in facilitating trust. The reason is simple: the disinterested "recommendation" of another user regarding the purchase of a particular service or product is much more effective than reading an advertisement or visiting a site, because these latter instruments are "paid for" by the companies, i.e. they are obviously designed to convince you to buy. Word of mouth is spontaneous, aiming only to advise you in your own interests. Indeed, we could say that people who advise us to buy something are actually taking a risk as they could be blamed if things go wrong! How can you stimulate word of mouth if it must be authentic and spontaneous to be truly effective? The answer lies precisely in the closing stages of the customer journey, namely in all those activities that involve customers after they have bought something. Managing your after-sales service well and continuing to keep the promise you made even after satisfying your immediate economic interests means turning the customer into a **promoter**.

Word of mouth is a true, selfless and altruistic action, aimed at offering a benefit and implying precise responsibilities. What we expect from a friend who recommends us a product or service is not just how good it is but also its flaws, the situations in which it will be useful and those in which we may encounter some imperfections. We suggest you communicate with your customers in exactly the same way, not hiding the true face of your organization behind an old-style mask of perfection. Getting back to the metaphor of love, alluring and "seductive" things

148 Love *how* you *do it*

are hardly likely to be defect-free. Remember that the ego, connected to the mind's rational processes, aspires to perfection while the soul, linked to the emotional sphere and the heart, seeks the truth which comes from an accumulation of knowledge that is won over time but also, and perhaps primarily, from our errors. This is why, in the chapter on branding, we focused on seeking and organizing elements that at first sight may appear as the flaws identified through the SWOT analysis.

Everything you communicate to the customer must be credible and empathetic; yet you must also make the benefits clear, otherwise those listening to you will ask themselves: "Why should I be interested?", "What does all this have to do with me?" Then focus your attention on what your offer can do for those who buy, setting all your descriptions in actual situations with which buyers can identify and in which they can imagine themselves.

To effectively communicate with customers within each touch point, considering their emotions and expectations, we have created a list of key concepts that you will need to keep in mind when designing the customer journey:

- **Friends not gangs** – When you try to expand your contacts and connections through your communication channels, bear in mind that you need to generate friendly relationships, not just a gang held together by material interests alone, but a community bound by values, goals, shared experiences and emotions.
- **Will not must** – Start from the idea of wanting to excite a sense of "wishing" in your customers, not of a "duty" to buy. This means that you will have to consider their freedom in choosing to join and stay with you.
- **I not my** – Remember that the buyers purchase your identity and you participate in theirs. It is not a question of giving or taking, but of offering and accepting something that will bring about new awareness through exchange.
- **We not you** – Always try to be inclusive; do not set yourself against others. Speak, write and create content bearing in mind you are on the same side as your listeners. Team up with customers, colleagues and even other companies operating in the same category, when appropriate.
- **Awareness not safety** – True safety lies in knowledge, which leads to evolutionary change. Help your customers increase their knowledge and, working on yourself and your organization, update the content often, refreshing any beliefs that do not aid you to journey into the future.
- **Solutions not problems** – Speak in proactive terms, a much more powerful concept than simply acting before others do. Proactive people and organizations always ask themselves, in every interaction with the customer and at every stage of the customer journey, a simple question: "What can I do to get the best for myself and others from this situation?"
- **Positive not naïve** – Optimism is not naivety. True optimists do not see good where no good exists, but are committed to seeking it. This allows them to move forward, seeking evolution without being anchored in complaints and excuses for not acting.

Love *how* you *do it* **149**

- **Relate not advertise** – Communicating is not about promoting oneself, but about encountering others. The basis of human beings' ability to speak is a relationship aimed at better comprehending the reality that surrounds us, to improve it for the benefit of all.
- **Resonance not visibility** – Instead of seeking visibility at all costs, of having everyone talking about you, activate contacts and relationships where you feel you share a vibe. The resonance of values will also trigger reactions in the media, but in the right channels and with the right tone.
- **Share not hold** – Ties are created when hands are open, ready to grasp each other, not when they are closed in a fist to hold onto something we are afraid of losing. Remember that when things seem to be going badly you need contacts and friends, not protection and defenses.
- **Thankfulness not showiness** – Be grateful rather than seeking consensus by showing off your achievements and the titles you've won. Every true winner needs support from others and is aware of it. Thus, the noblest form of celebrating one's successes is gratitude.
- **Pace not velocity** – We live in an ever-accelerating world, which often renounces reflection in exchange for speed, mistaking this for efficiency. Doing things well does not mean doing many things and, if you think about it, the market demands ever-higher quality. To keep pace with the times you need to find your own harmony, tune your gestures to a musicality that will guide your steps and that you can only find within yourself. As in a dance, customers will recognize your melody and follow your steps.
- **Enabling not empowering** – Help people to have access to new resources, information and knowledge, rather than using a "doped", self-referential language full of superfluous machismo.
- **Emotional not sensational** – Avoid the "wow" effect at all costs and speak to the heart. Surprises and sensationalism pass, while deep emotions remain and generate energy that lasts over time.
- **Multidimensional not self-referential** – Instead of always quoting yourself or passing off your ideas as facts, verify them by checking them against real data; accept and welcome opinions contrary to your own and be open to debate with those who think differently. It will be an opportunity for everyone to grow.
- **Simple not shallow** – Don't be superficial but produce genuine and clear communication based on reflection, research and coherence. Remember that simplicity is the result of complex processes, so do not avoid simplicity by confusing it with banality but pursue it and build it with care.
- **Real not perfect** – This is the most important advice. Whatever you do, don't forget to always be yourself. Even when consistency and transparency seem unprofitable, remember that there is no result or gain that can repay the loss of your soul. Your work and your business must serve your identity and your essence, not vice versa.

There is one last aspect that we would like to address before concluding the chapter and that is the concept of the **employee journey**, which unites with the customer journey and completes it.

We will give you a concrete example so you can clearly grasp it. Some time ago we contacted a start-up that handles home shopping in our city, to request a testimonial for our course for new entrepreneurs. One of the founders told participants about their initial difficulties, saying that the biggest mistake they had made was focusing exclusively on the customer's experience, neglecting that of their employees. In practice, everything had been optimized for those who wanted to shop online, but the same was not true for those who had to take the order, package it and deliver it. The indirect consequence was that the customer's experience also suffered because deliveries were often incorrect or delayed. The solution was to use the website and WhatsApp conversations (the company's main touch points) as tools not only for customers but also for employees, helping them to do their job as well as possible so that the customer would also reap the benefits.

Each phase of the customer journey, therefore, corresponds to a similar phase of the employee journey and each touch point must be designed with two interfaces: one for customers and the other for those who will have to interact with them.

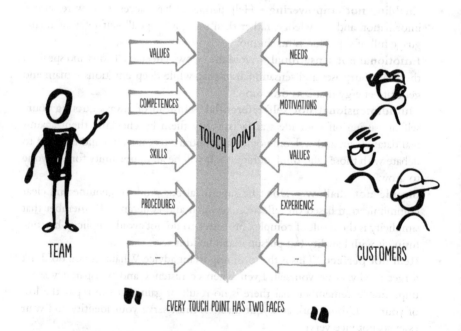

FIGURE 10.5 The two faces of touch points

Returning to the metaphor of love, we could compare the design of each touch point in the customer experience to the choice of a location for a romantic rendezvous between the people who buy and the person in the organization who takes care of them at that moment: an environment that accommodates lovers must be welcoming and comfortable for both. We call the sum of the customer journey and the employee journey the **value journey**.

Conclusion of the case study: a romantic movie with a happy ending

Working for an organization that has a huge positive social impact such as the Nazareno Cooperatives group is an honor and a privilege that our business sometimes allows us. Dealing with ethical marketing and sales, in fact, not only puts us in touch with "for profit" companies that have understood the strategic and competitive importance of investing in ties with their customers and with society, but also organizations such as the NGO that have been committed to ethics in their everyday activities for a long time but do not know how to reconcile them with market dynamics.

When approaching the Bistrò53 team, we first dealt with creating and generating a shared, coherent and acceptable market culture that enhanced its identity and aims. We worked together on the concept of "active solidarity" based on the idea that the market and profits, if well managed, can help finance and promote activities such as the employment of young people, the "International Festival of Different Abilities" and other initiatives in which the cooperative is involved and which require substantial funds. The chance to build a small restaurant in its headquarters also became an opportunity to open the cooperative's doors to locals, enabling many townspeople to see and directly experience how good and beautiful the cooperative's projects are.

Bistrò53's customer journey was conceived as accompanying many to discover a new and, in some ways, unknown reality. We, therefore, designed the park in which it stands as a "secret garden" that can be accessed by different routes, either on foot or by car. When positioning the car park, we chose to ensure that the cars were left at a comfortable distance but without ruining the atmosphere of the restaurant and the surrounding parkland with their presence. We also imagined that the guests would first see other patrons seated on the grass and hear background music that would help them enter the atmosphere, before arriving in front of the restaurant itself where everything, from the menus to dishes, would reflect the style and image of the location.

The planned results have been achieved, with a surplus revenue: in the first year of activity, the expected takings were exceeded by +7% and in the second year this positive trend further increased, with takings up by 23%, and a good prospect of reaching the break-even point in advance compared to the business plan. In a short time, the restaurant's social pages filled with followers and visitors. But the real value of the Bistrò53 project was to give dignity to the people employed there, who are now able to express their abilities through work.

What you have learnt and adding a piece to the Loving Business Model

The customer experience can be described within the customer journey. To design this, we firstly identified the phases of the relationship with customers, learning to isolate the most important touch points for each phase. We then worked on designing the touch points so that everything flows smoothly and in accordance with our goals. Using the tools learned in the chapter, design your customer journey by describing the different moments that make it up. For each one, identify one or more touch points, and then analyze them to see where improvement is possible or if you need to design new interfaces.

Notes

1 For example, think of a car manufacturer (B) with a network of dealerships in the area (B) that then sell to the final consumer (C).
2 In general, we advise you to consider all the *touch points* that refer to the initial scenes of the *customer journey*, or when you first receive customers, as strategic, as well as all the final phases when you take your leave of them. A good first impression will simplify your life and start your relationship off on the right foot, while a good "goodbye" will fix positive memories in your customers' minds that will tempt them to repeat the journey as soon as possible, i.e. to buy from you again.
3 As our colleague Marzia Mazzi (architect specialized in design aimed at people's well-being) said in the article "Marketing and Workspace" that appeared some time ago on our blog diariodiunconsulente.com, many errors like this are made quite unconsciously.

11

CONCLUSIONS

> A love that flames,
> by virtue kindled, always lights another if but its flame be outwardly revealed.
> *Dante Alighieri*

Is this the world you dreamed of as a child?

It is highly likely that as a child you daydreamed about what you would do when you grew up, where you would live, what your partner would look like and, in general, what your life would be like. It is fascinating and exciting to imagine a possible future because it allows us to create different scenarios, but also to experience unexpected contexts. Anyone who dedicates himself/herself to creating a business dreams of the future, and not just their own but that of all the people who will be involved in the organization they have in mind.

Not all your dreams will come true but almost all of them, even those fleetingly imagined, will have contributed to changing you, suggesting new paths and surprising outcomes. The same thing happens in business: maybe your results will not turn out exactly as planned but have no doubt that every strong idea based on love will generate some good for you and for others. Therefore, it is important to grasp the effects that each of your market actions can generate, with an open and conscious mind.

Being aware of your dreams and then committing yourself to realizing them can be difficult; many give up before even starting. "How will I reach my goal?", "What if I'm not strong enough?", "Where do I start?": these are just some of the questions that could worry you and keep you at the starting blocks. Such concerns may lead you to postpone making that vital first step, which many people claim is the most important and decisive for implementing any business project. However, the steps that follow also present a challenge; it will take courage, commitment

154 Conclusions

and dedication as well as method, capabilities and competences all the way. Being successful – in love as in business – is all a question of **movement**, continuous **change** and **adaptation**. In short, it is a matter of continuing your path. Indeed, we chose the name "Passodue" for our agency to remind ourselves that each of the "steps" is fundamental. We wish to give some advice to you and to those travelers who have decided to realize a project in their chosen profession:

- Keep a clear goal in mind but avoid being too rigid about the intermediate steps; rather, leave space for improvisation and adaptation to change.
- Travel light, with little baggage and plenty of space in your suitcase, so you can collect what is new and take it with you on the way.
- Discuss your relationship with fellow travelers without necessarily questioning it, encouraging dialogue serenely and, whenever possible, leaving no conflict unresolved.
- Get rid of toxic habits, limiting beliefs and any of the more brutal instincts such as anger, hatred and bad manners. Instead, always maintain a sense of respect and dignity towards yourself and others, attempting to face the darkest moments with elegance and irony.
- Nurture every relationship with expressions of affection: hugging, celebrating, spending time together. We are "analog" beings that need frequent human contact.
- Give up trying to please everyone or getting everything right. Choosing to take sides, even when it is painful, is a way of clearly defining one's position with respect to life.

But how do you find the courage to set off? The oft-quoted saying from Ralph Waldo Emerson is still valid and may suggest an answer: "Sow a thought and you reap an action; sow an act and you reap a habit; sow a habit and you reap a character; sow a character and you reap a destiny". Our advice to help you take the first step, therefore, is to start from the words you use to express your thoughts. Discuss your projects in a positive way, without fearing they will be copied or stolen; take responsibility for your choices and your dreams; avoid complaining and never blame others for what happens to you in your life and in your work; banish expressions relating to war, conflict or machismo from your business world. Enrich your jargon with words of love, creating a lexicon in which the target customers once again become people; the objectives are not targets but goals; a market is not to be conquered but to be won over and cared for, just as the product is not to be placed but to be offered and there are no hierarchies and grades, but levels of responsibility and service. Breathe with confidence and set off without focusing only on the results: along the way, you will learn to love yourself even in failure, while you could never forgive yourself for not having tried!

If you have the chance to return to the home where you grew up, perhaps using only your imagination, try to look through the window from which you observed the world when you were a child. Take a moment to ask yourself how you have changed and what has become of the dreams you once had. What have you achieved

Conclusions

or let go, and what else do you dream about now? As you seek these answers you will be forced to do some accounting. Triumphs, goals achieved and good times will be balanced against defeats and disappointments over the years. Don't worry or be scared if the latter seem to outweigh the positive things. This is not the spreadsheet of a life guided by love, nor even of a business inspired by it: you do not lose or win, you build and learn, you experience emotions, you evolve and grow, and you leave a legacy to those who will come after you or perhaps an example to follow. Then, as you look out that window, count how much gratitude you have felt, what relationships you have been able to weave, how many times you have given voice to your values, when and how happy you were or you made someone else, what you exchanged by offering and receiving value.

Activity – Finish your journey

We are at the end of the journey and you should have filled every space of the *Loving Business Model* diagram. You still have two last things to do, however, before you have finished. Download the grid that describes the interactions of all the elements and, in each intersection, write what the exchange can be. Just a keyword describing the shared value created at that level is enough. We have given you some examples in Chapter 3 but now we invite you to write down the reflections you have made on what you have learned so far.

The last effort we invite you to do starts from the idea that there can be no success without **gratitude**. Just like a person who has been awarded a prize or won a competition will take time to write a thank-you speech, we want you to do the same, mentioning the people and situations that have contributed to your success. Keep this text next to the *Loving Business Model* so that it is ready for the moment when you achieve your professional goals. Also remember to keep both the business model and the thank-you speech updated as life and business are constantly evolving. Find time to call some of the people mentioned in your speech and thank them directly for what they have done or are doing for you and your business: a joy shared is multiplied.

One step away from what is possible

Falling in love is characterized by an emotional impulse that overcomes all difficulties, allowing us to focus all our energy on what will come next, looking towards the future and ignoring any signs of difficulty in the present. This earliest phase is scattered with beguiling promises and we often believe they will lead us to resolve all our issues, with our emotional traumas wiped away, our shortcomings and deepest wounds removed. Disappointment originates when we discover that

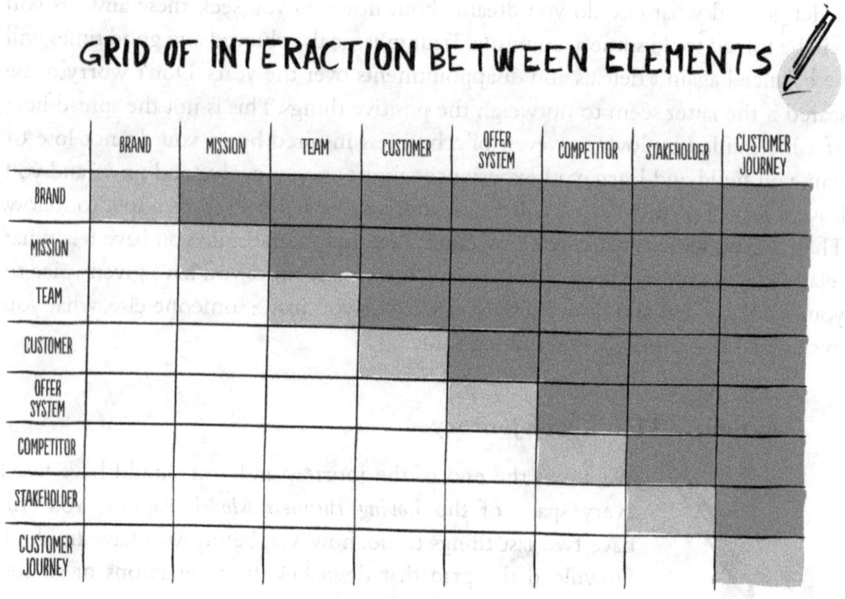

156 Conclusions

GRID OF INTERACTION BETWEEN ELEMENTS

	BRAND	MISSION	TEAM	CUSTOMER	OFFER SYSTEM	COMPETITOR	STAKEHOLDER	CUSTOMER JOURNEY
BRAND								
MISSION								
TEAM								
CUSTOMER								
OFFER SYSTEM								
COMPETITOR								
STAKEHOLDER								
CUSTOMER JOURNEY								

FIGURE 11.1 Grid of interaction between elements

nothing can come from outside that has not first germinated within us. Accepting that it is our responsibility to be happy is one of the most important discoveries we can make in our lives and probably quite traumatic. In fact, it corresponds to the realization that no one can achieve your goals for you.

Among the people you will come across in your work, you will soon discover that there are two categories: **asset seekers** and **meaning seekers**. A host of people have set themselves the goal of accumulating, of working to possess: their goal is well-having. On the other hand, we have others who are trying to give meaning to their existence by aiming at well-being and happiness. It is a question of choosing which side to take. For the former, ethics is seen as a hurdle in the path towards success; they prefer to find a shortcut to avoid being overtaken or even crushed. For the latter, it is difficult to imagine an alternative to using your heart and values to move forward. When the asset seekers mention love, feelings, reciprocity and moral principles, they are hoping to turn these words to their advantage, using a "fashionable" approach as people now agree that emotions help us to increase sales. The meaning seekers, on the other hand, do not exploit love and ethics when talking about the market but use the market, sales and marketing as tools for affirming love and humanity.

For the meaning seekers, the relationship with others is a necessary condition for happiness. Because just as there is no love without exchange, there can be no well-being without compassion and sharing with others. Overcoming selfishness and entering a dimension in which relationships generate value means accepting diversity, mistakes and failure, knowing there will be unforeseen events both for us and others: in a word, giving up control and accepting that we all have our limits.

Conclusions **157**

Partem claram semper aspice:[1] **actors of change**

The time has really come to end this journey. We are writing the conclusions in the same city in which we started writing the previous book: Boston.

We consider that part of *Passodue*'s mission is to cross cultures, i.e. to build a bridge between what is happening in the world's most advanced economy and our country, Italy, which possesses an unassailable artistic and cultural primacy despite its problems.

We hope you will stick to the road and continue the journey we started together in these pages. The more progress you make in your work and in your life, the more you can contribute to the evolution of those around you, of the market and of society overall.

We, like you, will not stop here, but as long as we have the energy and the opportunities, we will continue to work to show people that results can be achieved by remaining coherent with who they are and what they believe.

Your business is just one element in the greater value chain that the overall market represents, and then in society and all of humanity.

FIGURE 11.2 Actors of change

158 Conclusions

In your role as an "ambassador" for a business driven by love, you will meet opponents and people who will hinder or challenge you. When you are among such people you will need all your confidence, motivation, acceptance and flexibility as an **agent of change** because we believe that the market can only be saved by changing the hearts and consciences of individuals. The critical mass capable of triggering a domino effect of positive mutations will then be reached.

Companies are the social and economic institution from which this anticipated ripple of change can spread and grow.

Thus, the time has come to conclude these pages and return home. For a lifetime we believed that "home" was the place where you were protected and loved whatever happened, only now – at the end of this journey – we realize that it is the place to protect and love others whatever happens. We suggest you too, when searching for a refuge for your soul, go beyond the place where you just *receive* to those places where you can *offer* and *be*.

We hope you will be able recognize what you are looking for, find a way to reach it and never feel alone during the journey.

See you later...

Note

1 Always look on the bright side – *Passodue*'s motto.

FAQ – ANSWERS TO FREQUENTLY ASKED QUESTIONS

This section answers the most common questions we were asked during the writing of the book and the application of the tools presented. If you wish to contact us directly, you can do so using the contacts you will find here https://diariodiunconsulente.it/en/contacts/

- **Is it fair to exploit love to do business?** Business is exploited, not love, in the sense that business becomes a tool to talk about love and to do good not vice versa. Remember that the purpose of the economy is not profit – which is just a tool – but to create prosperity in the broadest sense of the word.
- **Can we teach people to love?** No, like trust, respect and other values, love cannot be taught. Without a creative act of will, nothing so important can be born in our hearts. What you can do is encourage the reflections and create that context in which a spark can generate love. That is precisely the purpose of this book.
- **Do you lose spontaneity by introducing a method to apply love to business?** Our goal is not to provide rules but to put you in a position to find your own authentic approach to *Engaging the Heart in Business*. Remember that having a method does not mean slavishly replicating the same gestures, but following a process whose result can be different every time because it is based on the style and values of those who have enacted it.
- **How do you artificially trigger love?** The spark is spontaneous but everything that comes before and after it must be guided and supported with patience and, once again, method and dedication. As happens in life, even in business, people can have an initial attraction to you, but then you will have to take on the responsibility to live up to their expectations and building the relationship with them.

160 FAQ

- **It is said that "all is fair in love and in war", could this not mean that the two fields are, in fact, similar?** We see love as the opposite of war because while the purpose of the first is generative, that of war is always destructive. Everything aimed at producing good outcomes, as in the case of true love, is morally acceptable and, therefore, permissible in the deepest sense of the term, while in our opinion the same is not true if the goal is possession, power or prevarication.

- **Love must be free; does this not distance it from the business world?** None of the actions that humans perform in their lives can be totally disinterested and free of some type of cost, whether economic or otherwise, but this does not diminish its morality and value. Remember that the objectives can be integrated; indeed, in doing so they strengthen each other. In true love, especially, pursuing your happiness corresponds to making your partner happy too.

- **Why predominantly use marketing tools and then talk about business models and other less related factors?** Our approach, as stated in the book, is inside-out; namely we worked to relate what we do with what we are, making the inside and outside of an organization consistent: By restructuring the relationship with the market through marketing, you can change the essence of a company. Of course, marketing is not the only field in which we can and must act, but it can help create operational tools that will generate success stories.

- **How do you measure the intangible and value results of an organization if you have said that not everything can be described in econometric terms?** In our opinion, there are three dimensions to consider: the outcomes for the organization, for those who are part of it and for those who come into contact with it from the outside. In the first case, it is possible to appeal to analyses on the increase in the value of the brand or on the reputation. In the second case, verifying the quality of the internal climate as explained in Chapter 9 can be helpful. The advantages and contributions towards society as a whole or the environment could be measured through instruments such as the balance score card, adequately adapted for the purpose. Regarding this, we refer you to specific texts like the one written by Prof. Alberto Bubbio entitled *Strategia aziendale: controllo, monitoraggio e valutazione*.

- **How were the numbers and statistics presented in the book generated?** In support of the theses presented in the book, we reported the results of surveys and statistics conducted by third-party bodies, all of which are referenced. Regarding the data relating to the case studies of *Passodue* customers, they are the result of a comparison between the figures available in the company before and after our intervention. The investigations and observations that allowed us to select the adopted tools, also allowing us to measure their effectiveness, were conducted through verifications and questionnaires that involved a selected sample of customers. For more information you can consult the page https://diariodiunconsulente.it/en/passodue-results/

- **Why are customers and teams studied separately from stakeholders if they actually share the same interests?** According to some interpretations of stakeholder theory, there is a division between primary stakeholders, that is, those that have a direct interest and on which the very existence of the organization depends, and secondary stakeholders that are not essential but can still influence and be influenced by the market action. Customers and teams are primary stakeholders who take on a central role in a marketing plan: this is the reason why they must be studied separately.

- **Why does the book address the identity and brand of the objectives and mission first, if this is placed at the top in Maslow's hierarchy of needs?** While considering Maslow's studies as an important reference, when organizing the chapters of the book and the various steps for building our operational model, we relied on the *be-offer-receive* model. Thus, it seemed natural to us first to help readers define who they are and what their true essence is after considering what they can offer in terms of mission to customers and society.
- **What is the difference between goals and motivations given that both inspire our actions?** A goal defines the "What" you want to accomplish while the motivation explains "Why". At the basis of motivations there are psychological needs, values and beliefs inherent to our identity. The goals instead appeal to concrete and specific needs, linked to a precise moment in time.
- **If the reciprocal appeal between my customers and me is triggered and they fall in love with me, can the answer to their material needs take a back seat?** Of course not, undoubtedly, they are more likely to forgive you a small mistake, but this does not mean that love lives only on intangibles alone.
- **Why, when analyzing customers, do we need to start from the products that have the greatest impact on turnover and not from those sold in the greatest quantity?** The inductive search for purchase motivations and, therefore, the identity of customers, investigates the value they find in the offer and which they can then generate for us. To give value centrality, it is best to start by selecting those products and services that produce the greatest profit, because it is the most visible indicator of the value collected. The quantities sold can also be linked to factors such as the life cycle and the cheaper purchase price thus skewing the analysis.
- **More than one category emerged in the example recognizing the customers' purchase motivations for the Feng Shui school: which should be given more importance?** Consider that when performing a marketing analysis that regards a number of people, rather than isolating a prevailing motivation, it is useful to put the recurring ones in a system, perhaps combining them together to outline multiple customer profiles.
- **Speaking of the reciprocal appeal, how should I behave if I have attracted the wrong customer?** Firstly, you have to reflect on the reasons that made that particular person feel attracted to you and why you perceive that person to be very different from the customer you had in mind. Perhaps there is some tangible or intangible element of your offer that speaks directly to him/her and shares his/her values? Have you made a wrong promise? Once

162 FAQ

customers have "crossed the threshold" of your business, you should always treat them as a guest of honor. Maintain good relationships with everyone, even with customers you consider "wrong". You can explain calmly that you are unable to satisfy their needs but ensure they will always speak well of you and your company.

- **Do your advice and tools apply to both the B2C and B2B markets?** In our opinion, this division of business is rather obsolete. When we talk about markets, we must always remember that they are populated by people. So, let's say this is a H2H book or human to human.

- **What is the added value that companies that adopt a** *Best Price* **strategy are able to generate, given that they attempt to focus customers' attention on the price and not on the value of their offer?** The value generated by these organizations consists precisely in knowing how to optimize the customers' purchasing power. In addition, these companies can "give more" because, for the same amount of goods purchased (at least in quantitative terms), they enable customers to pay a lower economic price.

- **Can the price strategy called** *Premium Price*, **which raises the economic price to give a higher value perception, be considered deceptive?** As we explained in the example of the artworks, when we are faced with an offer whose value is entrusted primarily to intangible elements, it may be necessary to use the price to help the customer to give the right value to what he is buying in order to reduce its information asymmetries. Companies use this strategy to offer more in terms of exclusivity, image and prestige, all elements that, although intangible, are the result of substantial investments and therefore expensive to obtain and generate real satisfaction in the buyer. To give them back some concreteness, it is necessary to use an adequate quotation.

- **Talking of promise, are we sure that a wider customer base like the one attracted by a more generalized proposal might not do better than the results of a sincere but attractive promise for a smaller catchment area?** Studies show the opposite is true; namely the results of the second strategy exceed, in a finite time, those of the first because the positive effects of negotiation facilitation (coherence helps the relationship), word of mouth and loyalty are added. If you want to go deeper into the topic, we suggest you read the book *The Blue Ocean Strategy* already mentioned.

- **In the chapter on competitors, you said that we must compete on value and not on price, but then price also features among the promises that a company can make to the market. How come?** Not all customers need the same things: some people, for instance, need an offer that optimizes their purchasing power. The companies that respond to this need are those that can promise price, which does not mean that they will always undercut competitors but only that their value lies in the particular efficiency they have in balancing the cost/benefit ratio. Purely price-cutting competition, on the other hand, is a different matter because it puts no emphasis on the benefit received but only on the purchase price, making the customer believe that the rest of the features of the offer are irrelevant.

- **Are only companies that promise a relationship the ones naturally close to the *Loving Business Model*?** No, even companies that promise Performance and Price can adopt a business model inspired by love; it is only a matter of making clear promises to their customers in a way that is conscious and consistent with the objectives set. As the designer and teacher Mario de Liguori reminded us, an example of a correct price promise is the 2011 Dacia Duster advertising campaign which tried to subvert the paradigm that low price must necessarily be synonymous with low quality, proposing a new luxury that becomes that of knowing how to make "intelligent choices" that go against the tide and without being influenced by the preconceptions of others.
- **What correlation is there between price strategy and type of promise? For example, are companies that promise price necessarily in the best price quadrant?** We investigated whether there was a perfect correlation between price and promise strategies, but the evidence did not lead us to define unique rules. Certainly, those who promise price will be on the left of the diagram presented in Chapter 7 to define the four strategies, given that they will use the price lever in a traditional way. Those who promise performance, on the other hand, will adopt a price positioning that tends to fall into the right side of the diagram. Focusing on the relationship means having a highly intangible offer; for this reason, those who adopt this strategy will fall into the lower quadrants of the diagram.
- **In love there should be no predefined hierarchies and roles, so why talk about leadership even in companies inspired by the *Loving Business Model*?** The suggestion to abandon a business model based on "command and control" in favor of one based on love does not mean removing the hierarchical company structures but adopting a leadership style consistent with the spirit of service, which takes into account the differences and centralizes respect for people and their emotions. Love does not disregard the diversity of roles. Think of the love that binds parents and children: each role is well-defined, but an emotional bond exists.
- **Looking at the diagram that illustrates the *Loving Business Model*, it would seem that the customer journey must include not only customers but also competitors, employees, context... Does this mean that I will have to design a journey for each of these actors?** The customer journey, as its name suggests, revolves around the customer. When designing it, however, we should consider all the other elements of our business. During the discussion in that specific chapter, we included those who interact with the customers and competitors in the organization. For simplicity we have left out the customer–context interactions (except for word of mouth) but certainly if you find it useful you can include it. The "extended" customer journey is what we have called the value journey.

164 FAQ

- **I am not clear about the roles within the customer journey, especially since you used the metaphor of the movie: who is the director and who is the star, given that the contact person can change within the buying process?** The customer is always the star and may be a single person or a "buying team". According to research by the Corporate Executive Board (CEB), on average, 5.4 people are involved in a purchasing choice and each of them will be the main player at a specific moment. You must know how to clearly identify who the customer is at each stage and what goals he/she has. The direction of the "movie" is the responsibility of the people in the company that deal with market relations; therefore, usually marketing strategists and sales managers. While the former will have contributed to writing the script, preparing the actors, setting up the sets and writing the parts, the latter as the stage directors will coordinate the actions on the set of the sellers and all those who interact with the customer.

BIBLIOGRAPHY

Achor, Shawn. *The Happiness Advantage: The Seven Principles of Positive Psychology that Fuel Success and Performance at Work.* Virgin Books, 2011.

Alberoni, Francesco. *Quel che conta davvero: valori per un'etica contemporanea.* Piemme, 2017.

Allen, David. *Getting Things Done: The Art of Stress-Free Productivity.* Penguin Group USA, 2017.

Arthur, W. Brian. "Increasing Returns and the New World of Business." *Harvard Business Review,* July–August 1996. https://hbr.org/1996/07/increasing-returns-and-the-new-world-of-business

Baccaglini, Alessandro. *La via dell'amore perfetto.* Le due torri, 2016.

Branca, Niccolò. *Per fare un manager ci vuole un fiore.* Edizioni Mondadori, 2013.

Brenkert, George G. *Marketing Ethics.* Blackwell Publishing, 2008.

Brizzi, Salvatore. *Officina alkemica. L'alchimia come via per la felicità incondizionata.* Anima Edizioni, 2008.

Brizzi, Salvatore. *La Via della Ricchezza: La Via della Ricchezza.* Anima Edizioni, 2017.

Bubbio, Alberto, and Dario Gulino. *Strategia aziendale: controllo, monitoraggio e valutazione.* IPSOA Innovative Management, Wolters Kluwer, 2017.

Capuano, Lorenzo. *Ti amo comunque. La frase che trasformerà per sempre la tua vita.* Anima Edizioni, 2010.

Casella, Sergio. *La morale aziendale. Un modello basato sull'etica per avere successo nel business.* Tecniche Nuove, 2014.

Casella, Sergio. *Vincere la paura in azienda.* Tecniche Nuove, 2019.

Casiraghi, Claudio. *Marketing etico. Un'opportunità per le aziende di oggi e di domain.* Guerini Next, 2014.

Castaneda, Carlos. *L'isola del Tonal.* Rizzoli, 1975.

Chapman, Bob, and Raj Sisodia. *Everybody Matters: The Extraordinary Power of Caring for Your People Like Family.* Penguin, 2015.

Chan, Kim W., and Renée Mauborgne. *Blue Ocean Strategy: How to Create Uncontested Market Space and Make Competition Irrelevant.* Harvard Business School Press, 2015.

D'Egidio, Franco. *L'impresa guidata dai valori.* Sperling & Kupfer, 1994.

166 Bibliography

De Liguori, Mario, and Francesco Zurlo. "How to Measure the Positive Effects on Wellbeing of Slowdown in Product Design." Paper presented at the *Letters to the Future* conference, Srishti Institute of Art, Design & Technology, Bangalore, India, November 13, 2018, 252–263.

Deaglio, Mario. *Un futuro da costruire bene: Ventiduesimo rapporto sull'economia globale e l'Italia*. Guerini e Associati, 2018.

Delers, Antoine. *Pareto's Principle*. 50minutes.com, 2019.

Di Montigny, Oscar. *Il tempo dei nuovi eroi*. Mondadori, 2016.

Diamond, Jed. *The Enlightened Marriage: The 5 Transformative Stages of Relationships and Why the Best Is Still to Come*. New Page Books, 2016.

Dilts, Robert B. *Visionary Leadership Skills: Creating a World to Which People Want to Belong*. Dilts Strategy Group, 2017.

Dyer, Wayne W. *Your Erroneous Zones*. Morrow Avon, 2001.

Folador, Massimo. *L'organizzazione Perfetta. La regola di San Benedetto. Una saggezza antica al servizio dell'impresa moderna*. Guerini Next, 2016.

Folador, Massimo. *Storie di ordinaria economia. L'organizzazione (quasi) perfetta nel racconto dei protagonist*. Guerini Next, 2017.

Gentile, Mary C. *Giving Voice to Values: How to Speak Your Mind When You Know What's Right*. Yale University Press, 2010.

Ghidini, Maurizio. *Amore ultimo scorso*. Alberto Maioli Editore, 1999.

Grant, Adam. *Give and Take: Why Helping Others Drives Our Success*. Reprint ed. Penguin Books, 2014.

Grant, Adam. *Originals: How Non-Conformists Move the World*. Viking, 2016.

Gray, Dave, Sunni Brown, and James Macanufo. *Gamestorming: A Playbook for Innovators, Rulebreakers, and Changemakers*. O'Reilly Media, Inc., 2010.

Hafrey, Leigh. *War Stories: Fighting, Competing, Imagining, Leading*. Business Expert Press, 2015.

Haidt, Jonathan. "Can You Teach Businessmen to Be Ethical?" *The Washington Post*, January 13, 2014.

Hersey, Paul, and Kenneth Blanchard. *Management of Organizational Behavior: Leading Human Resources*. 10th ed. Pearson India, 2015.

Hieatt, David. *Do Purpose: Why Brands with a Purpose Do Better and Matter More*. The Do Book Company, 2014.

Hillman, James. *L'anima dei luoghi: Conversazione con Carlo Truppi*. Rizzoli, 2004.

Hillman, James. *The Soul's Code: In Search of Character and Calling*. Reprint ed. Ballantine Books, 2017.

Honeyman, Ryan, and Tiffany Jana. *The B Corp Handbook*. Berrett-Koehler Publishers Inc., 2014.

Kelly, Simon, Paul Johnston, and Stacey Danheiser. *Value-ology: Aligning Sales and Marketing to Shape and Deliver Profitable Customer Value Propositions*. Springer, 2017.

Křivohlavý, Jaro. *Gratitudine, piccolo manuale per sorridere alla vita*. Città Nuova, 2012.

Macchiavelli, Niccolò. *Il Principe*. Libraria Editrice, 2018.

Mahajan, Gautam. *How Creating Customer Value Makes You a Great Executive*. Business Expert Press, 2017.

Masaru, Emoto. *The Hidden Messages in Water*. 1st ed. Atria Books, 2005.

Mastrocola, Paola. *L'amore prima di noi*. Einaudi, 2016.

McCarthy, Edmund Jerome. *Basic Marketing: A Global-Managerial Approach*. R.D. Irwin, 1962.

McKinsey Global Institute. *Measuring the Economic Impact of Short-Termism*, January 2017.

Morgan, John Michael. *Brand Against the Machine: How to Build Your Brand, Cut Through the Marketing Noise, and Stand Out from the Competition*. John Wiley & Sons, 2011.

Nash, John F. *Equilibrium Points in n-Person Games*. National Academy of the USA, 1950.

Bibliography 167

Noci, Giuliano. "Se Made in Italy fosse un brand sarebbe il terzo al mondo.". *Il Sole 24 Ore*, 27 August 2014.

Osterwalder, Alexander, and Yves Pigneur. *Business Model Generation: A Handbook for Visionaries, Game Changers, and Challengers*. John Wiley & Sons, 2013.

Pelligra, Vittorio. *I paradossi della fiducia: Scelte razionali e dinamiche interpersonali*. Il Mulino, 2007.

Pink, Daniel H. *To Sell Is Human: The Surprising Truth About Persuading, Convincing, and Influencing Others*. Canongate Books, 2013.

Poli, Erica Francesca. *The Anatomy of Healing: The Seven Principles of the New Integrated Medicine*. Anima Edizioni, 2017.

Poli, Erica Francesca. *The Anatomy of the Couple: The Seven Principles of Love*. Anima Edizioni, 2018.

Redfield, James. *The Celestine Prophecy: An Adventure*. Grand Central Publishing, 2018.

Redfield, James. *The Tenth Insight: Holding the Vision*. Corbaccio, Grand Central Publishing, 2018.

Rifkin, Jeremy. *The Zero Marginal Cost Society: The Internet of Things, the Collaborative Commons, and the Eclipse of Capitalism*. Reprint ed. St. Martin's Griffin, 2015.

Robbins, Tony. *MONEY Master the Game: 7 Simple Steps to Financial Freedom*. Giunti; Simon & Schuster, 2016.

Roberts, Kevin. *Lovemarks: The Future Beyond Brands*. PowerHouse Books, 2005.

Romagnoli, Gabriele. *Coraggio!* Feltrinelli, 2016.

Rosenberg, Marshall B., *Nonviolent Communication: A Language of Life*. 3rd ed. Puddle Dancer Pr, 2015.

Saint-Exupéry, Antoine de. *The Little Prince*. Mariner Books, 2000.

Sanders, Tim. *Love Is the Killer App: How to Win Business and Influence Friends*. Crown Publishing Group, 2002.

Sinek, Simon. *Start with Why: How Great Leaders Inspire Everyone to Take Action*. Portfolio, 2011.

Sinek, Simon. *Together is Better: A Little Book of Inspiration*. Penguin UK, 2016.

Sisodia, Raj, David B. Wolfe, and Jagdish N. Sheth. *Firms of Endearment: How World-Class Companies Profit from Passion and Purpose*. Pearson, 2003.

Sisodia, Rajendra, and John Mackey. *Conscious Capitalism: Liberating the Heroic Spirit of Business*. Harvard Business Review Press, 2013.

Stark, Andrew. "What's the Matter with Business Ethics?" *Harvard Business Review*, May–June, 1993.

Treacy, Michael, and Fred Wiersema. "Customer Intimacy and Other Value Disciplines." *Harvard Business Review*, January–February, 1993.

Verganti, Roberto. *Overcrowded*. The MIT Press, 2017.

Whyte, David. *The Heart Aroused: Poetry and the Preservation of the Soul at Work*. Industrial Society, 1997.

Williams, John. *Screw Work, Let's Play: How to Do What You Love and Get Paid for It*. FT Press, 2010.

Winters, Carol. "The Feminine Principle: An Evolving Idea." *Quest* 94, no. 5 (November–December 2006): 206–209, 215.

Yunus, Muhammad. *Banker to the Poor: Micro-Lending and the Battle Against World Poverty*. PublicAffairs, 2008.

Zoia, Luigi. *Cadere 7 volte… rialzarsi 8*. Mental Fitness Publishing, 2014.

Zygmunt, Bauman. *Liquid Life*. Polity Press, 2005.

INDEX

Note: Page numbers in *italics* relate to figures.

"5 Whys" technique 57
80/20 rule 75, 77, 83n8

ABC analysis 75
actions: Pyramid of Logical Levels 49, 50;
relationship with motivations and goals
56, 58, *58*, 62
actors of change 157–158, *157*
adaptation 44
affection 154
aging populations 7, 11
alibis, and corporate climate *132*, 133
Amazon 11, 42
apathy, and corporate climate *132*, 133
Apple 11, 16n4
appreciation, expressing 128
Aristotle 17n19
Arthur, W.B. 97
Aspen Institute 27n2
asset seekers 156
authenticity: mission and vision 63; and
objectives 59; *Passodue's* aims 135; and
values 57; word of mouth 147

Babson College 27n2
balance score card 160
banking sector 12
Bauman, Zygmunt 11
B Corporations 21
behavior: behavior/promise grid *111*;
Pyramid of Logical Levels 49, 50

being: and loving, links between 23–24;
Loving Business Model 34
being–offering–receiving cycle 33–34, *34*,
161; prosperity 66–67
belonging needs 90
benchmark analysis 101, 104–105
Benedict, Saint, and Benedictine
monasteries 14–15
Bentley University xi–xii, 13
Bertolucci, Bernardo 20
best price strategy 95–97, *96*; added value
162; customer loyalty, lack of 117n2;
FAQs 162, 163
Bezos, Jeff 42
Bistrò53 137–138, 145, 151–152
Blanchard, Kenneth 126
book: aim 1; chapter structure 4–6, *5*;
how it can help and how to use it 1–3;
organization 3–4, *4*; target audience 1
brand 31, 33, 53; character 43–44; as
communication tool 43; customer
journey 145, *146*; customers 71; and
defects 45–46, 148; engaging your soul in
your business 42–44; hypothetical launch
activity 51; Maslow's hierarchy of needs
161; offer system 87; people management
124; Pyramid of Logical Levels 48;
value 160
Brenkert, George G. 34–35
Brizzi, Salvatore 61, 135
Browning, Robert 83n1

Index **169**

Bubbio, Alberto 160
buck passing, and corporate climate
132, 133
business ethics *see* ethics
Business Roundtable (BRT) xi

capabilities: Pyramid of Logical Levels 49,
50, 51; and success 65
case studies 3, 4; competition 100–101, 102,
116–117; customer journey 137–138,
145, 146, 151–152; customers 69–70,
76–79, 80–83; data 160; goals 54–55,
67–68; identity 41–42, 52; offer
system 85–86, 89–90, 91, 98; people
management 119–120, 134–135
chameleonism and promises 107–108
change, signs of 7–12
Choi, Audrey 17n14
Circle of Trust 24–26, *25*; customer journey
140, 143
collaborators *see* people management
commodification effect: competition 105;
offer system 85–86
communication: brand 43; customer
journey 147–145; identity 43; mission
and vision 63; offer system 90, 97; people
management 128–130
competences: employees 122–123; Pyramid
of Logical Levels 49, 50, 51; and
success 65
competition 33, 100, 117; benchmark
analysis 104–105; building a genuine
promise 105–110; case study 100–101,
102, 116–117; cooperation 101–104;
FAQs 162–163; identifying and verifying
your promise 115–116; interpretation
of term 4; and love 102–103; people
113–114; positioning 111–112; processes
114–115; products and services 112–113;
value as basis for 110–116
competitive happiness 24
compliments, giving and receiving 128
conditional happiness 24
confidence, crisis of 10
Conscious Business Group 21
contact leads 142
context 31–32
cooperation with competitors
101–105, 117
corporate capital 99n5
corporate culture: checking your
131–133, *132*; employees 122;
valueholders 133
Corporate Executive Board (CEB) 164

credibility: communication 148; of
promises 107
criticism, expressing 128, 129–130
Cucinelli 14
culture *see* corporate culture
customer journey 33, 137, 152; analysis
example 145; case study 137–138, 145,
146, 151–152; designing your 143, *144*;
FAQs 163–164; genuine communication
147–151; *Love Mix* 36; movie scenes,
starring your customer 138–143; phases
138–139, *139*, 140–143; touch points *see*
touch points
customer-oriented companies 118n7
customers 33, 69, 83; analysis grid *80*; case
study 69–70, 76–79, 80–83; environment
124; FAQs 160–162; getting to know
your 74–80; journey *see* customer
journey; love 73, 80–83; reciprocal appeal
70–74, *73*; and stakeholders 160–161;
"wrong" 161–162; *see also* offer system

Dacia 163
Danshari 70
Dante Alighieri 153
decluttering *see* Danshari
defects 44–48, 52, 148
de Liguori, Mario 163
democratization 10
demographic change 7, 11
Dennet, Daniel 49
differentiation: competition 101–103, 107,
108, 116; customers 78, 79, 81–82; offer
system 86–90, 92; promises 108
dignity 154
Dilts, Robert 48
Disney, Walt 59
distrust *see* trust
diversity: changing world 12; employees 122
donations 67
Dreamers, The (movie) 20
dreams 153–155

economic crisis (2008) xvi, 9; and distrust
10; economics and ethics, integration of
13–14; *Giving Voice to Values* approach 18
economics 8, 9, 12–15
Einstein, Albert 9
Emerson, Ralph Waldo 154
emotions: customer journey 143, 149;
people management 120, 121, 125,
128, 133; use in communication 10;
valueholders 133
Emoto, Masaru 101, 117n1

170 Index

empathy 44
employees: business as a team sport
122–124, 135; journey 150–151; mission
vs motivations 124–125; quality of time
dedicated to 126, 128–138; resignation
123–124; time for growth of 126–128
environment *see* physical environment
error resolution 129
esteem needs 90
ethics 15–16; business and love, link
between 13–14; and business
performance 9; financial sector 12,
17n14; *Giving Voice to Values* approach
1–2, 18–20; and innovation 11;
and love, link between 2–3; and
sustainability 10
excuses, and corporate climate *132*, 133
externalities 99n6; offer system 94

Facebook 11
fear: corporate climate *132*, 132; and hatred
24; as opposite to love 25
feminine principles, spread of 10
Ferrari 53n3
FIAT 87–88; 103–104
financial sector 12
flexibility 154
Folador, Massimo 14
Francesca, Poli Erica 16n8
Franceschetti, Massimo 118n5
Franklin, Benjamin 39
freelancing 11
Freeman, R. Edward 13, 20–21
frequently asked questions (FAQs) 159–164
Friedman, Milton xi, 29

Gavioli, Roberto 59
game theory 13, 20
Gentile, Mary xii–xiii, 1, 16, 19–20, 43
Gestalt psychology 124, 136n5
Giving Voice to Values (GVV) approach
xii–xiii, 1–2, 16, 18–20, *19*
globalization 12
goals and objectives 32, 54, 68; case study
54–55, 67–68; customers 81; defining
your 61–62; employees 122, 125;
flexibility 154; formulation 59–61;
happiness and sustainability 64–66;
Maslow's hierarchy of needs 161; and
motivations 55–62, 161; offer system
91; people management 133; Pyramid
of Logical Levels 49, 50; survival vs
prosperity 66–67; *see also* mission; vision
Grant, Adam 30, 130

gratitude 155; customer journey 149; and
customers 81; and happiness 81, 90–91;
offer system 90–91; valueholders 133

happiness: as basis of being and loving
23; customers 70; Danshari 70; and
gratitude 81, 90–91; levels of 24; and
love 160; offer system 90–91; path to
22–26; people management 135; personal
responsibility for 156; secret to 49; and
sustainability 64–66
Harley Davidson 53n2
Heinz 53n3
Hersey, Paul 126
Hieatt, David 122, 124
hierarchy of needs 21–22, *22*, 24; FAQs 161;
offer system 89–91, 93; process 36–37
Hoffman, W. Michael 13
horizontal organizations 11
human–digital integration 11

identity 31, 51, 52; adaptation 44; brand
42–44; case study 41–42, 52; customer
journey 143, 148, 150; customers 71, 72,
73, 75; and defects 44–48, 52; Maslow's
hierarchy of needs 161; and motivation
58; Pyramid of Logical Levels 48, 49, 50,
51; and success 65
Illycaffè 14, 134
image 111, 112
inclusiveness and customer journey
148
inconsistency and promises 108
indifference, overcoming 147
information asymmetries: competition 102,
103; customers 162; offer system 87,
88, 93–94
innovation: changing world 11; Open
118n6; product- vs market-oriented
companies 105–106
Italian Association of Home Staging
Professionals 100–101, 102,
116–117, 118n11
Italy: business ethics 13, 14; culture
157; FIAT 87–88; product-oriented
companies 106

Jobs, Steve 16n4
justifications, and corporate climate
132, 133

Key Performance Indicators (KPIs)
75, 83n8
Kim, W. Chan 97

Index **171**

Lamborghini 53n3
leadership: FAQs 163; people management 120, 122–124, 126–131, 135; Situational 126–127; time use 130–131, *131*
Lehman Brothers 10
Levitt, T. 22
limbic system 16n8
love 1–2, 153–158; changing world 7–12; code 22–26; and competition 102–103; customer journey 147, 148, 151; customers 73, 80–83; and ethics, link between 2–3; FAQs 159–161, 163; and happiness 160; inclusive nature of 3–4; and lack of fear 15–16; mission and vision 63; and motivation 55; offer system 88–89, 92, 93, 95; origins in economics 12–15; pace and time issues 125–126, 130; people management 120–123, 133, 134; and reciprocity 25–26, 102; and success 64, 65; and trust, links between 24–26; *see also Loving Business Model*
Love Mix 35–37; and Pyramid of Logical Levels 50
Loving Business Model 26, 28–30, *31*; being–offering–receiving cycle 33–34, *34*; branding and identity 53; competition 101, 102, 117; customer journey 137, 138, 152; customers 74–75, 83; FAQs 163; goals, mission and vision 68; grid of interaction between elements 155, *156*; interaction between elements 37–38, *39*; *Love Mix* 35–37; marketing mix 34–35; offer system 89, 98; people management 125, 133, 135; pillars 30–34
loyalty: and competition 102, 109–110, 114, 117n2; importance 10; *Love Mix* 36; and promises 109–110

Maggiari, Massimo xix
manifesto 64, 68n4
market balance 94–95, *95*
marketing 34–35; mix 35; plan 3, 37–39
market-oriented companies 105–106, *106*, 114, 118n7
Maslow's hierarchy of needs *see* hierarchy of needs
maturity, and Situational Leadership 126–127
Mauborgne, R. 97
Mazzi, Marzia 152n3
McCarthy, Jerome 35
McKinsey 8, 136n11
meaning: need for 7–8; seekers 156

mechanistic models, failure of 9–10
microcredit 13
Mies Van Der Rohe, Ludwig 83n1
mission 32, 33, 54, 63, 68; case study 54–55, 67–8; competition 112; customer journey 145; customers 73, 74, 80–82; drafting your vision statement 64; employees 122, 124–125; Illycaffè 134; Maslow's hierarchy of needs 161; motivation 56; offer system 87, 91; and prosperity 66; and success 65; *see also* goals and objectives; vision
Montalti Worldwide Moving (MWM) 54–65, 67–68
Morgan, J. 42
Morgan Stanley 17n14
motivations 55–62; case study 67; corporate climate *132*, 132; customers *see* purchasing motivations; discovering your 57; employees 122, 124–125; and identity 58; mission and vision 63; offer system 90; relationship with goals and action 56, 58, *58*, 62, 161; relationship with needs 74; and values 57, 58
mutuality 15

Nash, John 13, 20, 93
Nava 53n3
Nazareno Cooperative Sociali 137–138, 145, 151–152
needs: customers 73, 75, 78; relationship with motivations 74; *see also* hierarchy of needs
Neuro-Linguistic Programming (NLP) 48
news 7
Numero Uno 53n2

objectives *see* goals and objectives
offer system 26, 32, 33–34, 85, 86–88, *88*, 98; case study 85–86, 89–90, 91, 98; competition 101, 103; customer journey *139*, 139; designing your 91–92; *Love Mix* 35; price as indicator of value 92–97; structuring the 88–92; *see also* being–offering–receiving cycle
Olivetti, Adriano 13
Open Innovation 118n6
opportunities (SWOT analysis) 45–47
optimism 148
Osho xv

pace *see* time
Panzavolta, Canzio 99n5
Pareto principle (80/20 rule) 75, 77, 83n8

172 Index

passion, and corporate climate *132*, 132
Passodue xiii, xvii, 135; banking sector 17n13; data sources 160; manifesto 57; mission 157; motto 157, 158n1; name choice 154
Patagonia 14
people: competition strategy 110, 113–114; *Love Mix* 36; management *see* people management; marketing mix 35
people management 119, 135; business as team sport 122–124; case study 119–120, 134–135; love 120–122; mission vs motivations of collaborators 124–125; pace 125–133; suppliers and stakeholders, managing your 133–134
performance promise 107, 108, *111*; customer journey 145; FAQs 163; people strategy 113; positioning strategy 111; processes strategy 114; products and services strategy 112
physical environment: *Love Mix* 37; marketing mix 35; people management 124; Pyramid of Logical Levels 49, 50
physiological needs 89
place: *Love Mix* 36; marketing mix 35
Plato 17n19
Poli, Erica 23–24, 90
position (*Love Mix*) 50
positioning grid 95–96, *96*
positioning strategy 110, 111–112
power price strategy *96*, 96, 97
praise, expressing 128
premium price strategy *96*, 96, 97, 162
price: and commodification 105; competition 102, 105, 110, 162–163; customers 123; lever 93, *94*, 94–96, 111–112, 163; *Love Mix* 35; marketing mix 35; offer system 86, 87, 89, 92–97; promise *see* price promise; strategies 94–97, 162, 163; supply and demand 73; and value, relationship between 92–97, *94*
price promise 107, 108, 109, *111*; customer journey 145; FAQs 163; people strategy 113; positioning strategy 111–112; processes strategy 114; products and services strategy 112
process: *Love Mix* 36–37; marketing mix 35; strategy 110, 114–115
procrastination 130–131
product: *Love Mix* 35; marketing mix 35; strategy 110, 112–113
product-oriented companies 105–106, *106*, 114
promises: behavior/promise grid *111*; building genuine 105–110; competing on

value 110–116; credibility 107; customer journey 145, *146*, 146; customers 162; errors regarding 107–108; FAQs 162, 163; identifying and verifying your promise 115–116; types 107
promise to market diagram *115–116*
promotion: *Love Mix* 36; marketing mix 35
prosperity 159; vs survival 66–67
purchasing motivations 71–74, *72*, *73*, *74*, 79–80; getting to know your customers 75, *76*, 78–79; and mission 80–82; prioritising 161
purchasing process 75–76, *76*, 79
purpose *see* goals and objectives; mission; vision
Pyramid of Logical Levels *48*, 48–51

receiving 26; *see also* being–offering–receiving cycle
reciprocity: customers 70–74, *73*, 81, 82, 161–162; employees 124; gratitude 81; and love 25–26, 102; and trust
reference models 18; *Giving Voice to Values* approach 18–20; love code 22–26; Maslow's hierarchy of needs 21–22; stakeholder theory 20–21
references 90
relationship promise 107, 108, *111*; customer journey 145; FAQs 163; people strategy 114; positioning strategy 112; processes strategy 114–115; products and services strategy 113
relaxation, and corporate climate *132*, 133
religion 11
reputation: competition strategy 109, 111, 112, 114; people management 124, 125; and promises 109; value 160
respect 154; people management 121, 124, 134; valueholders 134
responsible investments 17n14
Ricci, Rita Pederzoli 101
Rifkin, Jeremy 11

safety needs, offer system 89–90
Schultz, Howard 42
self-actualization needs, offer system 90–91
Seneca 54
Sinek, Simon 32, 56
Sisodia, Raj xiii, 8
Situational Leadership 126–127
Smith, Adam 20
social media 7, 10
Socrates xii
Sophocles 45

soul: engaging your soul in your business 42–44; soul days 131
Soul Pancake 81
spirituality 11
spontaneity 159; vs strategy 137–8
stakeholders 31–32, 160–161; people management 133–134
stakeholder theory 13, 20–21, 161
Starbucks 42
stock market 12
strategic games theory 13, 20
strategy vs spontaneity 137–138
strengths (SWOT analysis) 45, 46
submission, and corporate climate *132*, 132
success: elements of 120–122; and gratitude 155; happiness and sustainability 64–66
suppliers 133–134
survival vs prosperity 66–67
sustainability: changing world 10; dimensions of 64–65; and happiness 64–66
Sustainable Development Goals 17n10
SWOT analysis 44–48, *47*, 148

Talamo, Carlo 53n2
taxes 67
teamwork *see* people management
threats (SWOT analysis) 46
Timberland 53n2
time: checking your company's climate 131–133; collaborators' growth 126–128; customer journey 149; and love 125–126, 130; people management 125–133; quality of time dedicated to collaborators 126, 128–130; and success 120–121; for yourself and for your business 126, 130–131
tithing 68n5
touch points 138–139, *139*, 140–2; communication 148; controlled 142; designing 143, 145–147; employee journey 150–151; increase in 10; indirect 142; and promises 145, *146*, 146; strategic 142, 145, 152n2; two faces of 150–151, *150*
Toyoda, Sakichi 57
Toyota Motor Corporation 57
transparency 10; competition strategy 110, 114; customer journey 149; offer system 97; *Passodue*'s aims 135; and promises 110
Trevisani, Riccardo 43, 51, 53n1
trust: building 147; changing world 10; economics and ethics, integration of 14; ethics 2; financial sector 12; and love, links between 24–26; microcredit 13; people management 123, 135; and

reciprocity 25–26; and success 65; *see also* Circle of Trust

unconditional happiness 24
Unique Selling Proposition (USP) 108, 116
United Nations Sustainable Development Goals 17n10
United States: business ethics 13; Declaration of Independence 23; FIAT 87–88
UVA Darden School of Business 27n2

value (worth) 155; brand 160; case study 86, 98; competition 102, 103, 105, 110–116, 118n3; customers 161; *Love Mix* 35; offer system 87–98; people management 134; and price, relationship between 92–97, *94*, 162; reputation 160
value chain 133–134
valueholders 29, 133–134
value journey *see* customer journey
value price strategy *96*, 96, 97; case study 98
values (principles) 155; and authenticity 57; brand 43; case study 67; customer journey 145, 149; customers 71, 72, 73, 75, 82; mission and vision 63; and motivation 57, 58; offer system 90; people management 119, 120, 122, 133; Pyramid of Logical Levels 49, 50; resonance of 149; and success 65; SWOT analysis 45, 46; valueholders 133
virtuous circle 103, 104
vision 62, 68; case study 55; drafting your vision statement 64; motivation 56; offer system 91; and prosperity 66; Pyramid of Logical Levels 50; *see also* goals and objectives; mission
vocation 49
Volkswagen 12

Walmart 83n1
weaknesses (SWOT analysis) 45, 46
Whole Foods Market 14, 37–38, 83n1
willpower and success 120
word of mouth 38; customers 71; importance 10; as indirect touch point 142; *Love Mix* 36; offer system 93; and promises 109–110; and trust 147
work team 32; and stakeholders 160–161; *see also* people management

Yale School of Management 27n2
Yunus, Muhammad 13

Zoia, Luigi 21–22

Taylor & Francis eBooks

www.taylorfrancis.com

A single destination for eBooks from Taylor & Francis with increased functionality and an improved user experience to meet the needs of our customers.

90,000+ eBooks of award-winning academic content in Humanities, Social Science, Science, Technology, Engineering, and Medical written by a global network of editors and authors.

TAYLOR & FRANCIS EBOOKS OFFERS:

A streamlined experience for our library customers

A single point of discovery for all of our eBook content

Improved search and discovery of content at both book and chapter level

REQUEST A FREE TRIAL
support@taylorfrancis.com